Settlers in America from Norway & Sweden

SETTLERS IN AMERICA FROM NORWAY & SWEDEN
ELEANOR THOMPSON ASPHYXIATION &
MARIE WICK MURDER &
GUMMER TRIAL

EILEEN C. TRONNES NELSON, CP®

ISBN (Paperback): 979-8-9872734-1-8

ISBN (eBook):

Library of Congress Control Number: Pending

Notice: The information in this nonfiction book is true and complete to the best of my knowledge.

Settlers in America from Norway & Sweden:

Eleanor Thompson Asphyxiation & Marie Wick Murder & Gummer Trial.

Eileen Tronnes Nelson—(Paperback) Edition 2, October 28, 2023.

Eileen Tronnes Nelson—(eBook) Edition 2, October 28, 2023.

Deborah E. Nelson & Grandsons' Theodore & Amos (Photograph on Cover).

Vanessa Fettig, Art Teacher, Sketches of Eleanor Thompson, Marie Wick, William Gummer, H. W. "Hjalmer" Swenson, Ralph F. Croal, and Peter Levins.

Kacie Johnson, Curator: Ghost Tour, Bonanzaville, West Fargo ND (Oct. 2017) (I found Marie Wick portrayed at Ghost Tour.).

Table of Contents

In Memory of Marie Wick & Eleanor Thompson

IN MEMORY OF

MARIE PETRINE WICK

&

*ELEANOR THOMPSON

(*Eleanor's first name was Clara, but she preferred Eleanor.)

DEDICATION TO
NICOLE M. CHAMBERLAIN
(granddaughter) (proofreader/podcaster)

DEDICATION TO MY SONS, DAUGHTERS, & SPOUSES
DOUGLAS A. NELSON
DWIGHT D. NELSON (DARLENE)
DEBORAH E. NELSON
JULIE M. SCHANILEC (TIMOTHY)
ELEANORE M. TRONNES SORENSON (sister)
RONALD A. TRONNES, SR. (MARIE) (brother)

Sketches by Vanessa of
Marie & Eleanor

MARIE WICK AND ELEANOR THOMPSON
SKETCHES BY VANESSA

Introduction

Introduction

The first book of the series, *Settlers in America from Norway &*
Sweden: My Genealogy Techniques May Assist You, is the family history
of my Norwegian and Swedish ancestors found through genealogy
research. My hope is you will learn something from my experience and
research to assist with your family history research.

The second book of the series, *Settlers in America from Norway*
& Sweden: A Customized Itinerary Independent Travel 2018, is my
granddaughter, Jasmine M. Nelson and myself, Eileen Tronnes Nelson, traveling in Norway and Sweden.

The third and fourth books of the series, *Settlers in America from*
Norway & Sweden: Photos of Traveling in Norway & Sweden, is and
my granddaughter, Jasmine M. Nelson and myself, Eileen Tronnes
Nelson, photographs of traveling in Norway and Sweden. The original Keynote document is too large for one book, thus I divided the
travelogue book into three books.

The fifth book of the series, *Settlers in America from Norway &* *Sweden: Eleanor Thompson Asphyxiation & Marie Wick Murder &* *Gummer Trial*, is the family history of Marie Wick (18) who was murdered in the Prescott Hotel, 15 7th St. S., Fargo, North Dakota, and Eleanor Thompson (16) who died by asphyxiation of gas escaping from a defective hose in a Boarding House, 602 4th Ave. S., Moorhead, Minnesota.

My close relatives all deceased including my parents, Edna Mae Johnson Tronnes and Elmer Tronnes (Nielsville MN); my grandparents, Olga Victoria Johnson and Henning W. Johnson (Buxton ND); Bertha Møgedal Tronnes and Andrew Tronnes (Nielsville MN). I had no one to interview about family history and did not even know the names of great grandparents and other relatives. Thus, I did extensive research on my own of Norway, Sweden, Minnesota, and North Dakota records. I interviewed, Valerie Tronnes, a relative recently known to me, and a great great granddaughter of Andreas Tronnes (Andreas, Theodore, Edwin, Vernon), Andreas is also my great great grandfather (Andreas, Ole, Andrew, Elmer).

In 2018, my granddaughter, Jasmine M. Nelson, before studying in Europe, wanted to travel for eleven days near where the Tronnes/Møgedal families lived in Norway and the Johnson families in Sweden. Although, at the time, my research only revealed the general location where the relatives lived, after arriving in Stavanger, Norway, traveling along the southern coast of Norway, and departing from Goteborg, Sweden. A section in the first book includes photographs and more on our traveling in Norway and Sweden.

Family history is genealogy plus much more. Genealogy is not about just doing research, it is about telling the stories and ensuring that your ancestors' legacies live on for generations to come. Doing the research is fun but remember you have been chosen to tell their stories. ("Don't Die with Your Stories Still in You," No. 10, GotGe nealogy.com's Golden Rules of Genealogy, PO Box 10805, Oakland, CA,).

In memory of those relatives providing valuable information and now deceased Muriel Tronnes Sheridan (1927-2023), Vernon L. Tronnes (1924-2020), Larry D. Haugen (1945-2020), and Doris Teigland Smeby (1927-2016). Doris is not a relative but lived in rural

Grygla, Minnesota, near my great uncle, Randolph Thompson and my great grandmother, Johanna Maria Knutsdatter Møgedal. Doris was the sexton of the Valle Cemetery.

My genealogy research took a massive turn, when researching and uncovering the tragic death of Eleanor Clara Thompson and Marie Petrine Wick. This book is written to honor the teenage girls.

Eleanor Clara Thompson, 16-year-old from Gygla, Minnesota, died October 8, 1933, asphyxiation from a defective hose leaking gas at a boarding house 602 4th Avenue South, Moorhead, Minnesota.

Marie Petrine Wick, 18-year-old from Grygla, Minnesota, died June 7, 1921, brutally raped and murdered, at the Prescott Hotel, 15 7th Street South, Fargo, North Dakota.

Eleanor Clara Thompson is a cousin of my father, Elmer Tronnes. Her father, Randolph Thompson is a brother to my grandmother, Bertha Mogedal Tronnes.

Marie Petrine Wick is related to me through marriage. Marie's two brothers, Matt Wick and Elmer Wick married Eleanor's two sisters, Mildred Thompson and Beatrice "Betty" Thompson.

The following is the research I found on the Tønnes Tobias Rasmussen and Johanna Knutsdatter Møgedal Family (Mogedal, Vest-Agder, Norway), Randolph and Sophia Hilton Thompson Family, and the Hans and Katrina Brevik Wick Family.

Eleanor Thompson's Parents & Siblings

T he following is the research I found on the Tønnes Tobias Rasmussen and Johanna Knutsdatter Møgedal Family and Randolph and Sophia Hilton Thompson Family.

EILEEN TRONNES NELSON'S GREAT GRANDPARENTS TØNNES & JOHANNA AND MY GRANDMOTHER, BERTHA MØGEDAL TRONNES.

Tønnes Tobias Rasmussen born in Vest-Agder, Norway 1926-1885 (died in Norway)

Johanna Maria Knutsdatter Møgedal born in Helleland, Rogaland, Norway 1844-1926

Marriage 12 April 1866 Helleland, Rogaland, Norway

Children (6) all born in Helleland, Rogaland, Norway

Kørnelius Tønnesen Møgedal 1866–1909

Andrew Tønnesen Møgedal 1868-1954

Bergine "Gina" Olava Tønnesdatter 1870-1970

Bertha Møgedal Tronnes 1871-1949 (Eileen Tronnes Nelson's grand-mother)

Teodor Bertinius Tønneson 1875-1875

Randolph Thompson 1882–1982

Marie Wick's Parents & Siblings

**ELEANOR THOMPSON'S 2 SISTERS, MILDRED THOMP-
SON & BEATRICE THOMPSON MARRIED
MARIE WICK'S 2 BROTHERS, MATT WICK & ELMER
WICK.**

Hans A. Wick, born in Nordland, Norway 1876-1949

Katrina Olea Marie Brevik, born in Nordland, Norway 1880-1968

Marriage 1899 Perley, Norman County, MN

Children (7) all born in Minnesota

Arne Christopher Wick 1901-1959

Marie Petrine Wick 1903–1921 (brutally murdered in Fargo, ND)

Mathias "Matt" Andrew Wick 1907–2000 (Spouse Mildred Josephine
Thompson 1915-2009)

Kay Wick 1909–1990

Helen Olea Wick 1912–2000

Harold Philip Wick 1915–2000

Elmer Martin Wick 1917–1971 (Spouse Beatrice "Betty" Adella
Thompson 1922-2017)

Note: Another tragedy for Katrina Wick is her husband, Hans A.
Wick, passed away on March 7, 1949, on the same day as the funeral
for Katrina's mother, Gjertrud Marie Hoff Ottesson Brevik. Gjertrud
Brevik died March 2, 1949 (94-95 years Old).

Eleanor Thompson Asphyxiated 1933

ELEANOR THOMPSON ASPHYXIATED

Eleanor Thompson is a cousin to my father, Elmer Tronnes. Bertha Tronnes, my grandmother, is a sister to Randolph Thompson, Eleanor's father.

Moorhead Daily News [Moorhead, Minnesota], Vol. 50, Mon., Oct. 9, 1933, pp.1,6. Print.

———

HIGH SCHOOL GIRL ASPHYXIATED
IN MOORHEAD HOME
ELEANOR THOMPSON DIES
IN SLEEP AS FUMES FILL ROOM

———

BROKEN RUBBER HOSE CONNECTION BELIEVED
RESPONSIBLE FOR DEATH.

———

Coroner's Jury Says It was Accidental;

Girl Had Been Living With Sister (Mildred), Also Student.

———

[Eleanor is the name she always preferred and used instead of her first name, Clara.]

———

"Clara Eleanor Thompson, 16-year-old Moorhead high school junior was asphyxiated early Sunday in a room at 602 Fourth Avenue South [Moorhead, MN], after she had retired for the night without detecting the hiss of escaping gas from a broken connection.

Her sister, Mildred, a student at the Moorhead State Teachers college, found her in a dying condition about 2:15 a.m. Sunday. Eleanor died enroute in an ambulance.

Mildred, who had just returned from a dance, did not detect the odor of gas when she went upstairs, but when she opened the door of housekeeping room which she and her sister occupied, she saw the body lying on the floor beside the bed and a strong odor of the poisonous fumes met her.

Hold Inquest

An inquest was conducted today by Walter C. Wright, Clay county coroner and a verdict of accidental death by asphyxiation was reached, numerous witnesses were called to determine how the girl had met death and it was decided that a rubber hose connection had been accidentally broken. Members of the coroner's jury were Carl J. Peterson, Leonard Heart, J.D. Beckman, Thomas Curran, Gust Ekland, and W.H. Onstine. Witnesses were questioned by County Attorney James A. Garraty.

Mildred, testifying at the inquest said she and her sister had engaged the room from Mrs. Evelyn Evander September 3 and the two sisters kept house there while they went to school. They are daughters of Mr. and Mrs. Randolph [Sophia] Thompson, Grygla, Minnesota.

Saturday night, Mildred Thompson said she left for a dance with her friend Clara Levang and returned about 2:15 a.m. When she opened the door of the room saw the body of her sister on the floor and smelled the gas, she ran to the gas connection used by the girls in cooking meals and turned off the jet. The jet was sometimes left open, but a rubber hose attachment ran through the wall to a gas stove in the hall where the meals were cooked, and the gas at times was shut off at the stove.

Heard Hissing

She heard a hissing sound she said and that stopped almost completely when she turned off the jet. Then she ran into the hall screaming for help. Frances Eastman and Alice Koster, two other Teachers college students, occupied another room adjoining and they carried Eleanor from the room out into hall and then took her downstairs to the porch in an attempt to revive her in the fresh air.

Mildred ran to E.D. Tucker residence, 614 Second Avenue South, to call the doctor and waited there for him, returning with him to the Evander residence. An ambulance was called, but Eleanor died enroute to St. Luke's Hospital in Fargo.

Roscoe Brown, a patrolman testified that he and Henry Hammerud, another patrolman, received a call from Mr. Tucker about 2:45 a.m. and went to the Evander house. They arrived just as the ambulance was leaving. Dr. G.L. Goslee and Dr. J.M. Heimark were there. Brown said that he found the rubber hose connection had been broken off completely and was lying on the floor, but there was no gas escaping from the jet. Bed coverings were scattered on the floor, he said.

Was Dying

The two doctors testified that Eleanor was dying when they examined her. Dr. Gosslee said the girl apparently had been breathing the gas fumes several hours. Dr. Heimark said the odor of gas was very strong when he entered the room.

Mrs. Evelyn Evander, the landlady, said she had been home all evening and when she was retiring about 11 p.m. She heard a noise in Eleanor's room, but took no notice. She was awakened when Mildred came into the hall screaming 'She's been gassed, she's been gassed.'

Victor Tufford, 16, of Fargo, a cousin of the Thompson girls, testified he and Robert Ripley, another Fargo boy, had visited Eleanor earlier in the evening. Eleanor was sitting on the porch talking to several other girls and was getting ready to go out, Victor said. So the boys went upstairs to visit with Mildred for a while, then left on their bicycles. They met Eleanor and another girl on Sixth street and returned to the house with them, giving the girls a ride on their wheels. The boys visited their cousin and her friend in the room until about 9:25, meantime going down to the store to get some apples and candy.

Alice Koster and Frances Eastman, the other two student roomers, told of being awakened by Mildred and of helping carry Eleanor downstairs.

Was Old Connection

A.J. Schmitz, gas fitter for the Northern States Power company, said he examined the broken fitting Sunday and that it was his opinion the connection was broken by the day bed upon which the girls slept. The girls had to pull out the bed every night to make it up. The gas jet, he said, protruded several inches at right angles from the wall and the bed apparently had struck it and broken the rubber connection. The rubber was badly deteriorated, Schmitz said, and apparently had been used for several years. It had been broken before, he said, and had been given makeshift repairs with wire which was wound around the tube.

Eleanor was born at Grygla, [Minnesota] May 25, 1917 and attended grade school there. Because her sister was attending the Teachers' college, she came to Moorhead this fall to room with her and to attend high school here. She had been attending high school at Thief River Falls previously.

Surviving, besides her parents, are another sister, Corrine, a student nurse at St. Luke's hospital in Fargo, and two sisters at home, Beatrice, 10, and Marion, 8, and two brothers, Richard, 13, and Clifford, 5, at home.

The body will be taken to Grygla [Minnesota] where funeral services will be held Thursday, at 1 p.m. from the family home and at 2 p.m. in the Norwegian Lutheran church. Rev. S.T. Anderson, pastor, will officiate and burial will be in the Valley [Valle] Cemetery there [rural Grygla, Minnesota]."

OBITUARY

CLARA ELEANOR THOMPSON

"Eleanor Thompson was born May 25, 1917, in Lee township, Beltrami Co. [Grygla, Minnesota], passed away Sunday morning October 8, 1933 at Fargo, N. Dak. at the age of 16 years, 4 months and 26 days. Most of the girl's life was spent in this community, having lived with her parents on a farm about two and a half miles south each of here until the last three years, while the has been attending High School at Thief River Falls and Moorhead. Eleanor, [the name she always used] was a kind, good natured person, whose ever-smiling face and contented personality could induce the friendship of anyone who met her.

Funeral services were conducted at her home and at the Valle church where she was baptized and confirmed. Interment was made at the Valle church cemetery Thursday afternoon, October 12, 1933. Several hundred friends attended to bestow their last respects. The church was fittingly decorated and the array of flowers presented by dozens of friends from Thief River Falls, Moorhead, Nielsville, and Fargo was beautiful. The St. Petri Church [Nielsville, Minnesota] choir sang 'Under Thy Wings,' and 'God Be With You Till We Meet Again,' was sung by Olaf Anderson. The Rev. S. Anderson conducted the service and spoke in both the English and Norwegian language.

She leaves to morn her passing, her parents, Mr. & Mrs. Randolph [Sophia] Thompson, four sisters, Corrine, of Fargo, N.D., Mildred, Moorhead, and Beatrice and Marion at home and two brothers Richard and Clifford at home.

The Pallbearers were: Morris Haney, Gordon Rud, Matt Wick, Peder Windsnes, Kernel Paulson, and Olaf Anderson.

The entire community extends to Mr. & Mrs. Randolph [Sophia] Thompson and family their deepest sympathy."

———————

By request of the mourners we are publishing the following:

"Yes, Dear Eleanor, you have left us,

Left us, Yes, forevermore:

But we hope to meet our loved one,

On that bright celestial shore."

Moorhead Daily News [Moorhead, Minnesota], Vol. 50, Mon., Oct. 9, 1933, pp.1,6. Print.

Eleanor Thompson Research

ELEANOR THOMPSON
PARENTS: RANDOLPH & SOPHIA THOMPSON
RANDOLPH IS A BROTHER TO MY GRANDMOTHER,
BERTHA MØGEDAL TRONNES

I remember, my father, Elmer Tronnes, telling me it was his cousin, who was murdered in Fargo. I assumed she was a daughter of Randolph Thompson, but I did not know her name. In May 2017, John Hallberg, NDSU Archives found Randolph's obituary that listed a daughter preceding him in death and her name was Eleanor Thompson.

I researched Eleanor Thompson at the Clay County Historical Society in the Hjemkomst, Moorhead, MN. Mark Peihl, archivist found newspaper articles that Clara Eleanor Thompson (16) died from gas escaping from a defective hose in the boarding house at 602 Fourth

Avenue South, Moorhead, October 8, 1933. Thus, my father's cousin, I thought was murdered, was not murdered in Fargo. My research now focused on Eleanor Thompson. I learned that she did not like the first name Clara, and wished to be known as Eleanor Thompson. I am writing this book to honor and remember Eleanor Thompson my first cousin (once removed) (Elmer, Eleanor, Eileen).

Ghost Tour Bonanzaville

GHOST TOUR – BONANZAVILLE
WEST FARGO, ND, OCTOBER 2017
RESEARCH & TRANSCRIPT
by
KACIE JOHNSON (Curator, Bonanzaville)
(UND History Graduate) (NDSU Graduate Student in 2017)
I received the following transcript from Kacie Johnson after the Ghost Tour.

"Ghost Tour" at Bonanzaville

"*Guide, walking to the first location*: Most of the stories you hear tonight are based on real events that happened right here in North Dakota. We have several stops planned for the evening that will showcase North Dakota's dark history."

Ghost Tour Continued

GHOST TOUR TRANSCRIPT (MARIE WICK-GRYGLA, MN) – Continued

Three ghoulish figures each stand beside a thombstone in front of the Church in Bonanzaville. Guide leads group to stand around the three. The first one steps forward and begins to speak. She is dressed in 1920's garb, has a bloody wound on her head and is holding the nozzle to a fire house. Bloody ropes dangle around her wrists.

"*My name is Marie Wick*: I was 18-years-old the day I died (June 7, 1921). I was on my way to visit my aunt and Fargo was an overnight stop. I got a room at the Prescott Hotel. Later that night, a man came to my room and physically & sexually assaulted me, tying me to the headboard. Two women heard noise coming from my room, but did not investigate. The man left and I managed to get one of my wrists free, but he came back before I could fully escape.

Ghost Tour Continued

GHOST TOUR TRANSCRIPT (MARIE WICK-GRYGLA, MN)-Continued

He retrieved the brass nozzle from the fire hose in the hall and bludgeoned me to death with it. I managed to rip several hairs from his head, but I was still bound and he was too strong. After I died, he laid me out on the bed, covered me in a blanket, and wrapped my head in a towel. The next morning when I did not respond to the 6 am wakeup call I had requested, the hotel clerk, William Gummer, found me. Under pressure to solve my murder, authorities arrested Gummer. He was found guilty and sentenced to life in prison. It was not until 23 years later that my real murderer, Blackie Carter (aka Paul C. Welch) was found and Gummer was released."

The story has more twists and this book I am writing about Marie Wick.

Ghost Tour Continued

MARIE WICK, GRYGLA, MN – Continued

The preceding Bonanzaville "Ghost Tour" transcript is how I found out about the girl, I mistakenly thought my father said was his cousin, who was murdered at the Fargo hotel, now known to me as, Marie Wick. Marie Wick lived in rural Grygla, Minnesota, and probably attended the rural Valle School and Valle Lutheran Church with Randolph Thompson's children, who are my father's cousins.

A few years later, Marie Wick's 2 brothers, Matthew Wick and Elmer Wick married, Randolph Thompson's daughters, and my father's 2 cousins, sisters of Eleanor Thompson, Mildred Thompson and Beatrice Thompson.

NOTE: Marie Wick's parents, Hans Wick and Katherine Brevik Wick both immigrants from Nordland, Norway.

Synopsis

E leanor Clara Thompson (16), Grygla, Minnesota, asphyxiated from leaking gas, October 8, 1933, in a boarding house at 602 Fourth Avenue South, Moorhead, Minnesota. The house was about several blocks directly south of Moorhead Public Library.

Marie Petrine Wick (18), Grygla, Minnesota, brutally raped and murdered, June 7, 1921, in the Prescott Hotel, 15 Seventh Street South, in Fargo, North Dakota. The Prescott Hotel is a half a block south of Main Avenue near Island Park pool.

Eleanor Clara Thompson is the daughter of Randolph and Sophia Hilton Thompson. Randolph is the son of my great grandmother, Johanna Møgedal/Thompson. Randolph was born in Helleland, Norway. My grandmother, Bertha Møgedal Tronnes is a sister to Randolph Thompson.

In 1922, the Prescott Hotel clerk, William Gummer (23), Mayville, North Dakota, was found guilty of the murder of Marie P. Wick and spent nearly 24 years in prison, until his sentence was commuted in December 1944.

Marie Petrine Wick is the daughter of Hans Wick and Katrina Brevik Wick of Grygla MN. Hans and Katrina are Norwegian-born from Nordland, Norway.

In about 1901, Terence Martin sold the Martin Hotel to William Prescott. In 1913, Prescott sold the Prescott Hotel and went through several owners before S. A. and Anna Case. In 1922 the Prescott Hotel was sold to David Shields and became the Shields Hotel. The YWCA took over the building in 1942, it was torn down in 1977, and is now a parking lot. Lillian Frances Kjersten Smith of Nielsville, Minnesota, 2019 obituary states she stayed at the YWCA when she was an elevator operator in the DeLendrecie's Building across the street. I wish I would have known and could have visited with her about the Prescott Hotel.

State v. William Gummer Files Missing

S TATE v. WILLIAM GUMMER: ALL FILES, EXCEPT 500 PAGES OF SHORTHAND LANGUAGE NOTES, MISSING, EITHER MISFILED, OR TAKEN FROM THE NORTH DAKOTA STATE ARCHIVES IN BISMARCK.

All documents, except about 500 pages of shorthand language notes from the *State vs. William Gummer* case are missing from the North Dakota State Archives in Bismarck, ND. James Davis said all files and exhibits contained in the large file was either misfiled or someone took all the documents in Binder File 3744 1/2 in Large Files. C.C.B. No. 364 received from the Clerks of Barnes County District Court on February 27, 1922, and September 1928, all files and exhibits contained in the large file including photographs, blue prints, drawings, affidavit, correspondence, trial transcripts, parole board, etc. Thus, as a result of the missing files, I spent many years researching to obtain the information on what happened to Marie Wick and William Gummer.

The *Daily Times Record* mentions the prosecutor, Cass County State's Attorney William Green, had been a court reporter and fluent in shorthand language. Green wrote shorthand language notes during the investigation and discussions with William Gummer. I am assuming the 500 pages are Green's shorthand language notes. However, I am currently unable to transcribe William Green's shorthand language writing, but later may attempt to transcribe the shorthand notes and publish the shorthand pages in "Mystery of Shorthand Notes" in the series of my genealogy research.

North Dakota State Archives

T he North Dakota State Archives, Bismarck, ND, sent me a copy of the following from the William Gummer file:

"The North Dakota State Archives, Bismarck, ND

Received Binder:

Files as 3744 1/2 in Large Files.

C.C.B. No. 364

No. 00185 1/2

DISTRICT COURT,

Fifth Judicial District

Barnes County, N. Dak.

State of North Dakota, Plaintiff against

William Gummer, Defendant

Minute Book No. 3, Page 214 to 222 incl.

Judgment Book No. 13 Page 58-79-80

2-27-22

No. 3744 1/2,

State of North Dakota vs. William Gummer.

Received from L.E. Sansburn, Clerk of the District Court of Barnes County, North Dakota, the following papers in the above entitled use, for which we agree to become personally responsible:

All files and exhibits contained in large file and including photographs, blue prints,, drawings, affidavit, correspondence, etc.

Also transcript of testimony in Justice Court in said case.

Dated September 1928. Chas. Swenson, Attorney for Defendant. and

Received of Harry N. Olsby, Clerk of the district Court of Barnes County, North Dakota, the following papers: All files and exhibits in large filing cases under No. 3744 1/2 in the above entitled case, for which we agree to become personally responsible until the same shall be returned."

Cass County State's Attorney Birch Burdick

CASS COUNTY STATE'S ATTORNEY
AND
BARNES COUNTY STATE'S ATTORNEY'S OFFICE

Birch Burdick, Cass County State's Attorney, about the William Gummer file, and files 50 years and older are no longer stored in Cass County unless it is determined that the case may need to be accessed for some reason.

The Barnes County Clerk of Court said the file is no longer in Valley City, and that everything was sent to the North Dakota State Archives.

Penny Miller, Clerk, North Dakota Supreme Court found in the archives, *State v. Gummer*, 51 N.D. 445, 200 N.W. 20 (N.D. 1924) case, briefs filed by the prosecution and defense for the appeal. Penny Miller emailed me a copy of the briefs and the Gummer case.

Ted Smith, North Dakota Supreme Court Library, said the library does not have the North Dakota Brief Report volume on the *Gummer* case.

David Haberman, UND Law Library, Grand Forks, ND, said the law library does not have the North Dakota Brief Report volume on the *Gummer* case. The older books have been thrown out because of space constraints.

The North Dakota State Parole Board does not have any records on the William Gummer case. All files and documents were sent to the North Dakota State Archives. However, the North Dakota State Archives does not have the files from the State Parole Board. I am assuming these files would have been in the file box that is either misfiled or someone took all the files.

Newspapers

For this book on the trial of William Gummer for the murder of Marie Wick, I took pictures on my iPhone of all the newspaper articles on the 1922 Gummer trial in Valley City, North Dakota. I typed all articles for this book from the newspaper articles.

- *Bismarck Tribune*, Bismarck, North Dakota

- *Daily Times-Record*, Valley City, North Dakota

- *Daily News*, New York, New York

- *Fargo Forum*, Fargo, North Dakota

- *Moorhead Daily News*, Moorhead, Minnesota

- *Warren Sheaf*, Warren, Minnesota

Gummer Trial to be Opened Here Tomorrow

D AILY TIMES—RECORD [Valley City, ND], Vol. XVI—No. 205, Mon., Jan. 16, 1922, at p.1. Print.

GUMMER TRIAL TO BE OPENED HERE TOMORROW

Change of Venue Brings Case Before
Barnes County Jury

BRUTAL MURDER CASE IN COURT

Charged With the Brutal Murder of
Pretty Marie Wick in Fargo on June 7. Denies Guilt

"William Gummer, 22, will be brought before a Barnes County jury tomorrow on a charge of first degree murder in connection with the death of Miss Marie Wick, of Grygla, Minn, at Fargo on June 7.

The finding of the body of Marie Wick, 18, in a room at the Prescott hotel in Fargo, on June 7, 1921, and the brutal manner in which she had met her death, created a sensation throughout the northwest. The authorities were notified and started an investigation which resulted in the arrest of William Gummer on June 15. Mr. Gummer had been night clerk at the hotel at the time of the murder, and seemingly gave the authorities all the assistance possible in their effort to bring the perpetrator of the crime to justice. However, circumstances pointed to the fact that Gummer knew more of he crime than he had told and his arrest, on the complaint of States Attorney William Green, followed. The prisoner has stoutly maintained his innocence at all times, but after the preliminary hearing held in Fargo, at which time a mass of incriminating evidence was presented he was bound over to district court. His trial was to have been at Fargo in the Cass County term in November but Gummer, through his attorneys, asked for a change of venue claiming that, with the feeling in Fargo and vicinity it would be impossible to obtain a jury which would give him a fair and impartial trial. His request was granted by Judge Cooley and the case was transferred to the Barnes county term which opens here tomorrow.

States attorney William Green of Fargo will prosecute the case and the defense will be represented by W. H. Barnett and Clair Brickner of Fargo.

Sheriff Kraemer will arrive in the city on No. 3 tonight with the prisoner, William Gummer and Andy Brown, a material witness arrested by the state last September, who has been held in the Cass county jail pending the trial.

It is expected that tomorrow's session of the court will be occupied in full by the selection of the jury."

DAILY TIMES—RECORD [Valley City, ND], Vol. XVI—No. 205, Mon., Jan. 16, 1922, at p.1. Print.

———————————

Daily Times-Record Synopsis Every Day

P.R. Trubshaw, Editor, DAILY TIMES-RECORD [Valley City, ND], Vol. XVI—No. 205, Mon., Jan. 16, 1922, at p.1. Print.

"The Gummer trial opens up in this city tomorrow and will probably last for some time. There are about a hundred witnesses to be called in the case. It is the intention of the Times-Record to try and give a synopsis of the proceedings of this trial from day to day in the columns of this paper, but it is also our intention to leave out any testimony that in our judgment is unfit for publication. We do not believe in giving publicity to this kind of testimony anyway, but the other daily papers of the state coming into this city will have full reports of the case and it is only reasonable that our own subscribers will want something in the home paper. We had some time ago decided not to give any testimony in this case in our columns but under the circumstances we cannot very well refuse to do so—but it will be censored rigidly so that nothing will be published of an unfit nature."

P.R. Trubshaw, Editor, DAILY TIMES-RECORD [Valley City, ND], Vol. XVI—No. 205, Mon., Jan. 16, 1922, at p.1. Print.

Gummer Case Now at Courthouse

D AILY TIMES—RECORD [Valley City, ND], Vol. XVI—No. 206, Tues., Jan. 17, 1922, at p.1. Print.

GUMMER CASE IS NOW ON AT THE COURTHOUSE

WILLIAM GUMMER THE DEFENDANT AT THE BAR NOW BEFORE THE COURT TO PROVE HIS INNOCENCE OR THE STATE TO PROVE HIS GUILT. WHICH WILL IT BE?

"William Gummer breaks his silence and tells what took place in the Prescott hotel on the night of June 7th.

This is the question asked by those familiar with the details of the fiendish murder of Marie Wick, pretty seventeen year old girl of Grygla, Minn, who was raped and brutally murdered in a Fargo hotel where she had stopped overnight on a vacation trip into North Dakota.

The January term of court convened at the courthouse in this city this morning at 10 o'clock with Judge Chas. M. Cooley, senior judge of this district presiding. There are forty-four cases on the calendar outside of the Gummer case, which of course is the case of the most interest, not on to people here in Barnes county, to all the people of the state. Fifty jurors have been called in the regular panel and whether or not a jury for this case can be secured from this panel will depend very largely upon the jurors as to what they read or heard of the case. Nearly everybody reads a newspaper these days and there are few men who have not heard or read something of this terrible murder. This does not necessarily mean that all have formed an opinion the probable guilt or innocence of the defendant Gummer, but the crime was so revolting that it caused a wave of deep seated resentment to sweep over the state and what the people want of justice done to the one guilty of so foul a crime. There is a large array of witnesses for the state and the case will be fought to a finish on both sides.

Morbid curiosity to get a look at the young man who is held for this terrible crime, drew out a great big crowd of curious people last night to watch the incoming of train No, 3 on the Northern Pacific on which Sheriff Kraemer, of Cass county, was coming with is prisoner and the state's most important witness, Brown.

Gummer is rather a prepossessing looking young man, of 22 or 23, and does not look like a fellow who would be guilty of committing such a heinous crime. As he stepped from the train with the sheriff into the vast throng surging on the depot platform, a smile broke over his countenance but soon vanished as his mind got back to the ordeal that was before him. It is not the province of a newspaper to try the case in its columns before the evidence has been produced before the jury, and it will be our endeavor to keep any coloring out of our reports. The only one thing that the *Times-Record* wants to see is the person or persons who have been guilty of so brutally and heinously taking the life of this young woman in their desire to satisfy the cravings of their neatly lust, be brought to the bar of justice and convicted. We do not want an innocent party convicted but we do want the guilty ones convicted. We believe that the defendant in this case can and will receive a fair and impartial trial at the hands of the judge and jury composed of Barnes county citizens, and whatever the outcome of the trial may be, the verdict must be taken as the verdict of twelve honest men who have given the case deep thought and study and who will have rendered their verdict from the evidence submitted as they have seen it. It is a hard duty for any juryman sitting on a case of this nature, where the crime is so revolting and where the people of the commonwealth are demanding that the culprit be punished to the limit of the law.

The January term of the Barnes county district court convened at 10 o'clock this morning with Judge Chas. Cooley presiding. The case of State of North Dakota was called immediately. William Gummer was brought to the court room at 9:55 by Sheriff Larson. He appears to be in good spirits, was neatly dressed and, considering the length of time he has been confined, he has good color. He appeared to be only slightly nervous. It was not necessary to arraign the accused as he had pleaded not guilty before Judge Cooley in November term of the Cass county district court.

The selection of a jury was taken up immediately, John B. Gieske, 51, farmer of Rogers being the first juryman to be called to the box for examination. He was excused owing to his inability to understand the questions put to him. Frank Steidl, farmer of the Fingal district was next called and temporarily accepted. Chris Olson, 25, farmer of Ypsilanti was the third juror called and was accepted. Carl Rasmussen, the court juryman called, was excused to an admitted prejudice against the accused. Pius Stroh, farmer, of Sanburn was excused owing to prejudice against the accused. R. R. Kane, the seventh juryman called for examination was still on the stand when court was adjourned at noon. Mr. Kane is a farmer, 28, married with three small girls, the elder of whom is five years old.

Judge Chas. M. Cooley, the senior judge of the first judicial district, is presiding at the trial. The prosecution is being handled by State Attorney Wm. C. Green of Fargo, Cass co. States Attorney L. S. B. Ritchie of this city, is assisting Mr. Green in the selection of the jury.

The defense is represented by W. H. Barnett of Fargo, Clair Brickner of Fargo, and H. W. Swenson of Devils Lake. Attorney A. P. Paulson of this city is assisting the defense in the selection of jury.

Clerk of Court Harry Olsby called the roll of the jury men all were with the exception of P. J. Gauche of Oriska. At the completion of the jury roll call the jury box was filled and the examination of the jurymen began.

The court room was only comfortably filled, most people realizing that the day's proceedings would be taken up with the selection of a jury. All minors are to barred from the court during the hearing of this trial. Others will be admitted only until the seats are filled, when the doors will be locked. Only two women were present at the morning session.

Morris Gummer, of Mayville, father of the accused, appeared, in the court room at 10:55, taking a seat with the spectators and taking a very keen interest the selection of the jury. Mr. Gummer, Sr., is a small man physically, but appears to be quite keen as was indicated by the way he sized up the jurymen called up for examination.

Hans Wick, father of Marie Wick, the murdered girl, was in the court room at the opening of court. He is tall, well dressed, and takes a lively interest in the proceedings. He was seated at the back of the court room during the morning session.

That the case is widely known is evidenced by the fact that all the jurymen so far examined have stated that they had read of the case in various papers and has followed developments closely. However, there seems to be little prejudice either for or against the accused, the general attitude being that opinions, as to the guilt or innocence of the accused, have not been formed on the evidence submitted at the preliminary hearing, the minds of the members of the jury panel and the spectators being open to conviction on the merits of the case as presented at this term of court.

Questions asked by State Attorney Green in the examination of the jurymen lead one to believe that the case is to be decided on circumstantial evidence which the state will present to show that the crime could not have been committed by anyone other than the accused.

William Gummer, the accused man, is a young, clean cut man of 22 years. He does not appear to be a man who would be guilty of the crime with which he is charged and appears quite nonchalant during the examination the jurymen, giving them a quick glance when they are called to the stand and appearing disinterested during the examination, especially the older jurymen called. He watched the younger jurymen closely and seems to take an interest in their answers to the questions asked. The men who have been temporarily accepted for jury duty in this case up to the time of going to press are as follows:

Frank Steidl, Fingal, farmer, married.

Chris Olson, Ypsilanti, 25, farmer, married.

Olaf Olson, Kathryn, stonemason. 47, single.

R. R. Kane, Spiritwood, 28, married.

Benny Larson, Litchville, 42, married.

Lloyd Sampson, Valley City, 34, farmer, married.

J. N. Green, Valley City, 72, retired farmer, married.

Martin Conlon, Eckelson, farmer, married, former County Commissioner.

Wm. Flach, Sanborn, farmer, married.

Ernest Ladbury, Dasey, 24, married."

DAILY TIMES—RECORD [Valley City, ND], Vol. XVI—No. 206, Tues., Jan. 17, 1922, at p.1. Print.

Gummer Jury Complete

D AILY TIMES—RECORD [Valley City, ND], Vol.
XVI—No. 207, Wed., Jan. 18, 1922, at pp.1,4. Print.

GUMMER JURY COMPLETE AT PRESS TIME TODAY

GREAT CARE BEING USED IN SELECTION OF JURY-
MEN. AT NOON TODAY FOURTEEN WERE IN THE JURY
BOX PASSED FOR CAUSE. TEN WERE DISMISSED THIS
MORNING.

"If my boy is guilty of the dastardly crime for which he is on trial
there is no one in the state of North Dakota more anxious that he
should pay the penalty than myself." — Morris Gummer

"The session of district court opened yesterday afternoon to a
packed courtroom. Every available chair was filled and there was a large
crowd in the hall waiting for a chance to gt inside. The crowd was
orderly and quiet at all times and took a keen interest in the selection
of the jurors.

The selection of the jurymen was taken up at the point where it was
when court adjourned at noon R.R. Kane, 28, farmer of Spiritwood

was passed for cause, making the fourth juryman returned to the box. The next juryman to be called was Bennie Larson, 42, farmer, married, of Litchville. After being questioned and answering that he was not prejudiced either way he was passed for cause. Andrew Frostad, 34, married farmer, of Kathryn was examined and admitted a prejudice in the case as a result of reading published accounts of the preliminary hearing at Fargo. He was excused. Lloyd Sampson, 34, married, farmer of Valley City declared that he knew very little of the case, was not prejudiced and did not have any antipathy toward conviction on circumstantial evidence. He was returned to the jury box. Jas. Burchill, Luverne, farmer, stated that he had formed no opinion as to the guilt of the accused which would take considerable evidence to change. He was excused. N.N. Green, 72, retired farmer, of Valley City, stated that he had formed no opinion which would interfere in any way with his giving a fair and impartial verdict and was returned to the jury box, making the seventh talisman chosen. Martin Conlon, farmer of the Eckelson district and former chairman of the board of county commissioners, stated that he had formed no opinions which would be detrimental to his acting as juryman was returned to the jury box. Wm. Flach farmer, of Sanborn was passed for cause, making the ninth man in the box. Ernest Ladbury, 24, farmer, married, of Dazey, could see no reason why he would be unable to give a verdict as indicated by the evidence and was returned to the box. E. C. Thompson, 60, farmer, married, of Sanborn, was passed by counsel and returned to the jury box. Fred H. Getchell farmer, 42, married, after being examined was returned to the jury box. E. J. Holcomb, farmer, married, of Valley City was temporarily accepted and returned to the box. Harry Peterson, 29, farmer, married, Leal, was temporarily accepted as were S. O. Carlson, flour and feed merchant, 40, single of Litchville and Cornelius Pederson, farmer, married of Dazey, making sixteen jurymen passed for cause. At this point court was recessed until ten o'clock this morning. The Jurymen thus far selected were instructed by Judge Cooley to refrain from any discussion of the case on trial and to refrain from reading any newspaper accounts of the trial or case so far brought to light, and dismissed for the night.

Gummer, now 23 years old is more than six feet tall. He has long arms with hands of unusual size and is very powerful.

As an illustration of his strength, officials recite that on a recent occasion in the county jail when Gummer had the freedom of the corridors with several other prisoners he demonstrated to his fellow prisoners something of his power by lifting five men at once. Gummer told his companions to cling to the bars of the sliding door of a cell and turning his back to the door taking hold of it by iron bars about knee high, Gummer lifted the door with its human burden fully an inch and a half, or the extent of the play of the door.

Gummer said that he had been born and raised at Mayville. His father's home, he says, is inside the corporate limits of Mayville, though he operates a farm adjoining the town coming to that county in the pioneer days.

The prisoner explained that a scar on his forehead was given to him by his "kid brother" and he volunteered the information that he had four brothers and three sisters.

"You came in Fargo about a month before this thing happened didn't you?" Gummer was asked.

"I had only been in the hotel ten days", he responded.

Gummer said he spent all of the summer of 1920 in Fargo and that he spent the winter of 1920 and 1921 largely at his home in Mayville. Several years ago he took a special course at the Minot Normal school and he also has been a student in the Mayville normal. The prisoner chatted freely of his high school days and asserted pride in his record as a basketball player on the Mayville High school team the year that team went into the district tournament at Grand Forks being eliminated by the Petersburg High school. Petersburg eventually winning the state championship that season.

"We beat Petersburg twice before the district tournament," said Gummer, "but they had the best team."

During the progressive's of selecting the jurymen the defendant was very much at ease only at such times some man stated that he had very firm convictions as to the guilt of the accused, this very naturally had the effect of rather disconcerting him some.

The prospects are that the jury will be completed this forenoon and from present indications a very good jury will be selected and we are quite confident that Mr. Gummer will be given a fair trial on its merits as presented to the jury by both the prosecution and the defense.

CRIMINAL INFORMATION

In District Court, First Judicial District

State of North Dakota

County of Cass

The State of North Dakota, vs. William Gummer, Defendant

Wm. C. Green, State's Attorney in and for the County of Cass and State of North Dakota. In the name and by the authority of the State of North Dakota, informs this court that heretofore, to-wit, on the 7 day of June, in the year of our Lord One Thousand Nine Hundred and Twenty-one, at the County of Cass in the State of North Dakota, one William Gummer, late of the County of Cass and State aforesaid, did commit the crime of Murder in the First Degree, committed as follows, to-wit:

That at the said time on in the City of Fargo, Cass County, North Dakota, the said defendant, William Gummer, did, willfully, unlawfully feloniously and deliberately, without authority of law, with a premeditated design to effect the death of the said Marie Wick, and with malice aforethought, choking her the said Marie Wick, with his, the said defendant's hands, and by gagging, strangling, suffocating and choking her, the said Marie Wick, with cloths placed by him in the mouth and throat of the said Marie Wick and by him wrapped about her face, mouth and nose, and by striking, bruising and beating the said Marie Wick upon the head with a certain fire-hose nozzle of metal, then and there held in his, the said defendant's hands; as a result of which striking, bruising, beating, choking, gagging, strangling, suffocating and other acts last above described; all done by the defendant William Gummer in the manner hereinbefore set forth; she, the said Marie Wick, did at the time and place aforesaid die.

And so the said defendant, William Gummer, did, in manner and form aforesaid, willfully, unlawful, feloniously and deliberately, without authority of law, with premeditated design to effect the death of the said Marie Wick, and with malice aforethought, at the time and place aforesaid, kill and murder her, the said Marie Wick.

This against the Peace and Dignity of the State of North Dakota, and contrary to the form of the Statutes in such cases made and provided.

Dated this 1st day of November A. D. 1921.

WM. C. GREEN,

State's Attorney in and for Cass County, North Dakota.

State of North Dakota

County of Cass

Wm. C. Green, of said County and State, being duly sworn, on oath says that he is State's Attorney in and for Cass County, North Dakota; that he has read the above and foregoing information and knows the contents thereof, and that he is informed and verily believes that the facts set forth therein are true, and from such knowledge information and belief he states the same to be true.

WM. C. GREEN

Subscribed and sworn to before me this 1st day of November, 1921.

R. F. CROAL

Clerk District Court, Cass County, North Dakota.

(Seal)

Names of Witnesses Known to State's Attorney at the Time of Filing Information:

Fred A. Kraemer, James Milligan, James South, Richard Pickering, Otto Nelson, Casper Nelson, William Welsh, Frank Campion, Morton Syndness, Dean Spalding, Howard J. Hess, Thora Ness, Arnold Rasmussen, Jennie Halgenseth, Robert Richards, Silas Stamnes, Anna E. Lawrence, Dr. Paul H. Burton, Dr. Harry J. Fortin, O. J. Johnson, Hans Wick, Arnie Wick, Fred Lawrence, John Towers, Albert Rosenwater, Mrs. Margaret Bergstrom, J. T. Smith, Lawrence Jacobson, Roy Simmons, Mrs. Roy Simmons, John J. Meyers, Pedro Christianson, Mitre Dychuk, C. E. Matlock, A. A. Starkson, John Westin, Charles Fisher, Geo. LaLonde, John VanVorst, May Helaas, Wm. C. Green, Augusta Onsum, J. K. Bingham, R. F. Croal, C. C. Wattam, E. P. Still, R. P. Bennett, Mrs. Elmer Hilliard, Mrs. G. Gustenson, R. H. Flaugher, H. J. Hagen, Wm. Nelma, Jessie Manning, Al. H. Leimbacher, J. F. Holmes, L. W. Hamm, W. P. Larson, E. M. Brandies, Elvira Hippke, Lillian Rosholt, Geo. O'Brien, John Collins, Olga Rieck, Alice Kruse, Roe E. Remington, E. F. Moore, Wm. C. Dennis, H. A. Poague, Al. McDonald, Nora Nelson, A. A. Starkson, Albert Kincaid, Theodore Strand, John Worden, Albert Morrison, David Shields, Marie Cutting, Andy Brown, C. S. Knight, Geo. E. Morrissey, Alphina Braaseth, Florence Powell, Phronie Stiegel, F. B. Courtney, H. W. Jones, L. Moen, R. Hines, M. Keller, A. J.

Manners, Chas. E. Taylor, Geo. Raymond, E. Collins, Walter Briggs, T. J. Eaton, Mrs. R. Hinds, E. W. Madison.

———————

The morning session of court opened at 10:00. The court was filled fully half an hour before court opened and guards were placed at the doors to prevent any more spectators crowding in. There was only one woman present at the morning session.

Chas. Pollock of Fargo, arrived in court this morning to assist States Attorney Wm. C. Green in the prosecution.

At the opening of court five talesmen selected yesterday were excused from duty in this case under peremptory challenges. The jurors dismissed were Benny Larson of Litchville, Olaf Olson, Kathryn, Frank Steidly, Kathryn, J. N. Green, Valley City, and Harry Peterson of Leal.

Peter Lee, Pillsbury, farmer, was placed on the stand and stated that he was married and had a family of twelve children, seven of whom were girls. The elder of the girls is 25 years of age. He admitted a strong prejudice against the accused, basing his prejudice on the fact that the defendant stood accused of the crime and must have some connection with the death of Marie Wick. He was challenged by the defense and excused from service in the case.

Oscar Dahl, tailor, married, Valley City, stated under examination that he was the father of two girls, 10 and 18 years of age but that this fact would not influence his judgement in passing a verdict in the case. He stated that he had formed no opinion as to the guilt or innocence of the accused and felt that he could return an impartial verdict. He was returned to the jury box.

Tobias Thompson, farmer, married, Litchville, stated that he was the father of two boys and two girl, the elder of which was 5 years old. He stated that he had formed a decided opinion as to the guilt or innocence of the accused which would require much testimony to change. He had never served on a jury before. He was returned to the box.

M. P. Krogh, Valley City, Clothing Merchant, took the stand and stated that he was the father of one girl 16 years old, and two boys, the elder of whom is 18 years old. He stated that he had formed an opinion as to the guilt of the accused from accounts of the case which he had read and could not enter the jury box with a free and unbiased mind unless considerable evidence was introduced different from that which he had read or heard regarding the case. He was challenged by the defense and dismissed from duty in the case.

John Mortenson, farmer, married, 59, Luverne, stated that he had two girls aged 18 and 21 respectively, and three boys, aged 17, 20, and 22. He had formed but slight opinions of the case from what he had heard but these opinions of the case and felt that he could enter the jury box and give impartial consideration to the evidence. However, he was challenged by the prosecution. The court denied the challenge and he was passed for cause.

Peter Rumer, 51, farmer, married, Wimbledon stated that he was the father of three girls aged 12, 16 and 24. The fact that he was the father of girls about the age of Marie Wick would not influence his judgment. He has had previous jury experience. Opinions formed were slight and could be easily put aside. Was familiar with the rules of the court regarding the presumption of innocence until the accused had been proven guilty by the evidence. He was returned to the jury box.

C. H. Farrell, farmer, 40, married, Valley City stated that he had a little daughter 4 years old. That he had been a resident of the county for 30 years. Had never had previous jury experience. No opinions on the case had been formed. He was passed for cause.

At this point five more jurors were dismissed under preemptory challenges. The ones dismissed with Tobias Thompson, Litchville, Cornelius Pederson, Dazey, E. C. Thompson, Sanborn, S. O. Carlson, Litchville, and W. H. Price of Wimbledon.

Louis A. Sunde was next called to the stand for examination. Mr. Sunde is a farmer, is single, has four sisters aged 16, 20, 24 and 26. He stated that he had formed no opinion as to the identity of the murderer of Marie Wick and was familiar with the rules governing the consideration of evidence by juries. He was passed for cause.

G. W. Ohm, farmer, 55, Lucca stated that he was the father of four children, the oldest girl being 17 years of age. He feels that, while he had formed an opinion as to the guilt or innocence of the accused, that opinion could be easily put aside and he could enter the jury box with a fair and open mind. He stated that the fact that he had a daughter of the age of Marie Wick at the time of her death would not influence his judgment in this case. He was returned to the jury box, making fourteen in the box at the time court was recessed for the noon hour.

Up to the noon recess today 32 members of the original jury panel had been examined. Of these 24 were passed for cause and returned to the jury box and eight were excused for various reasons, the principle on being an admitted prejudice for or against the accused. Ten of those passed for cause have been dismissed under preemptory challenges.

This afternoon the courtroom was jammed and hall was filled with eager sightseers who wanted to get into the courtroom but could not do so on account of lack of room A large percentage of these were women.

J.W. Dunham, of Tower City, farmer, married, had three boys and one girl, 26 years old, was first in the jury box this afternoon. He said his opinion had been formed and it would take considerable evidence to remove the same. He felt that his mind was in as fit condition for a juryman and did not feel as though he would like to have his son's liberty held in the hands of jurymen with his mind formed as he had mind formed. The defense challenged him and Mr. Green examined him and stated that his opinion was not more decided than any other notorious case given much publicity. Mr. Dunham said he would decide according to the evidence presented and that he would give an impartial verdict. The challenge was withdrawn and he was passed for cause.

V. A. Broby, Nome, merchant, married. Had a daughter 14. He had a strong opinion formed from published reports of the case which would bias his mind and it would require a great deal of evidence to remove his opinion. The attorneys consulted the defendant and after a consultation the challenge of the juror followed. Prosecution examined the juror. He told Prosecutor Green that he might consider what he had heard outside of court in addition to the evidence submitted in court and that it would be hard for him to act as a fair and impartial juror. Defense challenge allowed and juror excused.

P. J. Gauche, Oriska, farmer, married, had two girls 16 and 11 and two boys 22 and 7. He said his opinion had been formed and the condition of his mind was not as a juror's should be and felt that he could not act as an impartial juror. The defense challenged, which challenge was allowed, and the juror excused.

Christ Minsch, Dazey, farmer, 20 years a resident of Barnes county said he had no knowledge of the case and had formed no opinion. Had no prejudice against the accused and he was married and had a boy 27. Passed for cause.

The following were dismissed under preemptory challenge: E. J. Halcomb, Valley City; Oscar Dahl, Valley City; C. H. Farrell, Valley City; Jos. Mortenson, Luverne.

Fred Haarstad, Nome, farmer, married, oldest girl 10, oldest boy 21. Had formed an opinion but it was not strong enough so that he could not make a fair and impartial juror. He was passed for cause.

Theodore Thilmony, Pillsbury, farmer, was married and had ten girls, ranging in age from 9 to 28. Cannot read. He had formed an opinion only through hearsay and that he could make a fair and impartial juror. He was passed for cause.

As we go to press at 3:30 they were still examining jurors and there is little likelihood that the jury will be completed this afternoon, There are fifteen men now in the jury box who have been passed for cause.

Thirty-nine jurors out of the regular panel of fifty have been examined up to this time.

Henry Helmers of Wimbledon, a farmer, has a girl 20 years of age, stated he had no opinion formed as to the innocence or guilt of the accused and that he did not know of any reason why he could not act as a fair juror. He was passed for cause. Four more were dismissed on preemptory challenge. There are as follows: J. W. Dunham, Tower City; Herbert Rutherford, Page; S. Baarstad, Nome and Martin Conlon, Eckelson.

Special—Jury completed and sworn in at 4 p.m.

THE JURY
Christ Olson.
William Flach.
R. R. Kane.
Lloyd Sampson.
Louis A. Sunde.
G. W. Ohm.
Peter Rumer.

Peter Helmers.

Christ Minsch.

Earnest Ladbury.

Fred Getchell.

Theodore Thilmony.

The press of the state is well represented in the court room during the Gummer trial which is before the court now. The *Forum* is very ably represented by H. D. Paulson. The *Forum* is maintaining a leased wire service and "Happy" is ably assisted in his by a telegrapher and a stenographer. H. C. Darland, formerly editor *The People Opinion* in this city, is covering the case for the *Courier-News* of Fargo. The *Grand Forks Herald* is being represented by John Conley. Mr Cooley is the nephew of Judge Chas. M. Cooley who is presiding at this term of court. The interests of the *Times Record* and *United Press* are being looked after by Lynn Cowell."

DAILY TIMES—RECORD [Valley City, ND], Vol. XVI—No. 207, Wed., Jan. 18, 1922, at pp.1,4. Print.

MORRIS GUMMER N. D. PIONEER

Father of Accused Boy Hauled Supplies During the Construction of the Northern Pacific. Notes Old Camp Sites in the City.

Morris Gummer, the father of the accused boy on trial now before a Barnes county jury on a case of first degree murder in connection with the death of Marie Wick of Grygla, Minn in Fargo last June, stated to a *Times-Record* representative last night that he had hauled supplies over the present route of the Northern Pacific railroad during the surveying of the route in 1872, camping on the river at the present site of Valley City. He is quite familiar with this portion of the state and says that he could pick out several former camping sites in the valley here if had time to look around, although the country looks considerable different now than at that time.

Morris Gummer is a man of 75 years of age. He owns and operates a farm in the Mayville district and is quite a pre-bred hog fancier, owning a number of exceptionally good Duroc Jersey hogs. He expects his wife and two of his sons to arrive in the city tomorrow morning. They will stay in the city during the trial of his boy. Mr. and Mrs. Gummer have been blessed with a family of eight children, five boys and three girls. John Gummer, 40 and Goodman Gummer, 24, will accompany their mother to the city. Arthur Gummer, 37, is the present postmaster at Gilford, Mont. Charles Gummer, 30, is looking after Arthur's land at Gilford. Mrs. Oscar Thomas, 30, of Fresno, Mont., is a daughter of Mr. And Mrs. Gummer, as is Mrs. Elmer Hildebrandt of Shaefer, N. Dak.

In speaking of the charge for which his boy is on trial Mr. Gummer states that to the best of their knowledge the boy knows nothing of the manner in which Marie Wick met her death other than was submitted as evidence at the preliminary hearing. He said that the accused has told both his father and his mother that he does not know who committed the crime and while he feels the seriousness of the situation he is sure that his innocence will protect him. Mr. Gummer states he believes the boy because he has never caught him any direct lie in his life. Mr. Gummer also said that **"if my boy is guilty of the dastardly crime for which he is on trial there is no one in the state of North Dakota more anxious that he should pay the penalty than myself. I have been a God fearing man and law abiding citizen all my life and have brought my children up in the same way. Such a heinous crime should be punished, whether committed by my son or not"**.

Mr. Gummer has every confidence in the ultimate acquittal of his son and feels that they are sure to take him back to the farm at Mayville at the conclusion of the trial.

Mr. Gummer stands up under the strain of the past few months well and does not show much sign of the mental suffering to which he has been subjected. He states however, that Mrs. Gummer is on the verge of a nervous breakdown and he is as much concerned about the effect of the trial upon her as he is to the ultimate verdict in the case.

Mr. Gummer, during his talk with the *Times-Record* representative, became reminiscent and spoke of the life on the prairie at the time he was hauling supplies through the camping site of Valley City. He said the valley made an ideal camping spot but the Indians were too numerous for comfort and "had a habit of wanting to add to their collection of hair." Mr. Gummer moved the surveyors to the present site of Jamestown and assisted in the laying out of the original townsite there, moving them on to Bismarck and assisting in the same work at that place. Mr. Gummer says he assisted in the raising of the first bridge to be built across the Red River.

Mr. Gummer is an interesting talker and has a fund of interesting anecdotes of North Dakota's early days and has quite an original manner of telling them."

DAILY TIMES—RECORD [Valley City, ND], Vol. XVI—No. 207, Wed., Jan. 18, 1922, at pp.1,4. Print.

Third Day Gummer Trial Examining Witnesses

D AILY TIMES—RECORD [Valley City, ND], Vol. XVI—No. 208, Thurs., Jan. 19, 1922, at pp.1,4,5. Print.

THIRD DAY OF GUMMER TRIAL SPENT IN EXAMIN-ING WITNESSES

Several Witnesses for the State on Stand Today. The trial is Now Getting Well Under Way and the Work will Proceed Rapidly From This On.

"Immediately after the final selection of jurors yesterday afternoon States Attorney Green read the information filed against Wm. Gummer, defendant, in the case of the State of North Dakota vs. William Gummer, a copy of which was published in the *Times-Record* yesterday afternoon. This included the reading of the list of witnesses for the state which was attached. After completing the reading of this document Mr. Green outlined the general plan of the case which the state will present in their attempt to prove through witnesses the connection of the defendant with the death of Marie Wick in Fargo on June 7 last, and establish beyond doubt the fact that he was guilty of the murder.

Mr. Green began his address by stating that the case would be opened by the placing of witnesses on the stand who would establish the identity of certain plans of the Prescott Hotel which would be placed before the court as exhibits for the state. He pointed out the fact that the crime with which Gummer stands charged the 7 day of June, 1921. The Prescott hotel is a three and one half story brick building situate on 7 street South in Fargo, N. Dak. The first floor is given over to the offices and lobby of the hotel and the other floors are used for guest rooms.

Marie Wick was a young girl of 18 years last spring. She was a pretty girl, of good form. She had lived her life on the farm with her parents near Grygla, Minn., until about a year before her death. She had a common school education and had been employed in a bank at Grygla. She left the bank about a year ago and went to Warren, Minn, where she entered a business college. After finishing her course she returned to her home and took a position with the Grygla Co-Operative Store where she worked until she left on her vacation trip. Miss Wick had an aunt living at Pettibone and she decided to visit her. She left Grygla accompanied by her father, and went to Warren. While there she obtained a $20.00 cashier's check from the bank and returned to Grygla with her father where they stayed with an aunt over night. This was Sunday night. On Monday morning her father placed her on the train for Warren where she would connect with the Great Northern train for Fargo. She made connection and arrived in Fargo that night about 10:00 o'clock. She had written to Arnold Rasmussen of Moorhead, who was an old friend of the family, asking him to meet her at the station as she had never been in a large city and was nervous about arriving there with no one to help her. Mr. Rasmussen got on the train at Moorhead and rode over to Fargo with her, walking from the Great Northern depot to the N.P. Depot where Miss Wick inquired as to the leaving of her train in the morning. They then went to the Prescott hotel. Mrs. Lawrence, proprietress of the hotel was at the desk and she assigned her to room 30. Miss Wick asked for a six o'clock call but Mrs. Lawrence told her that 6:30 would give her plenty of time to make the train and the call was listed at 6:30. At this time Gummer came in the office from upstairs and Mrs Lawrence asked him to show Miss Wick to her room. She was in the room for 15 minutes and returned to the lobby where Mr. Rasmussen had been awaiting her return. They left the hotel together and walked along Front street to Broadway and up Broadway to the Broadway Confectionery store which they entered and obtained some ice cream and played the automatic piano, Miss Wick appearing quite interested in the piano, never having seen one before. They talked about the folks at home and returned to the hotel, Miss Wick changing her call to six o'clock and going to her room. Mr. Rasmussen returned to Moorhead and met a young lady, whom he was going with, at the restaurant where she worked. He was with her from 10:25 until 1:50 when he went to his room and went to bed with his room-mate. He did not hear of the tragedy until late Tuesday afternoon.

Mr. Green then stated that "we will show you by witnesses that the prisoner, Gummer, called Fred Lawrence, son of the proprietress, the next morning, stating that he had repeatedly called Miss Wick and that she did not answer and that he thought "something was wrong in 30". They went up to the door of the room and tried to get in but could not. They then placed a small table against the door and Lawrence looked over the transom, seeing Mss Wick lying on the bed with some rags soaked with blood over face. They called a chambermaid who opened the door and they entered, finding that Miss Wick had been brutally assaulted and apparently dead. They notified the police officials and a doctor who came and examined the deceased, pronouncing life extinct. About this time Sheriff Kraemer and States Attorney Green arrived at the hotel and a minute examination of the room and body was made. Miss Wick was lying on the bed with about two-thirds of a pillow case stuffed in her mouth as a gag, this being bandaged in place with strips torn from bed linen. The gag and bandages were soaked with blood. There were several cuts on the face and head, so many in fact that the undertaker was obliged to use 150 stitches in closing them. There were thumb and finger marks on her throat which indicated hat she had been choked. There were several bloody finger marks on the wall of the room made by Miss Wick in her struggles. The right hand was securely tied but the left hand was very loosely tied and had evidently been freed and re-tied later. There was a dent in the plaster about four and one half feet above the floor, above the bed. The doctor's examination showed that she had been assaulted and raped, the two acts being apparently committed at two separate times, and that life had been extinct from 4 to 6 hours. This was at nine o'clock in the morning. Testimony will also show that her belongings in two suit cases in the room was undisturbed but that only a few cents in change were found in her purse in the room. The state will show by evidence submitted just who were in the hotel that night according to the testimony offered and will account for any single men who were guests at the time by placing them on the stand and having them explain their movements during the night. Married couples occupying rooms or others who are easily accounted for will not be called as the state has evidence showing their alibi. The state will show, through the testimony offered by N.J. Hagen, that Gummer was confused and decidedly nervous when showing Mr. Hagen to his room, number 31, at 1:15 a.m. The state feels that Hagen was assigned to this room to cast suspicion on him. All guests registered at the hotel that night have been accounted for with the exception of one Jas. Farrell, of Wilmer, whom the register shows had been assigned to room number 40. He has disappeared. The authorities were furnished with a description of this man by the accused but no trace of any person has been found. The state will attempt to prove, by expert witnesses, the connection of the accused with the signature of Jas. Farrell on the hotel register. The state will show the motive for the crime and the method of committing it. They will show by two reliable and competent witnesses that the two acts of assault and rape were committed at two separate times, one at about 12:30 and the other shortly after 4:00 o'clock. They will show by testimony that Gummer's various statements, made at different times on the same points, do not agree. They will show that he lied. They will show his attitude of mind on the night in question through statements he made to his friend, Andy Brown, when discussing the occupant of room 30. They will show by connecting these circumstances that the crime was committed by the accused and could not have been committed by any other."

During States Attorney Green's address to the jury the defendant kept his eyes down and seemed to lose a part of his nonchalant attitude. His face flushed at times and he seemed more nervous that he has been at any time thus far. As soon as Mr. Green concluded he leaned over and spoke for minute with his attorney H. W. Swenson.

Immediately after Mr. Green's address to the jury Dean Spalding of Fargo was called to the stand. He stated that he was a civil engineer and was familiar with the Prescott Hotel, having been in the hotel in June and having taken several measurements and helped in the drawing of plans of the hotel the latter part of October at the request of States Attorney Green. He did this work in conjunction with Mr. Hess of Moorhead. He stated that the plan of the hotel, as regards the arrangement of rooms and location of windows and doors, was the same in October as the time of the tragedy. Particular care was taken in the measurements in room 30.

Howard J. Hess, architect of Moorhead, was next placed on the witness stand and identified a set of drawings and plans as being the measurements taken by Mr. Spalding in October. Mr. Spalding made the drawings and Mr. Hess wrote them down. The plans were made from the measurements thus listed. States Exhibit No. 1 was entered as the plan of the second floor, exhibit No. 2 as the plan of the first floor, No. 3 as the plan of the basement, No. 4 as the plan of the first floor, No. 5 as the plan of the fourth floor and No. 6 which is on the second floor, to the building. On being questioned by the defense M. Hess stated that the shortest possible distance from room 30, which is on the second floor, to the office on the first floor was approximately 150 feet.

Before announcing the recess until this morning Judge Cooley told the members of the jury who were not drawn on the Gummer case that were excused from attendance in court until the completion of that case. Shortly before the recess the Judge had occasion to speak sharply to several spectators who were edging toward the door and tell them to remain seated until court was adjourned.

At this point recess was taken until 10:00 o'clock this morning.

———————————

The seats in the court room were filled before nine o'clock this morning and the halls of the courthouse were crowded with people wanting to get into the court room to attend the trial. The court room was cleared of all those who could not find seats and the doors guarded on order of the court.

Before court convened Christ Minch one of the jurors was before Judge Cooley to clear up some point as to his ability. He returned to the jury box as court opened.

At the opening of court counsel for the defense asked the court to order all witnesses removed from the court room. A conference between the prosecutor and defense was had with Judge Cooley at the conclusion of which State Attorney Green read a list of witnesses and asked that they leave the room. This request was complied with and they retired to the jury room adjoining the court room.

Hans Wick, father of the murdered girl was the first witness called for the state. He stated that he resided with his family on a farm near Grygla, Minn., which is about 40 miles north east of Thief River Falls. He has 6 children living at the present time the elder of whom is a boy 20 years of age. Marie was the next oldest child of the family and was 18 years old in April, 1921. He stated that she had a common school education and had worked in the Grygla State Bank. After leaving the employ of the bank she had attended the North Star Business College at Warren, Minn., from September 1919 to June 1920. After leaving the business college she was employed in Grygla as clerk at the Grygla Co-operative store. She was described by her father as being a very healthy, strong girl weighing 137 pounds. She worked in Grygla until Saturday, June the fourth when she decided to take a vacation and visit an aunt who lives at Pettibone, N. Dak. Her father took her to Thief River Falls on Sunday where they visited with Mr. and Mrs. Berg, who are relatives of the Wick's. He stated that he had given her a check for $20.00 the last time she had been at the farm but was not in a position to say just how much more money she had at that time. Monday morning Marie Wick boarded the Soo Line train for Warren where she would take the Great Northern train for Fargo. Mr. Wick stated that this was the last time he had seen his daughter alive. At this point the witness broke down under the strain of his emotion and was excused from the stand after only one question by the defense.

O. J. Johnson, vice president of the Grygla State Bank was the next witness called. He stated that Marie Wick had entered the employ of the bank on January first, 1919, and had continued there until June first, 1919. He stated that he was familiar with the hand writing of the deceased and identified the handwriting in a letter and check book stub as the writing of Marie Wick. The letter, envelope and check book were placed in evidence by States Attorney Green. Mr. Johnson stated that he had seen Marie Wick on Saturday, June 4, when she cashed the check which her father had given her for $20.00. She purchased a cashier's check with the money received from her father's check. She cashed a check drawn on her personal account in the bank for $20.00. This money she took with her. This personal check has never been returned to the Grygla State Bank for payment, according to Mr. Johnson's testimony. Mr. Johnson described Marie Wick as a very steady and industrious girl who tended strictly to her own business and was not in the habit of paying much attention to young men.

Mrs. Elmer Hillyard was the third witness called and told of taking the Great Northern train at Lengree, Minnesota, her home, on the morning of Monday, June 6. She stated that Marie Wick got on the train at Crookston, Minn. She sat in the same seat with Mrs. Hillyard and her mother. Mrs. Hillyard said that Miss Wick paid no attention to anyone in the coach but talked to her seat companions. Mrs. Hillyard said that, after discussing the different hotels in Fargo they decided to stay at the Prescott and Marie thought she would also stay there. They separated at the Great Northern station in Fargo, Mrs. Hillyard and her party taking a taxi to the Prescott hotel where they stayed that night. Mrs. Hillyard left the hotel at 5:30 the next morning and has never seen Marie Wick since leaving her at the Great Northern station that night.

The witness remembers Arnold Rasmussen getting on the train at Moorhead and joining Miss Wick in the coach. She stated that they had arrived in Fargo at about 10 o'clock and went directly to the Prescott hotel, arriving there at approximately 10:30. They were assigned to room 30 on the third floor by the proprietress, Mrs. Lawrence.

At this point, Hans Wick was returned to the stand by the prosecution and was asked if Marie had ever been in a larger town than Warren, Minn., in which he replied that she had not.

Arnold Rasmussen gave his age as 22 and stated that home was near Grygla, Minn., that he knew the Wick family, they living about two and a half miles from his home. He had known Marie Wick for the past seven years but had never gone with her or accompanied her to any parties or dances. At the time of the tragedy he was living at Moorhead and working for a contractor at that place. He identified the latter, formerly placed in evidence by States Attorney Green as the letter received by him from the deceased. The letter was read to the jury and court by Green. The letter asked Mr. Rasmussen to meet Miss Wick at Fargo on Monday evening as she expected to arrive about 10 o'clock on a Great Northern train. She considered this making quite a favor but felt nervous going to such a large city alone in the night. She stated that she had asked Rasmussen's sister, Laura, if it would be alright to ask this favor of him and she had said that it would. The balance of the letter referred to the lack of social doings around Grygla and was signed 'lovingly, Marie Wick."

Mr. Rasmussen stated that he got on the Great Northern train at Moorhead and rode to Fargo with Miss Wick. Miss Wick had as baggage a suitcase and small grip. The witness assisted her with this baggage at the Great northern station and carried the same to the Northern Pacific station, in company with Miss Wick, where they inquired as to the leaving time of the Northern Pacific train on which Miss Wick intended to leave in the morning. From there they went to the Prescott hotel where Miss Wick was registered by Mrs. Lawrence. The defendant, Gummer, came into the office from upstairs at this time and Mrs. Lawrence asked him to take Miss Wick to room 30 which he did. The witness waited in the hotel lobby for the return of Miss Wick about fifteen minutes and when she came down stairs accompanied her to the Broadway Candy Store which they entered and ordered ice cream. While in the candy store the witness dropped a nickel in the automatic piano and noted that Miss Wick was quite interested in the instrument, never having seen one before. They talked of mutual acquaintances at Grygla and returned to the Prescott hotel where Mr. Rasmussen left Miss Wick outside.

Jack Smith a taxi driver was standing on the sidewalk outside the Prescott hotel when the witness left Miss Wick. Mr. Rasmussen walked back to Moorhead and entered the Panchot cafe where he met Miss Jennie Helgenseth who was employed at that place and who the witness had been going with. The witness had a lunch and accompanied Miss Helgenseth to the Lenord house garage returning to the Panchot cafe about 1:50 a.m. The witness then went to the Skandia hotel where he roomed. On entering he saw three men and one woman in the lobby of the hotel. One of them he later identified as Silas Stamnes. One of the men in the lobby was intoxicated and the witness accompanied him from the hotel and to a taxi cab and returned to the hotel lobby within a few minutes. He spoke to those in the lobby about the intoxicated man and went directly to his room and went to bed with his roommate where he was until 7 o'clock in the morning, going to work at that time. He did not learn of the death of Marie Wick until 7 o'clock Tuesday evening. He immediately reported to Sheriff Kraemer in Fargo and delivered to him the letter which he had received from Miss Wick, told of his movement the previous evening and returned to Moorhead. Council for the defense tried hard in the cross examination to confuse Mr. Rasmussen but his testimony remained unshaken.

Miss Jennie Halgenseth was the next witness called. She stated that she was 20 years of age and that her home was at Abercrombie, N.D Evidence taken from her substantiated Mr. Rasmussen's testimony regarding his movements after meeting her.

At this point a bulletin board was brought in and set up in front of the jury. Plans of the Prescott hotel, entered as evidence yesterday by the state were arranged on the board for reference after which States Attorney Green explained the plans to the jury.

Harry A. Paogue, photographer of Fargo to the stand and identified certain photographs, entered as evidence, as being photographs of the exterior of the Prescott hotel, taken by him last week at the request of States Attorney Green. A few questions were asked him by counsel for the defense after which he was excused for the present.

Silas Stamnes 17 of Halstad, Minn., stated that he was in the lobby of the Skandia hotel when Arnold Rasmussen came in on the night in question. He saw him accompany the party he referred to as a 'stewbum' to the taxi cab. He had never seen him before and only for an instance that eve but had seen him many times since.

Robert Richards of Fargo was well acquainted with Rasmussen and was a roommate of his at the time of the tragedy. He remembered Rasmussen coming into the room on the night in question and going to bed. He did not see the clock but asked Rasmussen what time it was and Rasmussen told him it was 2:30 a.m.

Mrs. Anna E. Lawrence, proprietress of the Prescott Hotel of Fargo was next on the stand and identified the photographs of her hotel. She also identified exhibit No. 14 as the original register sheet of the night of June 6, 1921. She stated that she was familiar with the occupants of the room as registered by her until 11:45 that eve. She gave the names of the occupants and States Attorney Green wrote the names on the plans of the room as she gave them.

Following are the names of the occupants of the rooms to the best of the knowledge of Mrs. Lawrence:

20—Fred Lawrence, son of Mrs. Lawrence, proprietress of the hotel.

The room immediately north of room 20 is a parlor.

21—Not occupied on the night of the tragedy.

22—Mrs. Lawrence. This room is north of the parlor and was not numbered at that time.

24—Mr. and Mrs. E.T. Still and family.

34—A.H. Starkson, father of Mrs. Lawrence who is 79 years of age and who is now in a Minnesota hospital.

33—John Towers, a steady roomer at the hotel for the past three years.

32—Rose Walker, who had been at the hotel for five weeks steady.

31—No knowledge.

29—L. Jacobson, a transient.

28—Mrs. Flanger and son. Son was nearly blind. Both were transients.

27—Furniture was out of this room which was vacant and was being renovated.

26—No knowledge.

25—Vacant. A Mr. Bennett and wife had left this room of No. 8 that evening.

Second floor of Annex. Van Vorst and family occupied the room in the northwest corner of the Annex. A dressing room and writing room were also near this room. The dressing room and writing room was used by Mrs. Lawrence.

35—Private bath.

23—Vacant Door connecting with room 22 was not used.

First floor of Annex.

Large room office with one room which was used for storage. One of the rooms was an extra room and was vacant when Mrs. Lawrence left it.

One check room, one baggage room for storage. Also a maid's room occupied by Laura Nelson. Old dining room which was not occupied. The maid's room on the lower floor of the Annex was used by the Van Vorst family for a Kitchen.

Nos. 69, 70 and 71 were used by Mr. and Mrs. Simmes as housekeeping rooms.

67 and 68 were vacant.

Third floor."

DAILY TIMES—RECORD [Valley City, ND], Vol. XVI—No. 208, Thurs., Jan. 19, 1922, at pp.1,4,5. Print.

Editorial Daily Times-Record Newspaper

DAILY TIMES—RECORD [Valley City, ND], Vol. XVI—No. 208, Thurs., Jan. 19, 1922, at p.4. Print.

EDITORIAL

"We are mighty pleased that the jury now trying the Gummer case is composed wholly of men, no women having as yet had their names put in the jury box of Barnes county. We talk very much of equal rights and a lot of men loudly proclaim that they should be allowed to do jury duty, but those of finer feelings and culture do not want anything of this nature. Take the case in court for instance, it cannot help but be nauseating to hardened men, whose feelings and sense of modesty are not so fine as that of womankind. The disgusting details that must come out in a trial of this kind must be a course of embarrassment and annoyance to many men whose feelings are built upon finer lines than those who are the principals of a case of this nature. Equal rights may be what most women want but we cannot see where any woman would want to be mixed up in the average jury duty. We know very well we would not want our wife or daughter dragged into the jury box to listen to what they would have to at times. The Arbuckle case is another dirty mess that some women have to listen to as members of the jury.

Argument may be brought out that what is all right for the men is also all right for women, but it does not hold true. Men are built of rougher material than are women and can put up with a lot of this stuff that modest women would shun. At the trial now on in Barnes county courthouse women are striving to get in to listen to the rotten mess that will be presented to the jury and court and there is going to be some rotten testimony brought out that should bring blush to the checks of those who are sitting there listening to it. The editor is not claiming to be angel or anything of that sort in writing thus, he is just simply telling what he feels about this jury system and the connection that women will have with it in the future. Personally we are not going to listen to this case or any similar one, although as a newspaper man whose mission is life is to give that sort of news that will appeal to people we perhaps would have license to go up there and report the same did we so desire, but we have no inclination to do so. The public demands the news and we are going to give it to them under certain restrictions—all testimony is not fit to print will be left out of our reports. This editorial is inspired to show what a lot of morbid curiosity there is in a criminal case of this nature and we read time and time again where women get so "daffy" over a man who is awaiting trial for similar offenses as this defendant is, by sending flowers and candy up to the jail as a token of appreciation to him for the diabolical work and crime he is supposed to have committed.

When people get to such a state of mind that there is something wrong with them. Prisoners charged with heinous offenses should be given every opportunity to prove their innocence but this sending candy and flowers to them is rather sickening and decidedly silly."

DAILY TIMES—RECORD [Valley City, ND], Vol. XVI—No. 208, Thurs., Jan. 19, 1922, at p.4. Print.

———————————————

Gummer Jury All Farmers

DAILY TIMES—RECORD [Valley City, ND], Vol. XVI—No. 208, Thurs., Jan. 19, 1922, at p.4. Print.

GUMMER JURY ALL FARMERS

Jurors Drawn in Famous Case Men of Seemingly Good Judgment, But Men Who Will Not be Swayed by Sentiment.

"The complete jury drawn for the Gummer trial and sworn in at 4:00 o'clock yesterday afternoon are all farmers of the county and are mostly men of mature years. The average age of the jury is 40 years.

Chris Olson, 25, is a farmer in the Ypsilanti district, is married but has no children. He stated in examination that he knew very little of the case and had formed no opinion as to the guilt or innocence of the accused.

William Flach, 48, farmer south of Sanborn. He is a married man with a family and has formed no opinions on the case.

R.R. Kane, 28, farms a few miles north of Spiritwood. He is a married man and has three daughters, the elder of whom is 5 years old.

Lloyd Sampson, 34, farms north of Valley City in what is known as Getchell Prairie. He is married and has three daughters, the elder of which is 5 years old.

Louis A. Sunde, 33, farms northeast of Valley City. He is the only single man in the jury box on the case. Mr. Sunde has four sisters aged 16, 20, 24, 26. He stated that the fact that he had sisters about the age of the murdered girl would in no way effect his judgment.

G.W. Ohm, 55, is a farmer in the Lucca district. He is married and has four children. He stated in examination that he has one daughter of 17 but that this fact would not warp his judgment in the case on trial.

Peter Rumer, 51, is a farmer at Wimbledon, is married and has two boys 16 and 26 years old and three daughters 12, 16, and 24 years old. He has had previous jury duty and felt that he could lay aside any impressions he had gained through reading of the case and give a fair and impartial verdict.

Henry Helmers, 45, of Wimbledon, is also a farmer, is married and has a daughter 20 years old. He has gained no impressions of the case so far and felt that he could enter the jury box with a free and open mind

Christ Minch, 50, farms about 25 miles north of Valley City. His postoffice is Dazey. He has been a resident of the county for 20 years. Is married and has a son 27 years old.

Earnest Ladbury, 24, a farmer near Dazey is the youngest man serving on the case. He is married and has a baby boy.

Fred H. Getshell, 42, is well known in the city, having lived in the district all his life. He farms in Getshell Prairie, is married and has two boys 6 and 12 years old and one girl 9 years old

Theodore Thilmony, 54, farms in the Pillsbury district. Is married and has ten girls ranging in age from 9 to 28 years old.

Considering the jury as a whole it appears that they are all men of very sound judgment who are anxious to see that justice shall be done and will do their duty to the best of their ability, basing their verdict on the evidence submitted as they see it. William Gummer should feel that they will be fair to him in every way."

DAILY TIMES—RECORD [Valley City, ND], Vol. XVI—No. 208, Thurs., Jan. 19, 1922, at p.4. Print.

Sheriff Kraemer's Testimony Shakes Gummer's Nonchalant Attitude

DAILY TIMES—RECORD [Valley City, ND], Vol. XVI—No. 209, Fri., Jan. 20, 1922, at pp.1,4. Print.

SHERIFF KRAEMER'S TESTIMONY SHAKES GUMMER'S NONCHALANT ATTITUDE

EIGHTEEN WITNESSES EXAMINED UP TO NOON TO-DAY. EXPECTED STATE WILL BE THROUGH IN ABOUT FIVE DAYS

People Stand in Line For Two Or Three Hours Every Morning In Order To Get Seats In Court Room. Many Go Without Dinner To Hold Their Place For The Afternoon.

"Gummer appeared in court this morning bearing his usual non-chalant attitude and did not display signs of nervousness until sheriff Kraemer testified as to the minute particulars as to the conditions of the body when he found it. At this time Gummer appeared nervous and fidgety for the first time during his trial so far. He fumbled with his fingers continuously and swallowed and cleared his throat at frequent intervals. This nervousness increased when the bloody rags which were used as bandages and as a gag were introduced in evidence and passed around among the jurors. However he had regained a portion of his careless exterior before being led from the courtroom by Sheriff Larson, although his smile on leaving still showed trace of nervousness.

As soon as court recess yesterday noon about half of the spectators in the room left, the others remaining to hold their seats. As soon as those who had left were out others who had been waiting took their places and the house was again filled. They were waiting patiently for court to convene. When court was convened at two o'clock the upper and lower halls were jammed with disappointed people who could not get into the court room.

The first witness called to the stand was Sheriff Fred A. Kraemer of Fargo, Cass County. He identified the plans of the Prescott Hotel as evidence and certified the testimony of Mrs. Lawrence as to the occupants and various guests on the night of June 6. Mrs. Anna E. Lawrence was returned to the stand to testify as to the happenings in the hotel on the evening of the tragedy. The witness stated that when she was on duty Arnold Rasmussen and Marie Wick came in. A guest of the Hotel, Mr. Flaager and his blind son were in the hotel lobby when they entered. He stated that Marie Wick registered at the desk and paid her one dollar for the room for that night. At this point States Attorney Green entered a sheet of the hotel register as evidence and the witness identified this sheet as being a register sheet of the Hotel

Prescott on the night in question and also identified the signature of
Marie Wick. She stated that she personally gave the key to room 30 to
Miss Wick. At this point State's Attorney Green entered a key attached
to a brass plate in evidence. Mrs. Lawrence identified this key as being
one of the keys in the hotel at this time but stated that while the key was
attached to a brass plate baring the number 30, the key was not used for
that room. She did not know whether the key would unlock room 30
or not. She stated that after Marie Wick had registered she asked that
she be called at 6:00 o'clock in the morning but Mrs. Lawrence told
her that 6:30 would give her plenty of time to catch her train and Miss
Wick allowed her entry to be changed to 6:30. Mr. Green then entered
a call sheet as evidence and the witness identified this sheet as a call
sheet used in the hotel on the night of the murder and also identified
the entry for a 6:30 call as being her entry. The witness stated that the
defendant, Gummer, entered the room from upstairs and she told him
to show Miss Wick to her room which he did. Miss Wick remained in
her room about 15 minutes and returned to the hotel lobby and went
out with Arnold Rasmussen At about 11:00 Miss Wick again entered
the hotel alone She appeared confused in the lobby and the witness
told Gummer to show her to her room but Miss Wick stated that
she knew about her room and could find it alone. Before returning
to her room she asked that her call be changed to 6:00 o'clock. The
entry was changed by Gummer in the presence of the witness. Mrs.
Lawrence stated that she went to Howards Cafe shortly after this for
a lunch returning to the hotel at 11:40. Gummer was at the desk and
she asked him if Fritz, meaning her son Fred, had returned. Gummer
told her that he had and that she had checked up Gummer's entries
for the night. Mrs. Lawrence then went to her room on the second
floor. Before entering the room she looked down the hall and saw that
everything appeared to be all right. There was a light shining through

the transom of one of the rooms. She did not know whether her son Fred was in bed or not.

In cross examination the witness stated that the light she had noticed was coming from room 32 which was occupied by a Mr. Rosenwahler, who was a steady roomer in the Hotel. She stated that there were two lights in the hall. One a red light in the center of the hall between room 30 and the stairway and the other light was at the end of the hall. Room 31 was not occupied when she retired. She stated that 4 people had been registered after she had left Gummer in charge at the desk and at that time there were three rooms vacant on the second floor, one of which was the parlor. The witness then identified the signatures on the register of parties who had checked in in her presence. At this point Sheriff Kraemer was returned to the stand and stated that the defendant Gummer had admitted to him previously that he had registered those whose names appeared after Mrs. Lawrence retired.

Fred Lawrence, the son of Mrs. Lawrence, was next called to the witness stand and stated that his age as 27, that he was single, was engaged in the insurance business at the time of the tragedy and was living at the Prescott hotel, having room 20. Mr. Lawrence is now located at Wilmer, N.D., in the interests of War Finance Corporation. He stated that Gummer was on duty at the desk from 7:00 p.m. to 7:00 a.m. The witness came into the hotel on the night of June 6 about 11·30 and checked up on Mr. Gummer's accounts. He then retired to his room on the second floor shortly after. After he entered his room he returned to the hall and saw his mother and to the best of his recollections this was about 11:40. He retired and did not hear any untoward noises during the night. He was called by Gummer at 6:45. Gummer stated that he had been ringing the occupant of room 30 for 45 minutes and could not get her to answer and wanted

Lawrence to come down. Lawrence told him to look over the transom and if he could not awaken the guest to throw some cold water
in her face. Gummer called him again in a few minutes and stated
that he had looked over the transom and that the girl appeared to be
dead. Lawrence went down and returned to room 30 with Gummer,
climbed up on the table which Gummer had placed in front of the
door, and saw the body of Marie Wick with the hands tied to the bedstead and her face covered with bloody rags. Lawrence sent Gummer
back to the office to notify the police and called a chambermaid to
open the door. The chambermaid opened the door and entered, gave
a cry and rushed back out. Lawrence did not enter the room at this
time but closed the door and went down stairs. He told of the arrival
of the Doctor and the officers who came within a few minutes. Dr.
Harry J. Fortin examined the body casually and stated that the girl was
dead. Lawrence stated that the first time he entered the room was in
company with Doctor Burton. He accompanied officers Pickering and
Nelson to the rooms and after looking at room 30 they went to room
1. The door was locked but the occupant H.J. Hagan reached over
from the bed and let them in. Mr. Hagan was in bed and had only
his underwear on. The witness and officers searched the bed clothes
of Mr. Hagan. They found everything in order. The towels in the
room had not been used. Examination of room 29 occupied by L.
Jacobson disclosed the same condition. Examination of the rooms 35
and 49 showed everything O.K. In room 40, supposed to be occupied
by James Farrell there seemed to be nothing wrong but the bed was
already made up. Examination of various windows, doors and other
places of exit showed screens to be in place and fastened on the inside.
A window in the back of the Hotel on the first floor was open an
inch or two. This window was stuck owing to the looseness of a jamb
and required the efforts of two men to budge it. The bottom of the

window is about 5 feet from the floor. Of the two doors one was sealed and the other was locked with a pad lock on the inside. The witness stated that he had not noticed whether the fire hose nozzle, with which the state claims the girl was murdered, was fastened to the hose or not.

Mr. Harry Poague was returned to the stand and stated that he had taken photographs in room 30 during the morning following the murder. These photographs and enlargements were entered as evidence by Green and identified by the witness as being taken by him at that time. He further stated that he had taken the photographs in the presence of Sheriff Kraemer.

W.C. Dennis, photographer of Moorhead, stated that he had taken some photographs in room 30 at the request of State's Attorney Green and in the presence of Sheriff Kraemer. Theses photographs and negatives were entered in evidence and showed the bed and walls in the room as they appeared that morning. They also showed pictures of the bloody finger-prints on her arm but they were blurred.

The pictures entered in evidence and taken by Poague and Dennis showed in detail the bloody conditions of the room and walls and of the bed clothing. They are gruesome photographs and they give one a very vivid impression of the brutal way in which Miss Wick was murdered, and for which the defendant Gummer is on trial.

The next witness called was Richard Pickering, a Fargo policeman, who was called to the scene of the murder at 7:45 on the morning of June 7. He stated that Gummer and Fred Lawrence were at the desk when he came in. He asked what the trouble was and Gummer replied that the girl in room 30 seemed terribly cut up and that he thought it was a case of suicide. He noticed a key behind the desk. It was on a brass plate and not on a safety pin. The witness was shown the photographs of the room and stated that the appearance of the room was as the photographs showed them when he first entered. He then returned to the office and called up the police station and the acting Captain called the Sheriff. The witness stated that he then told Gummer that the girl had undoubtedly been murdered, to which Gummer replied that it was impossible as the door had been locked. On the cross examination the witness stated that when he entered the room there were pillows on the bed. At this point defense counsel asked for the photographs of the room and it was found that there were no pillows on the picture. When the witness was asked that, in view of this fact, if there were any pillows as he stated, could the photographs represent a true appearance of the room on that morning. The witness was decidedly confused by this and tried to evade a direct answer but when pinned down by the defense counsel stated that the photographs did not represent a true and correct condition of the room as he saw it but had to answer that they presented the general appearance of the room.

Otto Nelson, another police officer of Fargo, arrived on the scene at severn-thirty. Gummer and Lawrence were back of the desk. He noticed the key, which is produced in court, in the key rack back of the counter, and mentioned the fact to Gummer, and was informed that this key did not open room 30, and that the key regularly used for the room could not be found. He stated that he went to room 31 with Lawrence and then supported the previous testimony that Hagan was in bed when they arrived. He stated that he did not know Hagan but got his name while in the room. He also stated that Gummer told him that he had been busy at the desk until about 3:00 a.m. And that his chum, Andy Brown, was with him most of the time. Defense counsel in cross-examination referred to the previous testimony that Nelson had given at the time of the Preliminary hearing in Fargo in which he stated that he did NOT get Mr. Hagan's name before leaving the room and was asked to explain the difference in testimony. This he could not do. It was also brought to his attention that he had stated in the former hearing that he did not look over Mr. Hagan's belongings, while in the present testimony he stated that he had. This he was also unable to explain. Also at the preliminary hearing he stated that he had no conversation with Gummer regarding his movements of the night before while he stated yesterday that he had. The witness explained this by saying that Gummer had made the statement of his movements to Mrs. Lawrence in the presence of the witness.

Mr. James South, Deputy sheriff of Cass county stated that Pickering and Nelson were in the Prescott on the morning inquisition when he arrived. He looked in room 30 and then looked at the door a key which he got from the chambermaid and stated that this key was on a ring. He examined room 31, saw Hagan in bed as previously stated. He stated that 3 or 4 days later he found a hatpin bent at the end on a table near the water closet in the hall. Under cross examination the witness admitted that he had received the key with which he had locked the room 30 from Fred Lawrence who got it from the chambermaid and also that this key was on a safety pin instead of a ring. He further stated that when he found the hatpin three or four days after the tragedy was on the table in plain sight. At this point recess was taken until 10:00 this morning. Two sons of Morris Gummer were with their father in court this morning. These were John and Goodman. Mrs. Gummer is in the city but was not in the court room.

Locks on the courtroom doors were installed during the evening so that the doors would remain closed until the authorities were ready to let the spectators in.

When court convened this morning spectators were allowed to fill the court room under the judge's orders, who said that he would allow spectators to stand as long as they were quiet. The doors were kept locked until 9:30 and a jam of people in the hall and stairway was such that they nearly tore down the railings on the stairs.

Sheriff Fred Kraemer, of Cass co. was the first witness on the stand in the morning session and remained on the stand under direct examination and cross examination under 11:40. He stated that he had been called to the Prescott Hotel by the chief of police of Fargo and that he arrived there shortly before 8 o'clock on the morning of June 7, 1921. When he arrived the chief of police of Fargo and Deputy Sheriff South were in charge. He went immediately to room 30 which is located in the southwest corner of the second floor and is a room about 10x12 feet in size. There is a door in the north wall opening in to the hall and a window in the south wall. There is a door in the east wall opening into room 31. The room contained the usual dresser, washstand, chair and bed. The clothes of the deceased were lying on a chair, seemingly in the position in which the applicant of the room would have thrown them. Her stockings were hanging on the doorknob of the door to the room 31. States Attorney Green asked the witness if he had found a pocketbook among the belongings of the deceased and he stated that he had. Counsel asked what he found in this pocketbook. Counsel for the defense objected to this question on the grounds that it tended to prove the commission of a separate and different crime and the objection was sustained. This led to a lively verbal tift between opposing counsel at the end of which Judge Cooley said that the objection was still sustained. At this point States Attorney Green called the court reporter, Mr. Stone, to the Judge's bench to make a statement to the judge a matter of record. Attorney Barnett joined the trio before the judge and the matter was argued privately in his presence. At the end of which argument the judge overruled the objection. In answer to the question in dispute the witness stated that there were only a few cents found in the pocketbook. There were two suit cases, a suitcase and a small grip in the room in which the belongings of the deceased were arranged neatly and did not appear to have been disturbed. The witness then found a necklace in one of them. In describing the condition of the bed clothing and body, as it appeared to him on first entering the room witness stated that there were pillows on the bed and near the head of the body from which the pillow cases had been removed. He stated that the pillows were set aside and laid on the floor during the examination of the body and that the body was not disturbed in any particular other than the removal of the pillows and the withdrawal of the bed clothing covering the body. The bed clothing was again drawn over the body after the examination but before the photographs were taken but before the pillows were returned to the position to which they were originally found. Aside from these particulars as stated the photographs were identified by the witness as representing the true condition of the room when he entered. The witness stated that the towels which had been used in removing traces of the crime were found under the bed clothing. At this point a piece of the wall paper which had been cut from the wall of the the room and which showed a bloody smear or mark was entered in evidence by the set and was identified by the witness as having been removed at his request, but not by him. Another piece of wall paper showing finger prints was entered in evidence at this time and identified by the witness as having been taken from the wall of the room in question.

The witness was referred to the enlarged photograph which has previously been entered in evidence and said that it represented a true and correct condition of the body and bed as found by him. He said that the right hand and arm bandages folding the same had but few smears of blood on them. This arm was securely tied with seven or eight knots in what appeared to be piece of a sheet. The left arm was

not as well tied, there being considerable play in the bandage holding
it and the hand[,] arm, and bandage being covered with blood. The
face and head were also entirely covered with blood. The face and
head bound with a bandage or bandages torn from a sheet. These were
entirely blood soaked. The witness stated that while the head and face
were badly cut he did not find any cuts below the throat. There was a
large pool of blood on the carpet covering the floor underneath the
bed. The photograph taken of the bed and body was at this point
passed among the jurors. The witness stated that the only mark or
bruise he found on the body below the throat was a bruise or rather
an abrasion on the skin on the inside of the left shin about six or eight
inches in length. There were bloody smears on both the hips of the
body. These were very thin but quite distinct.

Court attaches brought in the carpet, pieces of flat paper, mattress
and the head of the bedstead which were in the room at the time of the
tragedy. These were entered in evidence by the state. The carpet was
arranged before the jury and witness in such manner as to show a large
blood spot near one edge. The witness stated that this carpet was the
one found in the room when he examined the premises that morning
and the spot indicated was made by a large pool of blood which was
not dry at the time he first examined the room. Next the pieces of felt
paper, three in number, were displayed before the court and identified
by the witness. These pieces of paper showed traces of blood which
had soaked through the carpet covering them. The state then returned
the carpet before the jury and witness and drew attention to a number
of thin white hairs which were stuck to the blood spot on the carpet.
Witness stated that these hairs were as found on the morning of the
tragedy with the exception of the fact that a few had been removed
to be tested by authorities to establish their identity. The witness also
stated that a number of these hairs had been found clutched in the

hand of the deceased the morning after the tragedy. The bedstead was brought before the jury and witness and identified as having been in room 30 on the night in question. The state called attention to the head of the bedstead and drew attention of the jury and witness to certain smears of blood and a dent in one of the uprights. The witness stated that the exhibit was in practically the same condition as found the morning of June 7. The mattress was arranged before the jury and witness and identified by the witness as being the mattress referred to in previous testimony. This mattress showed a large spot about ten by fifteen inches in size where the head of the murdered girls had rested. Witness stated that a slit in the mattress had been made by the authorities after the crime in their inspection of the mattress. Small blood stains on the mattress was made, said the witness, by the undertaker in removing the body with the exception of a very small stain on the west side of the mattress which was found in the room.

The witness stated that key to room 30 which was used by Miss Wick that night had been found.

An electric light bulb was introduced in evidence by the state and identified as having been found in the room by him. Several black smears on the bulb were stated by the witness to have been red smears when found, the color being changed to black by the application of graphite which was used by the authorities to get finger prints. These smears appeared to be blood stains and were as found except that a small portion had been scraped off in making tests, to prove that the stains were blood. This was passed among the jurors.

Sheriff Kraemer stated that the door connecting room 30 and 31 was locked. There were several holes in the door which had been plugged from the side of room 30. These were dusty on the room 31 side and showed no sign of having been disturbed. Witness stated that there were no signs of the door having been disturbed. Witness stated that there were no signs of the door having been opened as there was dust on the door and door frame and cobwebs connecting the door to the frame. The witness stated that there was an ordinary lock on the hall door of room 30 and that from the outside the door appeared to be equipped with a Yale lock but that the lock had not been used as examination showed the bang slot to have been removed from the door frame.

Sheriff Kraemer stated that he examined room 31 accompanied by States Attorney Green and that in the examination of the room and contents they found nothing out of the ordinary. Witness stated that he also saw Hagan in bed and that an examination of his clothes and person showed nothing out of the ordinary. He then examined room 35 which was occupied by a Mr. McKenzie and found nothing suspicious. He stated that Gummer told him later on that McKenzie had come into the hotel between 2 and 3 o'clock that morning. He also examined room 40 but found nothing out of the ordinary. He stated that Gummer had told him that the room had been occupied by James Farrell who had come into the hotel about 2 o'clock that morning. Gummer had described Farrell to him as being a man 30 years of age wearing a grey suit and cap and being about 5 feet and 8 inches tall, of quite tanned complexion. Witness did not remember as to whether Gummer had made a statement to him as to Farrell leaving the hotel but remembered that Gummer had stated that his chum, Andy Brown, had been with him most of the night. Direct examination was concluded at 11 o'clock and counsel for defense tried to shake Kraemer's testimony under cross-examination but were not very successful. The cross examination tended to fix definitely the time of arrival of various authorities and placed considerable stress on the examination given to room 31 and its occupant, again. The only point upon which Kraemer did not appear certain was relative to the finding of a Bible in room 31 which counsel for the defense claimed a maid had stated in the presence of the witness had a blood stain on it. Witness stated that he did not remember the statement but would not care to testify that the statement had not been made in his presence. When asked by States Attorney Green as to the Bible Kraemer said that he disposed of it by giving it to Green. Witness was excused at 11:40 having spent one hour and forty minutes on the stand.

C.E. Matlock, undertaker of Fargo stated that he was connected with Moore Undertaking Parlor and that Moore was the county coroner of Cass county at the time of the tragedy and that he, the witness, removed the said body from room 30 and prepared it for burial. He testified as to numerous cuts on the head and face of the body and stated that it required 100 to 170 stitches to close these cuts and estimated that the cuts totaled in length eleven inches. The only bruise or abrasion noticed below the throat was a bruise on the elbow of the right arm and referred to this as a slight abrasion of the skin. He did not refer to the abrasion on the left ? which Sheriff Kraemer had testified to. At this point the state introduced several rags in evidence and the witness identified them as having been used as gags and bandages holding the gags in place and also as strips used to tie the arms of Marie Wick to the bedstead. The part of the gag which was inside the mouth of the murdered girl was only slightly stained with blood which had evidently soaked in from the outside, the outside portion being completely soaked with blood. The bandages which held the arms were not badly soaked but were covered with blood stains, especially the one holding the left arm. These bandages were passed among the jurors for examination. They constitute the most gruesome exhibit so far introduced by the state. The night gown worn by the deceased was introduced and identified by the witness as being worn by Miss Wick at the time she was murdered. The night gown had been cut by the undertaker in taking it from the body. At this point court was recessed after the usual admonition to the jury until 2 o'clock this afternoon.

At the opening of court in the afternoon E. Matlock was returned to the stand. A few minor questions were put to him by States Attorney Green and he was turned over to the defense for cross examination. In the cross examination, he was referred to the photograph previously entered as evidence and asked if it represented a true condition of the body when he took charge. He replied that it did and stated that when he removed the body from the bed he cut the bandages holding the arms from the bedstead. He also stated that the cloths tied to the girl were not removed until he and Officer Milligan removed them at the morgue. These were exhibited again and the witness stated that they showed much blood at this time, than was on them when they were removed owing to the frequent handling of them while the blood was still moist. Referring to the bruises which were found on the right elbow he characterized it as a reddish abrasion about the size of a dime and appeared to have been bruised recently. He was excused from the stand and James Milligan deputy sheriff of Cass Co. placed on the stand. Milligan stated that he arrived at the Prescott hotel about 8:15 accompanied by States Attorney Green. He went immediately to room 30 and made a brief examination. He then went out and got the coroner and the Coroner's jury and was back in the hotel by 9 o'clock.

He stated that he assisted the undertaker in removing the body and that the bed sheets were wrapped around the body and then taken with it. Milligan afterwards took charge of the sheets. At this point the sheets were introduced as evidence. There was no blood on the upper sheet when the body was found according to Milligan's testimony, but the lower sheet was soaked where the head had rested but there was none around the body. Milligan stated that he was present when the bandages were removed from the arm and also stated that the left wrist was covered with blood but that the bandages around the left wrist was free from blood except where it had touched the wrist, the right bandage was free from blood except for couple of small spots.

At this point the blankets and bedspread were introduced as evidence by the state and identified by the witness as coming from the bed occupied by Marie Wick; also the blood soaked pillows were introduced. The witness corroborated previous testimony as to the general condition of the body when the examination of the rags was offered in evidence. Officer Milligan stated that he found the nozzle laying on the hose rack in the hall that morning and was referred to the plan and located on the plan the place in which the nozzle was found. He said that the nozzle was not fastened onto the hose but it was pushed in place and not screwed on. The nozzle was then introduced in evidence and identified by witness. He stated that when he found the nozzle he found spots of blood and flesh on it. He took the nozzle into room 30 and fitted it into the hole in the wall and saw that it had been made by the nozzle. He then delivered it to Casper Nelson at the Agricultural college for examination. This nozzle is made of brass about twelve inches long and five and three quarters inches in diameter at the large end which screws onto the hose.

There was no cross examination of Officer Milligan. Casper Nelson was the next witness called and stated that he was a chemist at the Agricultural college that he had examined the nozzle which had been entered in evidence and found traces of blood and human flesh on the same. During cross examination he stated that he could not say as to whether the blood was human blood or not.

John Powers, 71, of Fargo, stated that he roomed in the Prescott hotel in room 33. He stated that he had retired to his room at 11 o'clock on the night in question, that he did not hear any noises during the night, that he left his room about 8 o'clock the next morning leaving the hotel immediately.

The witness further testified that he did not learn of the murder until afternoon. Under cross examination he stated that on the night of June 6 he was at the Masonic temple until about 11 when he returned to the hotel passing thru the office and went directly to his room. He stated that Mrs. Lawrence and Gummer were behind the desk when he came in. He was excused.

Pedro L. Christianson stated that he was acting as foreman for Haggart construction company at the time of the murder and newly employed by the Kennedy construction company; that he was a roomer at the Prescott at room 46 which is directly above room 30. He stated that he retired about 12 on the night in question and went right to sleep and he heard no noise during the night. Arose at 5:45 a.m. And went to work and did not return to the hotel till 6:30 that evening. He first learned of the tragedy about 8:30 in the morning while he was working. Under cross examination he stated he had been at various places around town in the evening and had come back to the hotel about 11:30. When he came in Mrs. Lawrence and Gummer were behind the desk. He went directly to his room and wrote a letter before retiring. He was excused.

Clarence Jacobson, 25, stated that he was resident at Hunter, N.D. He had been at Bismarck until the night of the tragedy when he came to Fargo on the train which leaves Bismarck at 3:55 p.m. When he arrived at Fargo he went to Howards cafe and had lunch and then went to the Prescott hotel, registered and was assigned to room 27. After going to his room he found that the lock on 27 would not function and as he had considerable money with him and wanted door locked he went down stairs and got his room changed to 29.

He retired immediately and went to sleep. He was awakened in the morning by Gummer knocking on his door about 7:00 o'clock. He asked who was there and got up. Put on his trousers and let Gummer and the officer with him into the room. They searched the room. The witness stated that he heard no noises during the night. Under cross examination he stated that there were three doors to his and he tried them all and that they were all locked. He did not know that any of them lead to a bathroom or not. He was excused. He made a very good witness and answered up promptly.

Metro Dychuk was next called. He was a transient and arrived in the hotel Prescott at 10:15 p.m. that night. He was assigned to room 45 which is in the Northwest corner of the third floor. He went directly to bed and was not out of his room that night. He was awakened by some noise during the night but did not know what time it was. He got up and opened the window but did not hear any more. He retired again and arose at 8:30. Under cross examination he stated that going down stairs in the morning he met a man who questioned him as to whether he had heard any noise during the night. He later identified this man as deputy sheriff South.

Recess was called at this time. 24 witnesses have been called up to 3:45 this afternoon."

DAILY TIMES—RECORD [Valley City, ND], Vol. XVI—No. 209, Fri., Jan. 20, 1922, at pp.1,4. Print.

State's Examination of Andy Brown Surprises Opposition

D AILY TIMES—RECORD [Valley City, ND], Vol. XVI—No. 210, Sat., Jan. 21, 1922, at pp.1,4. Print.

STATE'S EXAMINATION OF ANDY BROWN SURPRISES OPPOSITION

Short Examination of the Prosecution's Star Witness a Big Surprise to the Attorneys for the Defense. State Evidently did not want to put all its cards on the table at this time. Brown is being held for further use by the state. Defense hardly knows how to cross examine Brown under the circumstances and he is let go with the request the he be kept in the city. State's Attorney William Green shot back that he would not be released from custody at this time.

H. J. Hagan, Former President of the Scandinavian American Bank of Fargo, on stand today. His testimony seems to be inconsistent. On di-

*rect examination he says Gummer was very nervous and fumbled when
he asked for his room key and then says he wasn't on cross examination.
Hagan will be recalled later.*

Court adjourned until Monday.

"The Gummer trial is going along steadily up to adjournment this
afternoon. In all thirty-six witness has been placed on the stand by the
state. The crowds are just as much interested as ever in the case and
the court room is filled to capacity, many standing up in the rear and
sides of the room. There have been no sensational developments up
to this time. The exhibit of brass nozzle used to beat the life out of the
innocent farm girl, was the main exhibit of yesterday, together with
the clothes and gag used to tie her up and gag her. These exhibits were
indeed of a gruesome nature and could not help but send a thrill of
horror thru the system of those who saw these exhibits and to kindle
the desire to bring the guilty one to the bar of justice so that he may
get the limit of the law—whatever that may be.

In the proceedings yesterday afternoon following the 8:30 recess the
prosecution disposed of witnesses quite rapidly. Six witnesses being
examined between 3:55 and 4:45 p.m.

The first witness called after the recess was R.H. Flaugher who is
76 years old and farms near Heaton, N.D. He stated that he and his
son came to Fargo on the night of June 6 on the Northern Pacific
train No. 8. His son, who is nearly blind, had been ordered by the war
department to go to Fargo for a physical examination and his father
accompanied him on the trip. This son is an ex-service man and lost
his sight while overseas. When they arrived in Fargo they first went to
the Waldorf hotel to try and get a room. There was a large crowd in
the lobby of the hotel in front of the desk and when they got to the
desk all the rooms had been taken so they went out on the street and
looked around and saw the Prescott Hotel sign. They knew nothing of

the Prescott Hotel but as it was the closest hotel sign in sight they went there and arrived in the hotel lobby about 10 o'clock in the evening. The witness stated that the defendant, Gummer, or some one who resembled him, was behind the desk when they came in and that Mrs. Lawrence was also there. They registered and were assigned to room 28. They sat in the lobby for some time and saw a young man and young girl come in, supposedly Arnold Rasmussen and Marie Wick. Miss Wick went to the desk and was registered by Mrs. Lawrence. The witness did not notice whether the girl went to her room or not but a few minutes later he noticed that the young man was still in the hotel lobby and was alone. A few minutes after this he noticed the young lady join the young man and go out with him. He stated that the girl came back to the hotel lobby about 11 o'clock and he saw her to her room. At his time Mr. Flaugher and his son went to their room and the witness stated that the girl and the defendant, Gummer, preceded them up the stairway. Gummer took the girl to her room according to the testimony of the witness and then showed the witness and his son to their room which was no. 28, going in with them and switching on the light, then showing them the location of the toilet room and switching on the light there, after which the defendant went down stairs. The witness then took his son back to their room and left him there, going down to the lobby for a smoke. It was about 11:30 p.m. When he returned to his room and retired. He arose at 6 o'clock, dressed and went down stairs arriving there about 6:10 and left the hotel about 6:30. The witness stated that there was no one in the hotel office at that time but Gummer.

Before taking the stand Mr. Flaugher asked that the questions be put to him quite loud as he was very hard of hearing. This fact explained the fact that he heard no noises during the night. After giving his testimony the witness was excused without cross examination.

The next witness called was the son of Mr. Flaugher, who stated that he 27 years old, was an ex-service man and had served overseas. Mr. Flaugher during his service in the United States army, was almost totally blinded, but is still able to distinguish objects and outlines faintly. He stated that he had been in the Prescott Hotel on the night in question as testified by his father and that he recalled going upstairs to their room and remembered that two persons, a man and a lady, proceeded them up the stairs, but was unable to distinguish their features. He retired about 11 o'clock and went to sleep almost immediately and did not awaken until approximately six o'clock the next morning. He substantiated his father's testimony as to their movements after leaving their room that morning. The witness testified that his hearing due to his affliction was unusually acute, but that he did not hear any noise during the night. The witness was excused without cross examination.

Charles Fisher of Moorhead, Minn., 62 years of age, stated that he had lived at the Prescott Hotel and occupied room 64 which is on the fourth floor. He had been in the hotel since March first, 1921. He stated that he had retired at 10 o'clock on the night in question and did not arise and was not out of the room until 9 o'clock the following morning. He stated that he had heard no noises during the night. He was excused without cross examination.

George LaLonde stated that he was at present living in New Rockford, was married and had one child. He had resided in Valley City from June 9 to September 1 last year. He came to Fargo on June 6 from Brainerd, Minn., and registered at the Prescott Hotel and was given room 49, which is on the third floor. He went to his room about 8:30 that eve and retired at 10:45 and did not awaken until 8:30 the following morning. He heard no unusual noises during the night and was not out of the room. He was excused without cross examination.

John J. Meyers, butcher, of Hebron, N.D., stated that he had lived at Hebron most of the time since 1915. On June 2, 1921 he left Hebron for Fargo going from there to Canada and returning to Fargo on May 4. On his return to Fargo he stayed at the Prescott Hotel and was assigned to room No. 42 which is on the third floor. The witness did not recall the number of the room but designated it as the second room on the right hand side of the stairway leading to the third floor. He was around Fargo with various friends all evening but came to the Prescott at 11:30 to get some money from Fred Lawrence that was owed him. Gummer was alone in the office when the witness came in. The witness stated that he had not been in the hotel between supper time and 11:30 and had no knowledge of the fact that there was a girl staying in room 30 that night. The witness stated that Gummer called Fred Lawrence on the phone and that he went upstairs and saw Lawrence in his room. He got the money from Lawrence went out, and sent a telegram to Bismarck, went to a restaurant and had a lunch, was around for some time with friends and started back to the Prescott Hotel. On his way back to the hotel he saw a friend, Carl Jaeger by name, in the lobby of the Waldorf and went in and talked to him in a few minutes. He then went to the Prescott, arriving there about 12 o'clock. Gummer was alone in the lobby. The witness retired immediately but did not feel very good and did not go to sleep for a little while and slept lightly most of the night. He came downstairs the next morning about 10 o'clock. He remembers there being a knock at his door and the door knob being rattled about 9 o'clock that morning but did not open the door. He stated that he did not hear any unusual noises during the night and did not leave his room between the hours of 12 midnight and ten o'clock a.m. Under cross examination he stated that on going down stairs the morning following the tragedy he was asked by a man in the lobby, when he later identified as Deputy Sheriff

Milligan as to what time he had got in the night before. The witness stated that on the following Monday he was arrested by officers in Fargo and placed in jail about 7 o'clock in the evening, remaining there until some time on Wednesday. Defense counsel asked under what charge he had been arrested. Prosecution objected to this and was sustained. The witness stated that he worked for a man by the name of Houser in Fargo for three days. States Attorney Green brought a pair of trousers before the witness and asked him if he had ever owned them or had ever seen them before to which the witness replied that he had not. The witness was then excused.

Albert Rosenwater of Powers Lake, N.D., stated that he had been idle since last May having been ill with sciatica rheumatism and had walked with crutches or two canes since March 1, 1921. He stated that he had been a resident in room No. 32 of the Prescott Hotel since May 1. On the night in question he went to his room immediately after supper, laid down on the bed and slept until 10 p.m., at which time he got up, went out to the N.P. Lunch counter and had lunch and was back in bed when the court house clock struck the hour of 10:30. The witness did not remember just when he went to sleep but does remember hearing the court house clock strike the hour of 11, and did not hear it strike 12, so suppose that he fell asleep some time between those two hours. He awoke about six o'clock in the morning, got up and was at the N.P. Lunch counter having breakfast by 7 o'clock. He stated that he had heard people in the hall about 6.30 that morning, or shortly before he left the room, but had heard no noises during the night. Questions asked by counsel for defense in cross examination brought out the fact that there was some difference in his testimony as to the time of retiring, between the testimony given at the preliminary hearing and at the present time. However this appeared to be immaterial. The witness stated that no one came into his room the morning after he awoke and that no one had accosted him until he returned to the hotel about 7:30 at which time an officer questioned him as to whether he had heard any noise during the night. He told the officer that he had not. He had no personal knowledge of any officer having been in is room to examine it at any time. He was excused.

At this point States Attorney Green entered in evidence a number of exhibits which had been introduced in testimony previously and passed them around among the jurors. All exhibits introduced previous to this time were entered as evidence with the exception of exhibits Nos. 9 and 17 one of which is the hotel register sheet of June 12 and the other being the check book of the murdered girl. This work occupied the remaining fifteen minutes of the afternoon session and court was recessed after the usually admonition to the jury, until 10 o'clock this morning.

_____

When court convened this morning the court room was jammed with interested spectators, the first of whom began arriving at 6:15 this morning.

Dr. Harry J. Fortin, of Fargo, was the first witness called to the stand. He stated that he had seen medical service with the service with the United States army. He was called to the Prescott Hotel on the morning of June 7 by Fred Lawrence and arrived there at 7:15. When he arrived Mrs. Lawrence and a police officer were in the lobby of the hotel and accompanied him to room 30 where he saw a young lady bound to the bed, her face covered with bloody bandages. The witness stated that he felt of her pulse and found the life was extinct. This was as far as his examination of the body went. He stated however that he did not notice that rigor mortis had set in. He further stated that violent struggle just prior to death would hurry the action of rigor mortis and that in his experience in the service showed him that rigor mortis might set in within half an hour after death. There was no cross examination of the witnesses and he was excused. Dr. Paul H. Buton, surgeon of Fargo, was called to the stand and stated he had practiced his profession for twenty-one years, that he was called to the Prescott Hotel on June 7, and arrived there about 9 o'clock, and went directly to room 30 and examined the body of Marie Wick. He stated that to the best of his knowledge, judging from his experience as a surgeon, the deceased had been dead from four to six hours, this opinion being based principally on the fact that rigor mortis had set in and that this condition ordinarily required four to six hours after death, but that a violent struggle might vary the time somewhat, but not to any great extent. He stated that the examination in room 30 as to the condition of the body was cursory. The witness stated that a more detailed examination was made by him at the morgue where he examined the wounds in the head of the corpse and noted that most of them extended to the bone. He found a fracture of the skull above the left ear and finger marks on the throat, and that the face showed signs of suffocation. The witness estimated that the condition of the body and his examination of room 30 that the deceased had lost about a quart of blood. He further stated that in his opinion death has been caused through the combined results of suffocation, hemorrhage, and fracture of the skull. He stated the gag would have had to be far back in the throat to stop passage of air to the lungs and cause suffocation. He also stated that the bruises left by the fingers of the assailant on the throat would indicate that there had been enough pressure used to cause consciousness. He stated that in his examination he found the progenitor organs badly ruptured, that the vaginal was full of blood and that the examination showed the deceased to have been a virgin prior to the assault. He stated that he found no marks below the throat which would indicate that the deceased had been bitten or torn about the breasts. He stated that the wounds around the head had been caused by a blunt instrument and when referred to the nozzle entered in evidence stated that it could have caused the wound. Under cross examination the counsel for defense spent considerable time on the question of how long it would require after death for rigor mortis to set in, but the witness reiterated his statement that to the best of his judgment four to six hours was the minimum time required, but admitted that the time of death was merely a guess, based on his past experience in cases of this nature. The witness stated that temperature had very little to do with the portion of times required for rigor mortis to set in. Attorney Swenson asked a question as to the possibility of suffocation being caused by the insertion of the pillow case in the mouth and throat, but this question was objected to on the ground that it introduced a question not supported by testimony previously, and the objection was sustained. Attorney Barnett asked the witness if in his experience he had any recollection of having seen a person with a mouth large enough to hold the pillow case without extending far enough into the throat to cause suffocation. The witness answered that in his opinion there were any number of men in the courtroom into whose mouths he could place a pillow case without causing suffocation, but added that the pillow case inserted in the mouth as previous testimony had indicated, with the blood soaked portion outside the mouth being bandaged over the nose, would cause suffocation. A question by Attorney Green in re-direct examination brought the answer, that the deceased might have lived if the pillow case had not been blood soaked.

Andy Brown was called to the stand by the state and brought into the court room by Sheriff Larson at 10:45. Spectators in the court-room manifested considerable interest in the witness around whom it is expected that a large proportion of the state's case will revolve. The witness stated that he was a resident of Fargo and had been held in the Cass county and the Barnes county jail at the instigation of States Attorney Green since September first. Two letters were introduced in court by States Attorney Green and identified by the witness as being in his hand writing. A document was introduced and identified by the witness as being written by him in States Attorney Green's office on the night of June 14. Fourteen postal cards were introduced and identified by the witness as having been written by him while he was being held in the Cass county jail. These exhibits were introduced in evidence by States Attorney Green with the statement that they were gathered for the purpose of comparing the hand writing contained therein with the signature of James Farrell on the register sheet of the Prescott Hotel on June 6. Time was given to counsel for the defense to look over and examine these exhibits and the defense counsel objected to the exhibit being entered in evidence on the ground that they were immaterial to the case being tried. The matter was argued before Judge Cooley who overruled the objection. During the time the exhibits were being examined the eyes of the witness, Andy Brown, and Gummer, met and both smiled. Gummer appeared to be slightly nervous during Brown's testimony, but had better control of himself than when the bloody exhibits were introduced yesterday. The state indicated at this point that they had concluded their direct examination which was somewhat of a surprise to the spectators and opposing counsel.

Under cross examination, Andy Brown stated that he had been interrogated three separate times by Deputy Sheriff Milligan, while being confined in the Cass county jail. He stated that Milligan came in one evening and asked him to fill out a blank with a number of questions but this he refused to do. The state objected to Andy Brown making a speech and relating his experiences while in the jail and this objection was sustained. Counsel for the defense seemed at a loss to know just how to cross-examine Brown and so excused him with the request that he remain in the city as they might want to call him again. States Attorney Green stated that the state had no intention of releasing the witness from custody at the present time.

H.J. Hagan, 61, former president of the Scandinavian American Bank at Fargo stated that he now lived at Seattle, Wash., had lived there about fifteen months and that he was in court as a voluntary witness. He testified that he came to Fargo on the night of June 6 on N.P. Train No. 4., arriving there about 12:55 p.m. He went to Waldorf, looked in the door and saw that the chairs in the lobby were occupied by several sleeping men and decided that all of the rooms were taken. He then went to the Prescott Hotel to see if he could get a room there. He stated that he was not familiar with the Prescott Hotel and had not been in the hotel for fourteen years, having stopped there only once and that time being fourteen years previously. He stated that he arrived at the Prescott two or three minutes after one o'clock that the lobby was very dimly lighted and that first he did not notice anyone in the lobby. He walked to the desk and saw a man whom he later identified as the clerk and defendant Gummer. He stated that he registered and that Gummer fumbled and appeared nervous when getting the key to his room out of the key rack. Gummer then took Hagan to his room, which was 31, carrying Hagan's grip and preceding Hagan up the stairs. The witness stated that Gummer appeared nervous fumbled considerable by putting the key in the key hole and had some difficulty in unlocking the door, went into the room and fumbled considerably in switching on the light. Before Gummer left the room he asked him to try the key on the inside of the door as the difficulty he had in opening the door led Hagan to believe that he might have the same difficulty in unlocking the door from the inside. Gummer tried the key and said it was all right. The witness was very tired and undressed immediately, washed and went to bed. In answer to a question by Green he stated that he had gotten some hot water to wash with from the bathroom across the hall which had been pointed out to him by Gummer. Hagan was asleep before 1:30 and was awakened in the morning by noises outside his door in the hall, between 7 and 8 o'clock in the morning. He heard no noises during the night. He stated that on awakening he called the office and asked them to advise an attorney in Moorhead that he had arrived in the city the previous night. This he did because he had been called to Moorhead to testify before the Clay county district court in a case which was to be tried on June 7 and he wished his attorney to be advised that he was within call. The party answering this phone in the office refused to make the call for Hagan and Hagan did it himself and returned to bed. Two men knocked at his door while he was in bed and he admitted them. He was not able to identify these men but stated that he presumed they were officers. They asked him whether he had heard any noise during the night and he told them he had not. After the officers' visit to his room Mr. Hagan got up, dressed and went out of the hotel to get his breakfast returning to the hotel about 12 o'clock noon when he stepped out, took his grip, and went over to Moorhead. Hagan reiterated his statement that he had heard absolutely no noise during the night and had not been out of his room after retiring at 1:30 and before being awakened by the officers in the morning.

Under cross examination Hagan stated that when he came in to the Prescott Hotel on the night in question Gummer was seated behind the desk and that it was necessary for Hagan to make some noise to arouse him. After getting Gummer's attention he made some inquiry as to the rates for rooms in the hotel, told Gummer that he wanted a clean bed, and asked for one of the rooms carrying the rate of $1.25.

He then registered. He did not recall having seen anyone else in the lobby while he was there. He stated that Gummer got the key to room 31 from the key rack. When questioned as to how much fumbling Gummer did in getting the key the witness appeared irritated but after several questions admitted that Gummer had produced the key without any more fumbling than would ordinarily be required in finding a key in a key rack which was dimly lighted and that it did not take Gummer more than two or three seconds to produce the key. After producing the key Gummer took Hagan directly to room 31. A number of questions brought out the fact that Gummer did not fumble when inserting the key in the key hole any more than person would ordinarily in a dimly lighted hall. Hagan also admitted that when entering room 31 he personally could not see the electric light bulb and admitted that Gummer did not fumble unduly in locating the bulb and turning on the light and the light was turned on by Gummer within an instant after entering the room. The final question asked of the witness was "did you ever have any conversation with a man named C.L. Thomas either in the lobby of the Hotel Prescott or in room 31?" Hagan replied "absolutely no." Hagan was excused at this point with the request that he be prepared to take the stand again this afternoon.

John Wertin, 68, of Fargo, testified that he was employed at the Herbst's Department Store, that he occupied room 65 on the fourth floor of the Prescott Hotel, that he retired at 9:30 on the night in question and arose about 7:30 the following morning, went down stairs, left the key to his room at the desk, told the officers there that he had heard no noises during the night and went his way. He was excused without cross examination .

Attorney Barnett had a bad cold this morning and had considerable difficulty in keeping his voice under control and he requested Judge

Cooley to call a recess at this time which the judge did, recessing the court at 11:35.

When court recessed at 11:55 this morning about two-thirds of the spectators remained in their seats, preferring to go without their dinner than to run the chance of losing their places in the court room. At 2 o'clock the court was jammed owing to the fact that it was reported around town that Hagan would be returned to the stand during the afternoon session, and it was estimated there were fully 400 people in the room. When the jury, attorneys and court attaches were in their places the jury roll was called and Judge Cooley announced that recess would be taken until Monday morning at 10 o'clock."

DAILY TIMES—RECORD [Valley City, ND], Vol. XVI—No. 210, Sat., Jan. 21, 1922, at pp.1,4. Print.

Preliminary Examination Over and Expected This Week Interesting Testimony

DAILY TIMES—RECORD [Valley City, ND], Vol. XVI—No. 210, Sat., Jan. 21, 1922, Mon., Jan. 23, 1922, at pp.1,4. Print.

RESUME OF TRIAL SO FAR

Preliminary Examination Over and Expected This Week Will Develop Interesting Testimony

"The first week of the Gummer trial closed on Saturday. The first two days were taken up with the selection of a jury and the examination of witnesses did not start until late Wednesday afternoon. Thursday and Friday the state disposed of witnesses quite rapidly and the material witnesses were not brought into court until Saturday morning. As Saturday was a short session their examination was very brief.

The state had introduced in evidence photographs of room 30 as found the morning following the tragedy together with the bloody rags with which the girl was bound, and shown plans of the hotel which will be used for reference in the examination of witnesses. They have also introduced the brass nozzle with which the girl was murdered and have entered certain exhibits with which they expect to prove the connection of Andy Brown with the signature of James Farrell on the hotel register. The majority of the witnesses called up to Friday night were people who had been in the Prescott hotel on the eve in question and whom circumstances showed could not have had anything to do with the crime. Their exams brief and they were brought here to testify merely as a part of the state's process of elimination, the state's avowed intention being to prove that the crime could not have been committed by anyone other than the accused.

When Andy Brown was called to the stand on Saturday morning those in the court room felt that the preliminaries were over and that the case against Gummer would soon be brought to light, but the examination of this witness was so brief that the only thing of importance divulged was the fact that the state would attempt to prove that Brown signed the name, James Farrell, to the hotel register. It is expected that the state will call handwriting experts to testify as to this phase of the case the first of this week. The examination of H.J. Hagan was also brief and the cross-examination of the witness merely showed that Hagan had placed undue stress on the nervousness of the defendant when he had registered and been shown to his room. The name of a mysterious C.L. Thomas was brought into the case during the cross examination of Hagan and it is expected that the defense will produce information regarding this man that will have considerable bearing on the case Hagan will be returned to the stand for further cross examination some time during the week.

Saturday's session, while short, showed that the state was just beginning their work of proving their case against Gummer and it is expected that the developments of this week will give a true insight into the commission of the crime."

DAILY TIMES—RECORD [Valley City, ND], Vol. XVI—No. 210, Sat., Jan. 21, 1922, Mon., Jan. 23, 1922, at pp.1,4. Print.

Sounds Demonstrated
Noises Awakened Her

DAILY TIMES—RECORD [Valley City, ND], Vol. XVI—No. 211, Mon., Jan. 23, 1922, at pp.1,4. Print.

SICKNESS OF STATE'S ATTY. GREEN CAUSES ADJOURNMENT OF GUMMER TRIAL

"After adjournment on Saturday States Attorney Green was taken sick and has been under the care of physicians and a nurse, and confined to his room since that time. His place in the courtroom was taken this morning by his partner, Attorney C.C. Wattam, of Fargo. Three witnesses were examined this morning. After their examination Attorney Wattam asked, that owing to the fact that Mr. Green was more familiar with the case, and that his doctor would not permit him to leave his room today, he would ask the court to adjourn until 10 o'clock tomorrow morning. As there was no objection from the counsel for the defense, Judge Cooley granted the request.

As the case progresses there is a noticeable increase in the number of women and girls in attendance in the court room. Spectators began arriving this morning before six o'clock and when court convened the room was jammed. The first witness called was John Van Vorst of Fargo, who stated that he had been night watchman at the Herbst Department Store for the past two years and held that position at the time of the murder of Miss Wick. The witness and family lived in the annex of the Prescott Hotel at that time. He stated, in describing the layout of the Annex that the bedroom occupied by himself and wife, adjoined room 30 of the hotel proper, a fourteen inch brick wall intervening. The bed of the Van Vorst's was placed with the foot of the bed toward the wall. The witness stated that he went on duty at Herbst's at 5:45 p.m., went home for lunch about 10 o'clock, met his wife outside of the department store and went to the hotel. He saw some people in the lobby but did not notice who they were other than that he recognized Mrs. Lawrence who was behind the desk. He then went to their apartment and had lunch. While he was eating Mrs. Van Vorst went out twice, and he supposed went to the lobby of the hotel to phone regarding a sick call which she was expecting. The witness left the hotel at 11 o'clock and returned to his duties at the store. When he left the defendant was behind the desk in the office. He returned to the hotel between 5 and 6 o'clock in the morning and stated that Gummer was in a chair behind the desk when he came in. The witness further stated that several days later he made a test of certain sounds alleged to have been heard by Mrs. Van Vorst. He made this test in company with Captain Welch and another man whom he did not know.

Sounds Demonstrated

The tests consisted of Mr. VanVorst walking on the roof of the annex while Mrs. Van Vorst, Captain Welch and the other man stayed in the apartment and listened to the sounds produced. The witness stated that there was a window in the apartment on the ground floor which was open. This was used by Mr. Van Vorst and the children in leaving the apartment at times owing to the fact that the outside door had been padlocked by Mrs. Lawrence. Under cross examination the witness stated that this door had been locked for at least two weeks prior to the night in question. The witness also stated under cross examination that when he had returned in the hotel between 5 and 6 o'clock of the morning following the tragedy the defendant Gummer had been seated in a chair behind the desk and was apparently dosing. Under re-direct examination the witness stated that when making the experiment on the roof of the annex he found that the roof was of graveled construction and that he had seen no sign of any tin. Mrs. Van Vorst was next called to the stand and substantiated her husband's testimony as to his movements that night as far as her knowledge went. She stated that on the night in question she had expected a call to the home of a sick friend and had arranged for Jack Smith, a taxi driver, to call for her and take her to this friend. When she returned to the hotel with her husband about 10:25 she had asked Gummer if anyone had inquired for her and had left word that she be notified if anyone did call. She returned to the lobby from her apartments within a few minutes to try and phone but the line was busy and she waited for a few minutes. While waiting Arnold Rasmussen and Marie Wick came in and Miss Wick registered. Mrs. Van Vorst returned to her apartment and had lunch with her husband returned to the lobby about 11:40. She stated that Gummer was at the switchboard at this time but that she paid no attention to his conversation on the phone. She was in the lobby about ten minutes and while she was there Fred Lawrence came in and spoke to Gummer. She then returned to her apartment and waited downstairs until 12 o'clock when she took her baby upstairs and put her to bed, retiring herself at 12:30.

Noises Awakened Her

The witness stated that she was asleep within a few minutes but was awakened shortly after going to asleep by some noise that sounded like a base ball being thrown against the wall intervening between her room and room 30. She stated that the floor of her apartment was considerably lower than the floor in room 30. After being awakened she heard a noise which sounded to her as though someone was walking on the tin and led her to believe that there was some one on the roof. She then heard a sudden noise which sounded like some one jumping and resembled a heavy thud. She stated that she had taken part in the experiments conducted by Captain Welch and a detective with Mr. Van Vorst walking on the roof and that the noises made by Mr. Van Vorst did not resemble the noises she had heard on the night in question. She further stated that certain experiments made with Deputy Sheriff Milligan in room 30 sounded similar to the noises she had heard resembling walking on tin, throwing a ball against the wall and jumping.

Under cross examination the witness stated that she had never been advised that Jack Smith had been at the hotel that night. The witness stated that she told her husband the morning following the tragedy that she had thought some one was on the roof but that her husband had told her that she was mistaken as there was no tin on the roof. She believed it, however, until the experiments by her husband and police officers had changed her belief.

J.T. 'Jack' Smith, taxi driver of Fargo, stated that he was at the Prescott Hotel between 10:40 and 10:50 on the night in question, being called there to get Mrs. Van Vorst, but stated that he did not go into the hotel but waited outside above five minutes, and as no one showed up he left. He stated that while he was there he saw a young man and young lady come to the hotel and stated that he later identified the young lady at the morgue as being the same person he had seen. However under cross examination he admitted that the slight glance he had given her when she came to the hotel was not sufficient to enable him to identify her after death.

Captain William Welch under examination, stated that he in the company with McDonald, another police officer, conducted the experiment on the roof of the annex and stated that Mr. Van Vorst had walked on the roof but that he himself had not been on the roof. Objection was made to Captain Welch testifying as to the statements made by Mrs. Van Vorst and the objection was sustained. After a few minor questions by counsel for defense, the witness was excused.

At this point Attorney Wattam asked for adjournment until 10 o'clock tomorrow morning and his request was granted, adjournment taking place at 11:45."

DAILY TIMES—RECORD [Valley City, ND], Vol. XVI—No. 211, Mon., Jan. 23, 1922, at pp.1,4. Print.

Continued Illness of Attorney Holds Up Gummer Trial

DAILY TIMES—RECORD [Valley City, ND], Vol. XVI—No. 212, Tues., Jan. 24, 1922, at p.1. Print.

CONTINUED ILLNESS OF ATTORNEY
HOLDS UP GUMMER TRIAL

"The continued illness of State Attorney Green prevented the continuance of the Gummer trial today and court is still adjourned pending his recovery. Mr. Green has been in poor health for some time and his present illness is due to overwork in connection with the prosecution of William Gummer. It will be remembered that Mr. Green was taken sick during the course of the Heaton trial in Fargo which necessitated the adjournment of that trial for two weeks. It is to be hoped that Mr. Green will soon be able to resume his duties, and advice from those in touch with him are to the effect that he will probably be in shape to take charge of the prosecution tomorrow."

DAILY TIMES—RECORD [Valley City, ND], Vol. XVI—No. 212, Tues., Jan. 24, 1922, at p.1. Print.

Green's Illness Delays Trial of William Gummer Attorney Green Suffers Relapse

DAILY TIMES—RECORD [Valley City, ND], Vol. XVI—No. 213, Wed., Jan. 25, 1922, at p.1. Print.

COURT HAS ADJOURNED UNTIL

10:00 A.M. MONDAY

Green's Illness Delays Trial of William Gummer Attorney Green Suffers Relapse

"Wm. C. Green, states attorney of Cass county, is still confined to his room under medical care, and court is still recessed pending his recovery. Report has it that he was feeling considerably improved last night but suffered a relapse during the night, his temperature rising, and his doctors will not allow him to leave the room as yet. Mr. Green has been working mighty hard for some time, having had two very important cases to prosecute in the past month, and was so run down physically that a cold which he contracted took a firm hold on him. It was feared at first that he was contracting pneumonia but this danger seems to be past now. It is hoped that he will soon be out be in shape to continue the case against Gummer."

DAILY TIMES—RECORD [Valley City, ND], Vol. XVI—No. 213, Wed., Jan. 25, 1922, at p.1. Print.

———————————

Gummer Trial Delayed by Illness

WARREN SHEAF [Warren, MN], Vol. XLIL—No. 4, Wed. Jan. 25, 1922, at p.1. Print.

GUMMER TRIAL DELAYED BY ILLNESS

"The trial of William Gummer the alleged slayer of Marie Wick, a young girl of Grygla, Minn., at a Fargo hotel last summer, has been delayed on account of of the illness of William C. Green, the state's attorney of Cass county, and also Judge Barnett, the attorney for the defendant. Charles C. Wattam, who is the assistant state's attorney of Cass county has gone to Valley City to assist Mr. Green in conducting the case. It is expected that the trial will be resumed on Thursday of this week. Thus it has fallen to the lot of two Marshall county [Minnesota] young men, William Green and Charles Wattam, to prosecute and convict the murderer of the pure and innocent girl of Marshall county and avenge her most cruel death. Mr. Green, the state's attorney is a son of Mr. and Mrs. F.A. Green of Stephen and

Mr. Wattam, the assistant attorney is the son of Dr. G.E. Wattam of Warren. Both were born and reared in Marshall county and are graduates of Warren High School. They will spare no effort to bring the guilty one to justice.

The whole state of North Dakota is aroused over one of the most heinous crimes ever perpetrated in the state and the court is packed every day during the trial. Step by step the prosecution is unfolding evidence, circumstantial in character, through which the state hopes to convict the young man charged with the horrible crime. Many witnesses have already been examined and many more will be called when the trial is resumed on Thursday."

WARREN SHEAF [Warren, MN], Vol. XLIL—No. 4, Wed. Jan. 25, 1922, at p.1. Print.

Summary of Former Court Proceedings

DAILY TIMES—RECORD [Valley City, ND], Vol. XVI—No. 223, Mon., Feb. 6, 1922, at p.1. Print.

WILLIAM GUMMER'S TRIAL IS RESUMED TODAY

Summary of Former Court Proceedings

PROGRESS MADE IN GUMMER CASE

Trial Halted on January 23 by the Illness of Green Had Only Reached the Preliminary Stages When Adjourned

"The trial of Wm. Gummer on a charge of murder in connection with the death of Marie Wick in the Prescott hotel in Fargo on June 7, 1921, was opened in the Barnes county district court on Jan. 17. States Attorney Wm. C. Green of Cass county led charge of prosecution and he was assisted in the selection of the jury by States Attorney L.S.B. Richie of this city. Chas. Pollock was also assisting him. The defense is represented by Judge Barnett and Clair Brickner of Fargo and H.W. Swenson of Devils Lake. Mr. Swenson is a brother-in-law of the accused. Attorney A.P. Paulson assisted the defense in the jury selection.

Preliminary Stages Over

The first two days of the trial was consumed in the selection of the jury and the jury was completed about 4:00 o'clock on Wednesday afternoon. The announcement of the completion of the jury was a surprise to everyone. After the selection of the jury the state entered the preliminary stages of the legal battle and began calling witnesses to the stand whom circumstances showed could not have committed the crime. Some 30 witnesses were examined during the first few days but in many cases the examination was merely perfunctory and tended to show the impossibility of the witness having any direct connection with the commission of the crime. The various gruesome exhibits found on the scene of the crime have been entered in evidence by the state and identified by witnesses. These exhibits tell a graphic story of the brutality of the murder and are a repugnant signs in the courtroom. The state had not produced a great deal of evidence connecting the accused with the crime up to the end of the fifth day of the preliminary stages requiring the attention of the court up to trial time. When court opened on Saturday morning, the 21, the placing of H.J. Hagan on the witness stand led the spectators to believe that the preliminary stages were over and that the state was about to start proving their contention that the crime could not have been committed by anyone other than the accused. The examination of Hagan was not long and he was turned over to the defense for cross examination. Cross examination by Barnett brought out some discrepancies in his direct testimony. The defense excused him while reserving the right to again place him on the stand. He will undoubtedly be returned for further questioning before the close of the case. The placing of Andy Brown, chum of the accused and material witness held by the state, on the stand and the short examination of him was a decided surprise to everyone and no less to the defense counsel. The state has announced their intention of showing the connection of Brown with the signature of James Farrell on the hotel register on the night in question. A handwriting expert by whom it is hoped to prove the connection, was in the city at the time of the adjournment. He will return to the city during the week and take the stand. Sensational developments in the case are expected thru the use of Brown, and speculation as to the connection with the crime is ? In the city. There are several points in the evidence so far presented to obtain a conviction of the defendant but the state has signified ? intention of straightening these ? out.

Defense Counsel Silent

The counsel for the defense have given no indication as yet to their plan of defense or as to the identity of the witnesses they will call to the stand. Neither have they indicated whether the accused will take the stand in his own defense. If he does not take the stand there is the danger of omission prejudicing the jury against him. If he does the state will be given the opportunity of cross examination him. What action will be taken in this matter can not be forecasted at this time. The defense as introduced the name of a mysterious C.L. Thomas into the case in the cross examination of Hagan. There is much speculation as to the identity of this man but it is not known definitely as to whether the introduction of his name has any direct bearing on the case or not.

The opening of court on the morning of the 23 found States Attorney Green unable to leave his room at the hotel and his place was taken in the courtroom by Assistant States Attorney Wattam who examined minor witnesses during the morning. On his motion for adjournment court was recessed until the next day, when it was continued for the following Monday. Mr. Green's continued illness demanded a further adjournment until today.

Great Interest Manifested

Owing to the wide spread publicity given the case, due to the unprecedented brutality of the murder a great deal of interest is being taken in the trial. As the preliminaries are over and the state is prepared to begin at once the proving of its claims the developments of the next few days will be watched with keen interest by the people of the state. The Times-Record will continue giving the full particulars of the evidence as presented, without prejudice for or against the accused and without coloring the testimony in any way. Feeling that our subscribers do not care to read the testimony verbatim as given we will continue giving a complete resume of the evidence as brought out in the examination of each witness. The court proceedings will be given up to 3:30 every afternoon, at which time we go to press, and will give you later information than any paper coming to the city.

————————

When court reconvened at 10 this morning there were not a great many spectators in the courtroom, due to the fact that the public was not certain that the case would be called. However, of those in attendance there was a larger percentage of women than in previous seasons. The officials of Cass county arrived in the city last night on No. 3. Gummer was brought into the court room and appeared as nonchalant as ever. He had the appearance of having been freshly laundered and seemed in good spirits. Before court opened he conversed for several minutes with his attorneys in a low voice. Mr. Gummer, Sr., with several members of the family were in attendance and took their former seats on the front row just outside the rail, back of the accused. Hans Wick, who had returned to Grygla, Minn., during the adjournment has not returned to the city as yet. Nels Hoff, uncle

of the murdered girl, and his son, Hans were in attendance and took
their usual seat in the unused jury box.

New Witnesses Filed by State

At the opening of court States Attorney Green presented two affidavits made by his assistant C.C. Wattam, and asked that two additional witness name be filled with the information. There being
no objection from the defense the names of Roy Murphy and E.B.
Charlson were annexed. Roy Murphy is the prisoner now being held
in the Cass county jail under sentence for the issuance of a fraudulent
check. He was in the Cass county jail during the confinement of the
accused, Gummer. The state is not willing at this time to disclose any
information regarding Charlson. Murphy will be brought to the city
tomorrow morning.

Previous Testimony Being Read

Motion by Judge Barnett to the effect that previous testimony in
the case be read to the jury was sustained and Attorneys Claire Brickner for the defense, and Charles Pollock, for the state, were instructed
to read all of the testimony as far transcribed. The testimony thus
far taken with the exception of the evidence brought out through
the examination of the doctors and chemists examined and a part of
the testimony relative to the condition of some of the rooms when
examined the morning following the tragedy This testimony covers
about 225 typewritten pages. As the attorneys are reading this at the
rate of about fifty pages per hour, a large proportion of the day's
proceedings will be taken up with this work. It is not expected that
the state will be able to introduce any further evidence until after four
o'clock this afternoon.

The state was undecided at the noon recess whether they would call
Deputy Sheriff Milligan as their first witness to testify as to the various
tests made in room 30 for the comparison sounds heard by Mrs. Van

Vorst during the night on which the crime was committed or whether they would first call George O'Brien, another material witness.

Andy Brown Nervous

A great deal of interest is being displayed in the prospective exemption of Andy Brown. Andy Brown, the chum of William Gummer, has been held by the state as a material witness in the case. States Attorney Green has indicated that the state will prove by the introduction of expert testimony that the signature of James Farrell on the hotel register on the night in question was signed by Andy Brown. If the state can prove their contention Andy Brown will no doubt face a charge of being an accessory to the crime which will place him in nearly as serious a situation as William Gummer now finds himself. Brown has an entirely different temperament than Gummer, being of a very nervous disposition and having less control of his feelings than Gummer. As the time for his re-appearance in court draws near he displays his nervousness more and more continually pacing his cell and corridor at a rapid rate which at time nearly approaches a dog trot. He evidently realizes the seriousness of his position and dreads the time when he will again take the stand for examination and cross examination.

States Attorney Green has recovered from his recent illness, the only effect being a slight difficulty in hearing. He resumes his work today with added enthusiasm and states that the trial will proceed quite rapidly from now on."

DAILY TIMES—RECORD [Valley City, ND], Vol. XVI—No. 223, Mon., Feb. 6, 1922, at p.1. Print.

Important Testimony Introduced Today

DAILY TIMES—RECORD [Valley City, ND], Vol. XVI—No. 224, Tues., Feb. 7, 1922, at pp.1,4. Print.

IMPORTANT TESTIMONY INTRODUCED TODAY IN GUMMER CASE

O'Brien, Witness For The State, Gives Important Evidence Today. He Says Nobody Was In The Office or Behind The Desk In Prescott Hotel Lobby at 12:15 on The Night Marie Wick Was Murdered. Is Very Positive on This Point In His Evidence.

George O'Brien First Witness

"When court reconvened yesterday noon the reading of the previous testimony was continued. This occupied the attention of the court until 8:30 p.m. At which time recess was taken. Court was called at 3:50 p.m. And the state called George O'Brien, 49, of Fargo, to the stand. The witness stated that he had lived in the Colonial apartments adjoining the Prescott hotel on the south. He testified that he was employed at the Gardner hotel as elevator man that his son Lee was employed at the same hotel as bell boy. That on the night of June 6 they quit work at 12 o'clock, midnight and went directly to their home in the Colonial apartments, passing the Prescott hotel in doing so. The witness stated that he had been in the Prescott hotel a great many times while living in Fargo and that he knew Gummer personally at the time of the tragedy. On the night in question he stopped in front of the Prescott hotel to light a cigar and that, after lighting his cigar he looked thru the window into his office and noted that the office and the lobby were quite dark, there being only one light lit, and that a desk light with a brass shade which was over the switchboard behind the desk. He further stated that on previous nights it had been customary for two lights to be lit directly above the desk. He stated that he looked at the clock behind the desk and saw that it was exactly 12:15. He further stated that there was no one in the lobby as far as he could see at the time. States Attorney Green asked the witness if he gone into the hotel to ask for a postage stamp to which the witness replied emphatically 'no.' On further questioning he stated that he had been in the hotel on the Wednesday night following the tragedy to get a stamp. He fixed the time of this visit by remembering that on Wednesday night his niece had arrived from Mandan and known that her parents would worry about her arrival, due to the tragedy a few nights previous, he had written them a postal card telling them that she had arrived safe. For the reason he knew that it was after the murder had been committed. He stated that he had gotten the stamp from Gummer and remembered a conversation with the accused in which he referred to the hotel register and asked Gummer if everyone in the hotel on the night in question had been checked up, to which Gummer replied that they had all been checked but one—a 'Mr. Farrell.' Gummer then gave him a letter to mail and the witness took the letter and his own postal card to the West Railroad mail box and mailed them.

Witness Sure as to Time

Under cross examination counsel for the defense asked the witness if it were not possible for him to be mistaken as to the time the postal mail was mailed to which the witness replied that it was not. Counsel asked if had the postal card and as being answered in the affirmative the witness was requested to bring it into court which he did. Further questioning brought out the fact that the postal card had been mailed at 12:30 Thursday morning. At this point the defense entered the postal card as exhibit for the defense No. 2. The witness on being questioned as to the height of the front window sill stated that it was about four and one half feet above the sidewalk, that the top of the desk was about four feet above the floor, but due to the fact that the window sill was about two feet above the floor the top of the desk was approximately six and one half feet above the level of the sidewalk. On being questioned as to the arrangement of the office in the Hotel Prescott the witness stated that he remembered a big arm chair behind the desk which Gummer ordinarily sat in.

Son Substantiates Father

Leo O'Brien, 18, son of George O'Brien was next called to the stand and corroborated his father's testimony regarding their walk home, noticing but one light in the Prescott hotel and noting that the time was exactly 12:15. Only a few minor questions were asked the witness under cross examination but did not shake his testimony as given.

Deputy Sheriff James Milligan stated that he had examined all the windows and doors in the hotel on the morning of June 7 shortly after having been called to the hotel by Fred Lawrence. Much questioning brought out the fact that all the windows proved with screens were found locked from the inside. The witness stated that there was no possible means of exit by way of the window of room 40. He stated that the hall windows in the Van Vorst apartment of the annex was closed an all other windows not provided with screens were closed. He further stated that he examined the windows for signs of any dust or marks of any description and that all windows were dusty and showed plainly that they had not been used as a means of exit from the hotel. The witness stated that he examined the outside of the hotel particularly the fire escape and a ladder which led from the fire escape to the roof of the annex. These he found to be covered with dust and slime with no marks showing. He also stated that the roof was more or less dusty and that his walking on the roof left foot prints but that there were no other footprints found by him other than his own. He stated that there were no other unusual, reasonable means of exit than those, which he had followed.

Milligan Again On Stand

Officer Milligan stated that he was in the basement of the Prescott hotel on the morning of the seventh, accompanied by Gummer. That in the few days following he had visited the basement many times but had seen nothing unusual until the Monday following the crime. He stated that he had been down there on Sunday evening and saw nothing out of the way but that he was down again about 9 o'clock Monday morning and found a pair of trousers lying at the bottom of the stairs The trousers were then shown to the witness and his attention called to certain stains on them which he identified as being there when the trousers were found. A hole, evidently made by cutting out a piece of the material was shown the witness who stated that this hole had not been in the trousers when they were found. He stated that the defendant was still employed in the hotel at the time the trousers were found.

Questioned as to the finding of the stains on the Bible in room 31, Officer Milligan stated that he had noted the stain at the time, that he had examined other similar Bibles in various rooms of the hotel and found no other stains on them. Questioned as to the condition of the walls thru out the hotel the witness stated that they had all appeared badly stained and that the stains had the appearance of having been caused by the crushing of bed bugs.

Witness Tells of Tests

The witness stated that he had been in room 30 on the day which Mrs. Van Vorst had testified certain experiments had been made and that nothing in the room had been changed between that day and the morning of the discovery of the body. Strong objections to the introduction of testimony were made by the defense but the objection, after being argued, was overruled. Officer Milligan, on being questioned as to what he did during these experiments, stated that he shook the springs of the bed violently trampled over the pipes which ran along the floor next to the wall and slapped the bed once with a flat iron bar.

The witness testified that on the morning of the seventh he had examined the body of Marie Wick and found that the bandages covering her face did not cover her eyes, when the body was found, they were wide open. He further stated that there had been no change made in the lock of room 30 during the ten days following the commission of the crime and that he had tested the key which is produced in evidence in court and found that it would not unlock the door. He stated that he had opened the door between room 30 and 31 himself and that he had noticed that it has not been opened for some time. The door between these two rooms was locked and no key could be found fitting the lock. The witness opened the door using a master skeleton key of his own. In addition to the lock the door which was an ordinary pine door had been fastened with a nail. The steam pipes led from room 30 down thru the room below which had been occupied by May Melaas, one of the employees of the hotel, and the witness stated that there were quite a hole around the pipes where it went thru the floor of room 30 and ceiling of the room below. This pipe led right by the head of the cot in the May Melaas room. The witness stated that there were no trains going west out of Fargo between the arrival of Northern Pacific train No. 4 and a Great Northern train which leaves at nearly morning

Cross Examination Not Completed

Under cross examination the witness stated that he did not know whether any west bound trains on the night of June 6 were late or not and could not say just what time they had left Fargo. Under questioning Officer Milligan stated that there were two possible exits from the hotel without going thru the office, one is a window in room 63 which leads to the roof of the annex and then by way to the ladder to the fire escape and down, the other being thru the Van Vorst apartment on the first floor and out thru the window. Examination brought out the fact that there was sufficient room between the door and door jam between rooms 30 and 31 to push an ordinary case knife between them. He further stated that the nail which held the door was driven into the door jam about one or one and a half inches, that it was necessary to use a pair of pliers in removing it and that after opening the door he had replaced the nail in the hole. Judge Barnett asked the witness if his attention had been called to stains, resembling blood stains, on the door of room 31 leading to the hall to which Milligan replied "not that I recall". The attention of the court was drawn to the fact that it was then five o'clock and upon the statement by Judge Barnett that he could not finish the cross examination of the witness yesterday Judge Cooley ordered a recess until this morning.

Greater Number Women Present

When court convened at 10 o'clock this morning the room was filled and with a greater percentage of women than at any previous time during the trial. Gummer's family had their usual places and were accompanied by several people from Mayville and surrounding district. Hans Wick was not in the courtroom this morning but is expected to arrive during the day.

Deputy Sheriff David Milligan was returned to the stand for further cross examination and stated that he reached the Prescott at eight o'clock on the morning of June 7, that Sheriff Kraemer and Deputy Sheriff South were there when he arrived and that he went directly to room 30. He went out a few minutes and called the coroner and coroner's jury, returning to the hotel in about 45 minutes. Going to room 30 and remaining there about 30 minutes. He made the experiments in room 30 on the afternoon of the 7 and was alone in the room while making the tests. On being questioned as to what he did in room 30 he stated that in going in he went directly to the bed and placed one knee on the mattress and shook the bed, walked around to the other side, and in so doing trampled on the two pipes which ran along the wall by the floor, stepping on the upper pipe and allowing his foot to slip off onto the lower one, then placing his knee on the side of the bed nearest the wall, shaking the bed, and again walking around the foot of the bed, trampling on the pipes again and making the noises produced the first time. At this point Judge Barnett asked that the head of the bed, which had been entered in evidence, be brought to the court room. The witness testified that he struck the corner of the bedstead with a flat piece of stove iron. Bailiff Moordale was sent in search of an iron to use in striking the bed and the witness struck the bed to reproduce the noise as produced in the test, but stated that the iron used in the test was entirely different from the one which he used in the courtroom. The jury was shown the dent in the bedstead which the evidence had shown was there when the room was examined the morning after the tragedy. The witness said he had not tried to produce another dent when doing the test in room 30 but had only tried to reproduce a sound which the making of the dent might have produced. Counsel for the defense asked the witness if he thought he could find an iron such as had been used in making the test and he replied that he thought he could if he had the time. Judge Barnett informed him that he would be given time to find one. The witness stated that the window of room 30 was closed while making the test but that the door had been opened. Officer Milligan was in room 30 the morning of the seventh and found that the room was not made up, that the room showed indications of having been slept in, that one towel had been used and that there was water in the wash bowl. He was in room 31 after the body had been removed from 30 some time after 9:30 in the morning and reiterated his previous testimony regarding the condition of the room. Barnett asked Milligan if his attention had ever been called to blood stains on the hall door of room 63 to which Milligan replied that it had not. He was excused to be returned later with an iron such as he had been used in the tests in room 30.

Walter Jennings of Fargo said that he was assistant chief clerk of the U.S. Railway mail service and explained the system of dating mail taken directly from the mail boxes to the cars between St. Paul and the first mail division on the N.P. at Jamestown, saying it was customary for the mail clerk to date all mail taken in this way with the date on which left the initial terminal, or St. Paul. He was shown the postal card written by George O'Brien which O'Brien had testified he mailed at 12:30 the morning of the ninth. The postal card described carried the post dated mark of June 8. And the witness stated that, agreeable to the custom in the use in the mail service this card would be mailed on No. 1 on June 9.

Bloody Pants Accounted For

Roscoe Hines, of Fargo, said that he had lived at the Prescott hotel from October 27, 1920, to March 27, 1921, that he was an employee of the packing company and identified the pants shown in court as being a pair he had owned and thrown away some time about the first of March, but could not say whether the blood on the pants were there at the time they were thrown away at not. Under cross examination be stated that his job in the packing plant consisted of killing and assisting in the skinning of cattle and that considerable blood was gotten on his clothes in this work. Mrs. Hines, his wife, stated that she had thrown the pants away, on the advice of her husband, the last of February or the first of March, 1921, and that she had thrown them either at the foot of the stairs in the basement or behind the meat box in the basement. She stated that her husband's clothes were generally bloody at the knees of his trousers and the sleeves of his shirts and underwear.

Al. H. Leimbacher, Fargo, was the manager of the Gardner hotel and was one of the coroner's jury called to take part in the inquest held over the body of Marie Wick. Questioned as to whether he had any conversation with Gummer at the time of the inquest he said that he had. He told Gummer that he was in the hotel game and asked Gummer if he had been asleep at any time during the night of the tragedy to which Gummer replied that he absolutely was not. He also asked him if he had any visitors during the night or anybody had been with him to which Gummer replied that he had been alone all night. He asked him if it would be possible for anybody to have left the hotel either thru the office or down the back stairs and out the back hall without the knowledge of Gummer to which Gummer replied that it would have been impossible. Under cross examination Mr. Leimbacher reiterated his testimony regarding his conversation with Gummer and gave it word for word as given in the direct examination.

Mrs. Van Vorst was recalled to the stand and said that she could hear anyone walking in the halls downstairs when she was in her bed room upstairs but that she had not heard any one in the hall down stairs on the night of the tragedy after hearing the noises in room 30. Cross examination brought out the fact that the window in their apartment downstairs which had been used by her husband and children as a means of exit from the building was locked ordinarily but was not locked the night Marie Wick was murdered. After several questions as to certain particulars of the arrangement of rooms in her apartment she was excused.

Miss Melaas' Testimony Important

May Melaas, 41, chambermaid at the Prescott, whose home is at Ulm, Minn., stated that her rooms in the Prescott were room 72 and a room adjoining, that they were in the southwest corner of the building on the first floor and that her bedroom was directly under room 30. Miss Melaas said that she was in between the hours of 8:30 and 9 o'clock on the night Marie Wick was murdered and that she slept until just a trifle before four o'clock in the morning, fixing the time of awakening by the fact that the court house clock struck 4 shortly after she awoke. She said that she a noise in room 30 just a minute after four o'clock which resembled a noise made by some one jumping out of bed in room 30. She said that it sounded as though the occupant in room 30 had jumped out of the bed, struck the bed several times with what she supposed was a shoe, walked around the room and struck the bed a few more times. She then heard the party open the door and go out, close the door and go down the hall the front way to the office. She did not hear any one going down the back way after the noises had been produced. She unlocked the door to room 30 for Fred Lawrence the following morning, using a pass key, which was attached to a safety pin, went inside and came out immediately, left the door open went up to room 41 and made up the room and returned to the office to leave the key to room 41. She then returned to room 30 at the instigation of Fred Lawrence and locked the door. This was about 7 o'clock and two officers were in the office of the hotel when she left the key to 41.

Under cross examination Miss Melaas reiterated her statements as to her movements after awakening at 6 o'clock the morning after the tragedy. Counsel for the defense tried to shake her testimony as to the room she had made up before locking room 30 but she stated that while she was not absolutely certain the fact that room 41 was occupied by a steady roomer and it had been customary to make this up first in the morning, she thought that, 41 had been the room she had visited.

Irrespective of which room she visited, the bed had been used and more than one towel had been used but there was no dirty water in the room the witness supposing that the occupant had used the towels in the bath room. On being asked if she had ever told Mrs. Lawrence and a friend that she had heard no noises during the night, thinking that some one was in trouble and wishing to protect them the witness stated that she had not made any such statement to Fred Lawrence. Under redirect examination Miss Melaas stated that she could always hear anyone walking in the old dining room which adjoined her rooms. Under recross examination the witness said that she had heard the phone in room 30 ring two or three times shortly after she awoke at 6 o'clock.

Hagan Admits Previous Convictions

H.J. Hagan was returned to the stand for further cross examination and stated that he was a voluntary witness in the present case but admitted that he was present at the request of State Attorney Green. Judge Barnett asked Hagan if he was the same Hagan who had been prosecuted and convicted of a charge involving irregularities in the management of the Scandinavian-American Bank of Fargo. This question was objected by State Attorney Green but the objection was overruled. Hagan said that he did not know the status of the case at this time.

Barnett asked, 'Do you, or do you know whether you were convicted of the charge?'

Hagan said 'I presume so'.

Barnett said, 'Well did you or did you not furnish bonds for your appearance in court for a second trial on this charge?'

Hagan said, 'I presume so.'

Barnett, 'You "PRESUME." You didn't.'

The witness was excused.

Cross Examination of Brown Halted

Andy Brown was returned to the stand at the request of Barnett for further cross examination and testified that he had written the states' exhibits, Nos. 55, 56, and 57, which are letters, and wrote two of the names appearing on states' exhibits No. 58 which is a copy of the Prescott hotel register. Barnett asked him:

'Did you write the name "James Farrell" on states' exhibit No. 14?'

This exhibit is the hotel register of June 6. The question was objected to on the grounds that such a question had not been included in the direct examination and the objection was sustained. Brown was excused.

States Attorney Green requested that, as the next testimony to be given was of a technical nature and would require some time, that recess be taken. This was done at 11:45 with the instructions to the jury that with the instructions to the jury that the afternoon session would convene at 1:30 instead of two o'clock.

When court convened at 1:30 p.m. The court room was jammed, the public hearing that the case was well under way and turning out in a large number.

May Melaas Did Not Hear

John Van Vorst was returned to the stand at the request of Barnett and stated that he returned to the hotel Prescott at 5:30 the morning of the seventh, that he entered thru the main door in front and walked thru the old dining room which adjoins room 72 and walked very close to the wall. This is the room occupied by May Melaas and the witness walked thru the dining room before she awoke in the morning. May Melaas stated under cross examination this morning that she could easily hear any one walking thru this room but that she had not heard any one in the room between 4 o'clock and 6 o'clock on the morning in question.

Sheriff Kraemer was returned to the stand and asked a couple of questions to straighten out the record on some previous testimony.

T.J. Caton, Minneapolis, teacher, hand writing expert and publisher was the next witness called and stated that he conducted a commercial school in Minneapolis about ten years ago and had since been publishing a work on rapid writing. He is a graduate of the Spencerian school of penmanship and has been recognized as a handwriting expert for the past 30 years, testifying in numerous cases the last forty years.

He had been requested last November by Assistant States Attorney C.C. Wattam to examine the specimens of handwriting contained in states' exhibit No. 14 which is the hotel register and No. 58 which is the segment written by Brown in Green's office. The witness stated that he had no indications at that time of the nature of the case. He informed M.M. Wattam that he could not give an opinion on the handwriting without the presentation of more specimens. He was then furnished with various letters and postal cards entered in evidence by the state and compare then with the signature of James Farrell on the hotel register sheet. The witness stated that.

Brown Signed James Farrell

'My opinion is that one and the same person wrote all specimens examined including the signature "James Farrell" on the register sheet Mr. Caton stated that it was necessary to have abundance of specimens for comparison in case of disputed hand writing. These testimonies must be undisputed samples of the handwriting of the person suspected. A black board was brought into the court room for the purpose of demonstrating methods of expert comparison. Mr. Caton said 'In the handwriting in dispute there are several letters which do not follow the mathematical standard for hand writing.'

The witness said that the notable letters in the signature of James Farrell and the specimens examined are the letters "r-a-f-w and the combinations rr and ell', these letters showing a striking similarity between the signature of James Farrell and the different words in the specimens presented. The 'R's' are exceptionally well made when used in the center of words but the writer had evidently formed the habit of completing a word with a horizontal stroke instead of a right curve and this applied in the undisputed hand writing of Brown as it also contains a stroke which may be called an eccentric stroke, the entail stroke extending across the entire field of the letter. This capital 'W' in Willmar and other words in the writing of Brown show a striking similarity. The small letter 's' is described by the witness as being formed in an unusual manner which is almost identical when superimposed on the undisputed handwriting with the 's' as written by Brown. Counsel for defense desires time in which to study his testimony in regard to specimens of hand writing and advised him that he would be recalled for cross examination tomorrow.

Fred Lawrence was returned to the stand and questioned briefly as to the occupant of room 41 before being turned over to Bartlett for cross examination. Lawrence stated that May Melaas did not make up room 40 the morning following the murder. When questioned regarding his conversation with the accused when they looked over the transom of room 30, the witness reiterated his previous testimony. Barnett asked Lawrence if he had made up or counted the cash in the till on the morning following the tragedy but the witness said he did not remember whether he had or not and that he did not remember Gummer telling him that he had been required to make change during the night, using two dollars of his own. The witness did not remember this but did not deny it. Asked as to his conversation with May Melaas on the morning following the murder he stated that he had asked Miss Melaas if she had heard any noise during the night and she told him that she had not. Under redirect examination he stated that Miss Melaas was very nervous and excited for several days following the tragedy.

Attorney Green Takes the Stand

States Attorney Green requested that the presentation of further evidence required the settlement of certain points of law by the judge asked that a recess be taken. This was at 3 o'clock and Judge Cooley ordered a recess until 3:45 p.m.

Following the recess States Attorney Green will take the stand to testify as to certain admissions made to him by Gummer in the few days following the murder of Marie Wick and the statements made by the accused before and after his arrest. The examination of Green will be conducted by Assistant States Attorney C.C. Wattam."

DAILY TIMES—RECORD [Valley City, ND], Vol. XVI—No. 224, Tues., Feb. 7, 1922, at pp.1,4. Print.

Attorney Green and Sheriff Kraemer on Stand

DAILY TIMES—RECORD [Valley City, ND], Vol. XVI—No. 225, Wed., Feb. 8, 1922, at p.1. Print.

GUMMER ADMITS LYING TO OFFICER

BLOOD ON PANTS NOT HUMAN BLOOD

Accused "Tried Out" all Single Women in Hotel

Judge Cooley Advised Women This Morning That Testimony To Be Introduced Would Not Be Very Edifying But That Some Plain Facts Would Be Stated. He Said That It Would Be An Opportune Time for Any To Leave Who So Desired—Many Left But a Few Remained.

4:30 p.m. State Rests Case.

"During the recess the attorneys for both sides argued the question of what admissions or statements by Gummer were admissible to the presented in evidence. This argument took place in the Judge's chamber before Judge Cooley. While court had been recessed until 3:45 p.m. The attorneys had not completed their confidential argument and court did not convene for some time afterwards. At 3:55 Attorney Barnett appeared at the door of the Judge's chamber and called the accused in to take part in the confidential talk of the attorneys before Judge Cooley.

Attorney Green on Stand

Court reconvened, following the recess, at 4:15 with States Attorney Wm. C. Green on the stand, being questioned by Attorney Charles Pollock. Mr. Green stated that he had been a stenographer for the supreme court for three years, and had been court reporter for five years following, and since that time had been assistant states attorney and states attorney for Cass county. He told of a meeting in the private office of Sheriff Kraemer in the Cass county court house about 3 o'clock on the afternoon of June 14, 1921, at which time the witness, Sheriff Kraemer and E.M. Brandias, an operative for the Burns Detective Agency, had been present. They called Gummer into the office and Brandias questioned the accused. This was before Gummer had been accused of the crime or had been arrested. He said that Gummer had not been threatened in any way during the questioning and that no promises had been made to him. That they merely told him that his movements on the night in question had not been explained to their satisfaction and asked him to go over them again. A question interposed by Barnett elicited the information that Gummer had not been advised in any way to tell the truth and nothing but the truth. The witness described the movements of Gummer after he met Northern Pacific train No 8 at 10 p.m. Most of the testimony had been taken down in shorthand by Mr. Green at the time of the examination in Kraemer's office. Gummer had told of registering the various guests and taking them to their rooms and his statement in this respect was practically the same as testimony offered by other witnesses. He had stated that he took Marie Wick to her room going ahead of her up the stairs. When she left the hotel with her friend Rasmussen he had noticed she was a good looking well built girl. He also stated that when she returned the second time she appeared bewildered in the lobby but got her key and went to her room alone. She called the office at about 11:15 to see if her call had been changed to 6 o'clock. Gummer stated that he had no conversation with her but left the lobby Gummer had stated that he was alone for about 15 minutes with his chum, Andy Brown, came in, and visited with him for awhile.

Gummer Tells of "Jazz Parties"

They talked about some calsomining which was to be done in the hotel and which Brown planned on doing. After finishing the conversation about calsomining Brown asked Gummer if there were any 'wild women' in the hotel, and Gummer told him of the girl in 30, saying that there was a swell looking Jane in 30. The accused had described the girl as appearing to him to be a good, green country girl. After some conversation as to Andy Brown's affair with a girl he was going with Brown got up to leave but Gummer asked him to stick around as it was lonesome to stick around as it was lonesome sitting their alone. Attorney Green, in his capacity as witness, detailed a lengthy statement by Brown which was not completed at the time adjournment was taken. This statement had to do with various affairs Gummer had had with different girls or 'Jazz Babies' who had stayed at the hotel at various time and detailed Gummer's visit as described the accused to the various rooms occupied by these girls, giving instances of his conversation and, as he expressed them 'Jazz Parties' with the different 'wild women' of his acquaintance. The stories of these 'jazz parties' as described by Gummer are unfit for publication in any form but showed quite vividly the ordinary state of mind of the accused while on night duty in the hotel and impressed the spectators with the fact that the accused was not of a very choice moral character.

Women composed about a third of the total number of spectators. When the story of Gummer's escapades begun to get strong a few of the women had the good grace to leave the court room but a good percentage of the prominent women in the city were there evidently didn't want to miss anything and stayed until court adjourned at 5 o'clock.

When court convened this morning there were but few women in attendance, yesterday afternoon's proceedings evidently scaring them out. Judge Cooley announced that this morning's proceedings would not be given in the choicest language and any ladies present could take advantage of that time to leave. A few women left but there were still a few in the courtroom when testimony was started. The ladies in the Gummer party were not in attendance this a.m. Hans Wick arrived in the city last night and took his usual place in the unused jury box this morning.

The reading by States Attorney Green of the transcript of admissions made by Gummer in the sheriff's office on June 14 only required about fifteen minutes to complete.

Sheriff Kraemer Tells of Conversation With Gummer

Sheriff Kraemer was placed on the stand and said that he was present a part of the time on the afternoon of June 14 when the admissions read by Green had been made, but was not there when the meeting was finished. He saw Gummer at six o'clock that evening when Gummer had supper at Sheriff Kraemer's home. He had a conversation with Gummer after supper in the jailor's quarters in the Cass County jail at which time Mr. Syndness was present. The sheriff opened this conversation by telling Gummer that he did not believe the accused had told them the truth as to his movements the night Marie Wick was murdered. Gummer replied that had not told the truth in all particulars. Gummer stated that when he had said that he met train No. 4 about 1 o'clock that night he had lied as he did not meet the train. He also said that he had called up Marie Wick on the phone about 11:30 that night instead of Marie Wick calling him as he had previously stated. He said that he had called her up to josh her and see if she was at all sporty but that she cut him short and hung up on him. He also told the sheriff at this meeting that he was the first one in the hotel, to the best of his knowledge who knew that Marie Wick was dead and stated that he had been in room 30 shortly after 6 o'clock on the morning of the seventh. He said that he had phoned to the room at 6 o'clock that morning but did not receive any answer. After waiting a few minutes he again rang her phone and on receiving no answer went up stairs and rapped at her door but received no reply. He then went down stairs, swept out the office, took the skeleton keys which were hanging on a hook, went back to the door of room 30, rapped and received no reply, unlocked the door, went into the room about three steps, saw that the girl had been murdered, went out, locked the door, and returned to the office where he stayed for several minutes before calling up Fred Lawrence on the phone. He explained the fact that he had never told this before to the fact that he knew a man in Mayville who had discovered a person who had been murdered and reported it immediately and had been held by the coroner's jury as being implicated in the murder. The accused, Gummer, felt that he might be held in connection with this murder if it were known that he discovered the body when alone. Sheriff Kraemer testified that Gummer had admitted to him that he had sized up Marie Wick when he had taken her to her room and had told him that he felt that he desired intercourse with her. Gummer had also told Sheriff Kraemer that he told his chum Andy Brown about finding the body previous to the time Lawrence had been with him. Between the morning of the murder and June 14 Gummer had maintained that he met train No. 4. On June 8 Gummer had told the Sherif that he had been awake all night, that the stairs would squeak and that he would have heard any movement on the stairs during the night. Later he told the sheriff that he had been dosing a part of the night. At 4 o'clock that morning the accused had said that he had turned off the light on the second floor and did not notice anything wrong. Gummer had never told the officials anything about calling Marie Wick on the phone at 11:30 or being in the room at six in the morning until the afternoon and evening of June 14.

Under cross examination Sheriff Kraemer said that from the day of the murder until the accused was placed under arrest on the fourteenth he had been in the sheriff's office every day and had seemingly given the officers every assistance in their search for the murderer. Sheriff Kraemer admitted that the only information he had as to Gummer's being in room 30 was from Gummer himself. He also admitted that in the two instances Gummer had lied Gummer had voluntarily corrected his misstatements himself without officials having any previous proof that he had lied. Gummer never refused to answer any question which the officials put to him nor did he ever make an effort to evade their questions.

Under redirect examination Sheriff Kraemer stated that it was very difficult to get answers to their questions from Gummer but under recross examination when asked by Attorney Barnett.

'What question did you ever ask him which he hesitated in answering to the best of his ability' he answered that he did not recall any particular questions and admitted this his impression in this respect must have been wrong.

States Attorney Green Again on Stand

States Attorney Green was returned to the stand and told of a meeting with Gummer, at which time Brandias, Kraemer, Sydness, and Milligan had been present. Mr. Green stated that he and Mr. Brandias had been in the jail talking to Brown when Gummer came in, that they left the jail about 10 o'clock, met No. 4 at 1 o'clock and went with Officer Milligan to a cafe, had lunch and returned to the jail about 2 o'clock on the morning of the fifteenth. In answer to a question interposed by Judge Barnett Mr. Green stated that Gummer had not been arrested at that time but had been taken into custody by Sheriff Kraemer and was being held without warrant for further investigation. When the party returned to the jail Gummer was lying on a cot and was told to get up. At this interview the majority of the questions were asked by Brandias. As regards Gummer movements in finding the body the statements of the accused were about the same as had made during the interview of the afternoon. He told to his conversation with Marie Wick at 11:30 that night in which he asked her if she was going to bed, to which she replied that she was, and the accused then asked her if he couldn't help put her to bed. At this point she hung up. He also told the officers that O'Brien had come into the hotel that night and asked him for a stamp with which to mail a postal card and stated that he had given Mr. O'Brien a letter written by Fred Lawrence to mail at the station mail box. This statement was contrary to the evidence submitted by Mr. O'Brien and corroborated by other witnesses to the time he received the stamp from Gummer and mailed the postal card and letter which Gummer gave him. It has been shown that this occurred on the night of June 8 and morning of June 9.

Gummer Admits Lying

At this interview Gummer admitted that he told the officers a lot of lies regarding his movements but claimed that these lies did not amount anything.

The accused also stated that on the night of June 12, six days after the murder he had been in the basement of the hotel during the night but had not gone to a back part of the basement to investigate a water leak as it was spooky back there and he was scared to go back. He had stated that he slept well every night following the murder with the exception of two nights when he slept on a cot in the hotel.

The accused stated at that time that he did not care to go with any more women for awhile after the murder and had decided that his affairs with different women might get him in trouble. When asked by States Attorney Green if he could remember any single or unmarried girl or woman ever stopping in the hotel while he was there whom he had not 'tried out', the accused stated that he did not recall any and admitted that he had tried them all out. The accused had admitted telling Andy Brown of the girl in room 30, and telling him that she would be a dandy 'to Jazz'. To which Brown replied that 'She's another one for your list, Bill.' He also admitted telling Brown of finding the body in the morning before he had notified Fred Lawrence but asked Brown not to repeat it as it was known that he, Gummer, was quite a 'Jazz Hound,' and they might 'get him for it'.

Dr. W.P. Larson, a professor in the University of Minnesota, said that he was a specialist in the testing of blood to determine whether it was human blood or not and explained which are of a quite technical nature. He had examined the stain on the Bible found in room 31 but stated that there was not sufficient blood on the Bible to determine whether it was human blood or not. He gave it as his opinion that the bloody stain was caused by bloody mucous from some one's nose. He had explained the blood stains on the trousers entered in court and stated that these were not caused by human blood and that the sample of blood examined was of such quantity as to exclude any possibility of error in the test.

Sheriff Kraemer was recalled to the stand by Green and identified the Bible as being the one found by him in room 31. This identity was established by Kraemer's signature on one of the levels of the Bible.

Court was adjourned at 11:45.

Afternoon Session

The courtroom was crowded this afternoon when court reconvened. The first witness to take the stand was a stenographer who had registered at the Prescott Hotel on the night of October 23, 1920. She had stopped on her way home and arrived there about 10:30. She had gone to the Howard Cafe for lunch and then went to the Waldorf and Dakota Hotels for a room. The clerk at the Dakota got her a room by phone to the Prescott Hotel. She went there and registered between 12:30 and 3 in the morning. She was registered by Gummer and left a call for seven o'clock in the morning. After leaving the call she stated that Gummer had tried to engage in conversation with her and made no effort to take her to her room and she waited 10 or 15 minutes while he attempted to get her to talk. She did not remember any of the conversation as she paid no attention to him. She finally asked him to show her to her room, which he did. Then arriving at the room she waited in the hall for Gummer to turn on the light. He did so but did not come out of the room. She stepped just inside the door and Gummer stood in front her her and again tried to start the conversation and asked her if she had any 'jack' to which she replied 'she did not'. He then asked her if he could take off her shoes. She immediately requested him to leave the room. Gummer did not call her in the morning.

Under cross examination by Judge Barnett she was asked if she had waited ten or fifteen minutes in the hotel lobby for Gummer to take her to her room. She replied she had. When she was asked 'do you think you know how long ten minutes is?' she replied that she did and Judge Barnett asked her to cover up her wrist watch and tell him when the ten minutes was up. This she did and she announced that the ten minutes were up. It was only a little less ten minutes. The witness was then excused.

T.J. Caton was returned to the stand for cross examination and a black board was brought into the court room. Attorney Claire Brickner conducted the cross examination. The witness explained the method of making the chart which was produced in court, explaining that the letters shown were made by tracing the originals on tissue paper. While the examination was in progress F. Leland Watkins of Fargo, and Prof. Langum of Bismarck, hand writing experts for the defense, were brought into court and took seats near the counsels table. A objection was made by Attorney Green to the line of questioning in the examination. The court sustained the objection.

In questioning Mr. Caton it developed that several of the letters, the form of which he considered characteristic of those Andy Brown had written were characteristic of other handwriting produced. This was shown by reference to other signatures on the hotel register sheet and it was shown that many of these letters he showed to be characteristic of Andy Brown's undeveloped hand writing. The letters being formed in many instances entirely from the letter which the witness had referred to. The examination of Caton took up the time of court until 3:30 when recess was taken.

After recess Alfred Kincaid was put on the stand to testify as to the statements made to him by Gummer in which he said that Gummer had told him that he had been awake all night the night of the murder.

Morton Sydness will be called to the stand to testify to his examination of the finger prints found in the room. Mr. Syndness is a finger print expert.

E.B. Charlson and Roy Murphy, the two witnesses who were added to the information Monday morning will also be called to the stand to testify as to the conversation they had with the accused and as to statements he had made to them. The state confidently expects to complete their case against Gummer tomorrow noon. Counsel for the defense have given no indication of their method of defense."

DAILY TIMES—RECORD [Valley City, ND], Vol. XVI—No. 225, Wed., Feb. 8, 1922, at p.1. Print.

Gummer and Brown to Take Stand

DAILY TIMES—RECORD [Valley City, ND], Vol. XVI—No. 226, Thurs., Feb. 9, 1922, at p.1. Print.

GUMMER AND BROWN TO TAKE STAND

Judge Barnett In His Address To Jury Expects To Show Gummer's Movements On Night Marie Wick Was Murdered In The Prescott

Barnett Claims Statements By State's Witnesses Greatly Exaggerated

Defense Claims It Was An Impossibility For Brown To Have Signed Farrell's Name On Register.

"In the proceedings following the recess yesterday afternoon E.B. Charlson said that he lived in the Addison Flats in Fargo where Andy Brown also roomed. That he got up at 6 o'clock on the morning following the murder and went down stairs about 6:30. As he was coming down the stairs he saw Brown coming into the flats. Brown was dressed in his good clothes and had the appearance of having been out all night. The witness spoke to him said 'Good morning', but Brown did not reply. Brown went directly to the telephone and put in a call and had a telephone conversation with someone. The witness stated that Brown seemed very nervous and preoccupied.

Roy C. Murphy, who stated that his real name was R.C. McDermott, said that he was serving time in the Cass county jail on a charge of impersonating an officer and that during last December he was not confined to his cell but had the run of the jail as a trustee. He told of Attorney Brickner calling at the jail to see Gummer. He, Murphy, told Brickner that Brown wanted to see him and Brickner asked him to bring Brown down and said that he would talk to him as soon as he finished with Gummer. The witness did this and was called away for few minutes. When he returned Gummer and Brown were together and he heard Brown say 'Bill, you stand pat', and Gummer replied, 'You stand pat, I am.' After few minor questions in cross examination the witness was excused.

At this point state rested. It was not expected that the state would complete their evidence until the close of court for the day, or until this morning and their announcement was unexpected at that time. The counsel for the defense stated that they unprepared to continue at that time and adjournment was taken until this morning. This was at 4:30.

Case for State Re-Opened

At the opening of court this morning the case for the state was re-opened, by agreement between opposing counsels, and Barnett recalled Sheriff Kraemer to the stand for their cross examination as to the action of the officials when getting the admission from Gummer which were testified to yesterday and the day before. The calling of Kraemer was entirely unexpected and it was necessary to wait for half an hour before he could get to the court room. At the start of the cross examination Attorney Green objected to the line of questioning on the ground that it was competent and was immaterial. This objection was argued in the court room and finally sustained by Judge Cooley. Barnett then asked that the judge and attorney retire to the Judge's chambers in order that a statement by him might be read into the records in the absence of the jurors.

In order to get the testimony which Judge Barnett evidently wanted as to the treatment of the accused by the officials when making these admissions it would have been necessary to him to call Kraemer as a witness for the defense and they would have to abide by his answers to their questions. If he had denied any mistreatments to he accused the matter would have been closed and the defense would have been unable to enter any contradictory testimony.

States Attorney Green was placed on the stand for further cross examination as to happenings at the 2 o'clock meeting when Gummer had made certain admissions and Mr. Green reiterated his former statements when under direct examination.

Claimed Accused Coerced

He was asked:

'Isn't it a fact that at some time during this meet at the jail the lights were snapped on and off?'

To which Green replied:

'Not prior to the time the admissions were concluded.'

Green was excused.

As the state had reopened their case by permitting the cross examination by Barnett they then again rested and Barnett began his address to the jury at 11:05. It will be the object of the defense to show by testimony the complete details of the movement of Gummer during the night of the murder.

The defense will show by further testimony that statements made by the witnesses for the state and accredited to the accused have been greatly exaggerated.

It will be shown that different witnesses for the state had made gross misstatements.

That all of the truth regarding the different angles to the case known to the various witnesses so far examined had not developed thru the examination.

Gummer Helped Officials

That the accused spent most of his time during the week following the murder in the presence of the Sheriff or his deputies, assisting them in the unraveling of the mystery and that all of the facts regarding the case out of which the officials had knowledge came from Gummer himself. That Gummer had made certain misstatements but that he had corrected them voluntarily.

The state has tried to prove by the introduction of expert testimony that Andy Brown signed the name of James Farrell to the hotel register sheet but the defense will prove by two expert witnesses just as well qualified in these matters as the witness for the state, that the name was not signed by Andy Brown and will prove that it would have been impossibility for Andy Brown to have signed the name.

Gummer and Brown Will Testify

The defense will put Andy Brown on the stand and he will testify as to his movements on the night in question and will state that he did not sign the name of James Farrell.

Judge Barnett also stated that the defendant, William Gummer, will be placed on the stand to testify as to his movements during the night and his subsequent action.

F. Leland Watkins, professor and manager of the Dakota business college in Fargo stated that he had made a study of the comparison of hand writing for the past 29 years and that in that time he had testified on matters of disputed hand writing between 75 and 100 times. He stated that the first time he had been approached on the present case he had been approached by States Attorney Green who showed him the hotel register sheet, states exhibit No. 58, which is a list of names written by Brown in Green's office in order to supply them with a specimen of his hand writing, and also states exhibit No. 57 which is a letter written by Brown. The witness could not state just when this meeting was but remembered examining the exhibit at that time. The witness stated that he had examined the various exhibits presented in court and compared the hand writing of Brown with the signature of James Farrell and gave as his opinion that the person who wrote the letter, post card and exhibit No. 58 did not sign James Farrell and further stated that it was his opinion that Andy Brown had no connection with the James Farrell signature. The blackboard was set up and Mr. Watkins explained his reasons for giving this opinion. He was still on the stand when court adjourned at the dinner hour and will probably be on for some time this afternoon.

During the examination of Watkins, T.J. Caton, the hand writing expert for the state, took a position by the jury box where he could watch the explanation given by Mr. Watkins.

———————

Court convened at 2 o'clock with F. Leland Watkins still under direct examination. In a lengthy and technical explanation of the characteristics of the specimens of the hand writing examined by him, and upon which he based his opinion he made the statement that there was very little similarity in the manner in which Brown formed the letters in his admitted hand writing and the manner in which the letters were formed in the disputed signature. In answer to a question by Barnett:

'Do you find the signature of "James Farrell" any of the character-istics found in the admitted hand writing of Andy Brown'?

The witness replied, 'No'.

Barnett then asked:

'Is it not a fact that there are more or less tremor shown in copying an unfamiliar work or signature?'

Mr. Watkins replied:

'This is a fact.'

Barnett—'Is there any such tremor in the signature of '"James Farell?"

Watkins—'No.'

After the direct examination and cross examination of Mr. Watkins, Prof. Langum of Bismarck, another hand writing expert for the defense will be placed on the stand to tell of his various exhibits and give his opinion as to whether Andy Brown signed the name "James Farrell" or not. This will no doubt occupy the time of the court until the closing hour."

DAILY TIMES—RECORD [Valley City, ND], Vol. XVI—No. 226, Thurs., Feb. 9, 1922, at p.1. Print.

Experts In Hand Writing Take Up Day

D AILY TIMES—RECORD [Valley City, ND], Vol. XVI—No. 227, Fri., Feb. 10, 1922, at p.1,4. Print.

EXPERTS IN HAND WRITING TAKE UP DAY

The Gummer Trial Drags While Experts Are Being Examined.

"In yesterday afternoon's session F. Leland Watkins was on the stand under direct examination until the 8:30 recess and was excused without cross examination until today, when the state will question him as to the statements he had made.

After the recess George M. Langum penmanship teacher and hand writing expert for the defense, from Bismarck, was placed on the stand, and after giving his opinion as to the possibility of Andy Brown having signed the name of James Farrell, started a lengthly explanation of his reasons for arriving at that conclusion. This occupied the attention of the court until the closing hour. He will be cross examined this morning.

When placed on the stand George M. Langum stated that he had at one time taught penmanship in the Commercial school owned and operated by T.J. Caton, the handwriting expert for the state, in Minneapolis and was familiar with the methods employed by him. He stated that he had been studying specimens of handwriting submitted for some time and from this study had formed the opinion that it would have been impossible for Andy brown to have written the signature of James Farrell.

Disguising Writing Causes Tremors

He said that he had noted, in his experience with students and other, that when anyone tried to change their style of writing or attempted to disguise their handwriting, there was easily distinguishable a perceptible tremor in the formation of the letters. The person so writing did not write with the easy stroke and fluent manner usually issued in writing and the letter so written appeared cramped. He further stated that the signature of James Farrell showed that it had been written in a fluent and confidential manner and showed no indication of tremors and was not in any way cramped while the undisputed handwriting of Andy Brown, throughout, showed a cramped style. As there was no indication of his style in the signature, and as an attempt to disguised his handwriting would accentuate this characteristic, it would have been impossible for Andy Brown to have written the signature. The witness then proceeded to give a detailed explanation of the examination of the specimens of handwriting submitted and the manner in which he had arrived at his conclusions.

At the opening of court this morning the courtroom was filled but not crowded as formerly owing to the blizzard and the fact that the evidence being produced is of a technical nature and not very interesting to spectators.

George M. Langum was returned to the stand for further direct examination and he continued in his explanation of the reasons for forming his conclusions that Andy Brown did not write the signature of James Farrell on the register sheet of the Prescott Hotel. This was continued until 11:20 when he completed his direct testimony. A ten minute recess was taken at the completion of Mr. Langum's testimony and following the recess F. Leland Watkins was placed the stand for cross examination by States Attorney Green.

The witness said that, at the time he examined the various exhibits, produced in evidence, and shown to him by Green, his examination of them was only casual and only took about a half hour. This applied to the hotel register and exhibit 58, the sheet written by Brown in Green's office.

In the direct examination of the witness Mr. Watkins had confined himself almost exclusively to the comparison of the specimens of handwriting found in exhibit 58 and the disputed signature. States Attorney Green asked him in cross examination, if the specimens found in exhibit 58, which is acknowledged to have been written by Brown in the presence of Green and Sheriff Kraemer, would be as fair a standard for comparison as the specimens found in exhibits 55, 56, and 57, which are letters written by Brown previous to the time of the murder and before he had any knowledge of any disputed signature.

Comparison Fair

The witness replied, 'Taking into consideration the fact that they are the same words I would say that it was a fairer comparison.' He further added that the characteristics of a person's handwriting would not change under any circumstances without showing evidence of the attempted change and that he could not see where the date of the writings, whether before or after the writing of the signature, would make any difference. After much questioning by States Attorney Green, the questions being asked from all angles of the matter, be finally admitted that the letters written prior to the time of the murder would be a better means of comparison, but qualified that statement with the one that this would only apply if all the letters contained the signature were found in the specimens and in the same relation to the other letters in the signature.

The witness described Andy Brown as being an eccentric Perlman, who showed an inclination to allow his handwriting to degenerate.

The witness stated in direct examination that, owing to the different method of connecting the capital "J" with the succeeding letter in the name James and the fact that Brown's writing showed that he had never connected his letters thus in any specimens examined, it would have been impossible for Brown to have written the signature. A great deal of time was taken in an effort to get the witness to say that he had not meant that it was impossible but that he had meant that it was his opinion that it was impossible.

Mr. Watkins was still on the stand at the noon recess and it is expected that it will take some time to complete the cross examination of him. When he is excused George M. Langum will be placed on the stand for cross examination and it is evident that the larger portion of the afternoon's proceedings will be taken up with this expert testimony."

DAILY TIMES—RECORD [Valley City, ND], Vol. XVI—No. 227, Fri., Feb. 10, 1922, at p.1,4. Print.

_____

Defense Putting on Hand Writing Experts Past Two Days

P .R. Trubshaw, Editor, Daily Times—Record [Valley City, ND], Vol. XVI—No. 227, Fri., Feb. 10, 1922, at p.2, Print.

"The Gummer case is drawing near the end. The defense has been putting on hand writing experts the past two days and we presume that Gummer and Brown will soon go on the stand. The defense will not have been many witnesses. It is hardly possible, however, that the case will be finished this week."

P.R. Trubshaw, Editor, Daily Times—Record [Valley City, ND], Vol. XVI—No. 227, Fri., Feb. 10, 1922, at p.2, Print.

Former Policeman Testifies He Saw Man Leave Prescott Hotel The Morning Of The Murder

D AILY TIMES—RECORD [Valley City, ND], Vol. XVI—No. 228, Sat., Feb. 11, 1922, at p.1. Print.

UNKNOWN MAN LEFT PRESCOTT AT 2 A.M.

Former Policeman Testifies That He Saw Man Leave Prescott Hotel On The Morning Of The Murder But Was Unable To Identify Him.

T.J. Caton Again On Stand For State Refutes Testimony Of Experts For The Defense.

"The cross examination of F. Leland Watkins yesterday after-noon got Mr. Watkins riled up at times but in the main did not shake his contentions voiced during the direct examination. The court room was jammed in spite of the inclement weather, the majority of the spectators evidently expecting that the accused, Gummer, or his chum, Andy Brown, would be placed on the stand. However, it was evident early in the afternoon that the day's proceedings would be fully occupied by the testimony of the handwriting experts. The cross examination of Watkins was completed at 2:30 and the usual recess was taken.

After recess George M. Langum was placed on the stand for cross examination. He said that he had only testified in two court cases as a hand writing expert, and these two cases were held in Mandan. When asked if the presence of tremors in handwriting was an indication of attempted disguise or forgery the witness stated that it was. His attention was directed to the signature of Mrs. Elmer Hillyard and family on the register sheet and admitted that this signature showed the presence of tremors, as did the signature of R.H. Flaughter and son. There was no tremor possibilities in the signature of H.J. Hagan. When asked if the tremors would be apt to show in the writing of an assumed named the witness said that they would.

Tremors Do Not Show

His attention was then called to the signature of Ed. Smith and wife, immediately below the James Farrell signature. This man is one who is married but who registered in this manner in company with a prostitute under an assumed name. There were no tremors perceptible in the signature. Neither were there any visible tremors in the signature of James Farrell, either in the signature on the hotel register or in the names as written by Andy Brown in the presence of Green and Kraemer. The witness stated that the correct way to spell Willmar was with two ll's also it is spelled 'Wilmar' on the register and was so spelled by Brown when writing the name in Green's office. The witness also said that specimens written before the tragedy were the best comparison and stated that, while he had used exhibit 58 in demonstrating his conclusions for the jury, he had done this as exhibit 58 was more legible and easier for the jury to see, but that he had also examined the other exhibits in making the comparison of signatures, had based his conclusions on all the evidence at hand. Mr. Langum also said that the capital letter **W** was peculiar and distinctive and formed a good basis for comparison. That the initial, or cross stroke might be omitted by the writer frequently and that Brown did not write a uniform capital **W** in his other writings, but stated that it was his belief that the ink spot or broadening of the stroke in the initial stroke was not the result of hesitation on the part of the writer in writing the Signature.

Man Seen Leaving Hotel

H.B. Howard was the first witness called to the stand by the defense this morning. He stated he had been a police officer in the city of Fargo at the time Marie Wick was murdered and that his beat included that part of the city wherein the Prescott Hotel is located, that while walking his beat on the night of the murder he walked through alleys between the Prescott Hotel and the Waldorf Hotel and continued east across the street. When he was about midway across the street he heard the front door of the Prescott Hotel open and, on reaching the sidewalk, he looked back and saw a man coming out the door. This man continued north, up the street, until he was in front of the Waldorf where he sat down in one of the benches in front of the hotel. The witness continued on his rounds and when he next returned to the street the man had disappeared.

Questioned under cross examination the witness reiterated his direct testimony and said that he was able to fix the time of the night as being just a minute or two before his time to report which was 2 o'clock. He was unable to give any other description of the man than that he was about a middle sized man, and stated that he did not note the manner in which the man was dressed. When asked if he had ever seen Andy Brown the witness said that he had not.

Owing to the fact that T.J. Caton resides in Minneapolis and was anxious to return to his home the opposing counsel had agreed that the state should place him on the stand for redirect examination under rebuttal and allow him to leave. Upon permission being granted by the court this was done and Mr. Caton took up the balance of the morning in explain his reasons for differing in opinion, with the experts for the defendant. He was still on the stand at the time of the noon recess and will probably be on for some time this afternoon.

In explaining his reasons for his opinion he prefaced his remarks with the statement that he had been present while F. Leland Watkins and George M. Langum were giving their testimony and that he had afterward studied their testimony and would explain his reasons for differing with statements they had made. He further stated that it would require many departures from the form of Brown's undisputed handwriting to base a conclusion such as they had given. He also said that he had confined his examination of the specimens written previous to the time the disputed signature was written and that he considers the states exhibit 58 of no value in the comparison of signatures. He felt that the great majority of hand writing experts would agree with him that any writing done in the presence of officers, when it is assumed that the writer knew the purpose of the writing, would be of little value for the purpose of comparison and should only be used used for the purpose of establishing characteristics.

11 Letters Out of 52 to Compare

He found three capital letters of a possible 26, making 11 letters out of the possible 52, and confined himself to those 11 letters as much as possible while making the examination and forming no conclusions. In this examination he examined all exhibits with the exception of 58.

Mr. Caton said: 'The experts for the defense stated that they found all of the capital 'J's' disconnected from the letter following but my examination shows that there are only two capital 'j's' in all of the specimens of handwriting submitted and both of these are connected to the letter following. There is only one 'Ja' and these letters are connected. There is a 'Jc' and these lettered are connected. In exhibit 58 the 'J's' are not connected to the letter following. He further stated that the 'Ja' In James and the 'Ja' found in the letter were 'strikingly similar'. In the connecting of small letters kindred to capital 'J' he found that Brown did connect these letters in some instances and did not in others and that under these conditions it would be impossible for the experts for the defense to state positively that Brown could not have signed 'james'. He continued with the various letters found in the signature, placing particular stress on the capital letter 'W' and the small letters 'r, s, and m', saying that he could see no reason for the statement that Brown could not have written them, inasmuch as several specimens of these letters were found which were very good reproductions of the letters as they appeared in the disputed signature.

When court convened this afternoon Mr. Caton was still on the witness stand. After Mr. Caton left the stand the defense put F. Leland Watkins and George M. Langum, two hand writing experts back on the stand for testimony in rebuttal and cross examination by the state.

These two men will undoubtedly be the only two on the stand this afternoon. The hand writing exerts testimony will undoubtedly be finished this afternoon and it is believed the case will proceed very rapidly from now on.

Owing to the fact that Monday is a holiday which is observed by the court, a recess was taken until 10 o'clock Thursday morning."

DAILY TIMES—RECORD [Valley City, ND], Vol. XVI—No. 228, Sat., Feb. 11, 1922, at p.1. Print.

Closing Days of Famous Case Will Bring Out Interesting Evidence

D AILY TIMES—RECORD [Valley City, ND], Vol. XVI—No. 229, Mon., Feb. 13, 1922, at p.1. Print.

GUMMER TRIAL RESUMED TOMORROW

Closing Days of Famous Case Will Bring Out Much Interesting Evidence. Jury May Get Case Sometime Thursday.

"Owing to the fact that yesterday was Lincoln's birthday, which makes today a legal holiday, there will be no court until tomorrow morning. During the recess the various court officials and attorneys are resting at their homes for the final efforts in the case. Judge Charles M. Cooley is at Grand Forks over the holiday and the attorneys are spending the holiday at their homes in Fargo.

It is expected that the case will be given to the jury either Wednesday night or some time Thursday. The attorneys for the defense have indicated that they will only call a total of seven witnesses. Three of these, the two handwriting experts and H.B. Howard, the former Fargo police officer, have been disposed of. There remains to be examined Mrs. Anna Lawrence, who will testify for the defense and tell the method employed by those in the hotel in entering rooms when it was found impossible to awaken the guest. Then there is a Mr. Sorlie, a private detective who has been employed in the defense and will testify regarding certain points in the case which the defense wish cleared upon. The defense have also indicated that they will place the defendant, William Gummer, on the stand and it is expected that the examination of him will consume considerable time as will the examination of his chum, Andy Brown, whom they will also call to the stand. The state has indicated that their rebuttal testimony will be brief, as they are confident of the outcome on the evidence already presented, and they will not take up much time on this phase of the case. States Attorney Green has also said that his argument to the jury will not take much over two hours. The argument to the jury by the defense may take considerable time, but this is problematical as they have not stated what their argument may cover. Taking all these things into consideration it is evident that the twelve men who have been selected to decide the fate of William Gummer will be given the instructions of the court during the third day of the trial this week, and the defendant should know their judgment before the end of the week. A great deal of interest is being shown in the final days the trial as it is known that Gummer and Brown will both be on the stand, either tomorrow or Wednesday, and many people are interested in the evidence which they will present, both in direct examination and cross examination. The tiresome handwriting testimony has been completed and the final days will be certain to bring out much important evidence owing to these facts the courtroom will be crowded to capacity during the closing days of the trial."

DAILY TIMES—RECORD [Valley City, ND], Vol. XVI—No. 229, Mon., Feb. 13, 1922, at p.1. Print.

Andy Brown Takes Stand for Defense

DAILY TIMES—RECORD [Valley City, ND], Vol. XVI—No. 230, Tues., Feb. 14, 1922, at pp.1,3. Print.

ANDY BROWN TAKES STAND FOR DEFENSE

Mrs. Lawrence Testifies That She Found a Footprint Near Fire Escape At the Prescott Hotel the Day After the Murder.

"When court convened at 10 o'clock this morning the court room was only partly filled but before many minutes standing room was at a premium.

Mrs. Anna Lawrence was the first witness called to the stand and said that she has been in, or around, the Prescott hotel for a week or more following the murder. When she retired on the night of June 6 there were five rooms vacant on the second floor of the hotel. Of these rooms 21 and 23 were not used unless the hotel was full. Room 27 had a poor lock and a guest who had been assigned to that room had transferred to 29, leaving 27 vacant. Room 35 had been occupied until Northern Pacific train No. 8 left that night but was vacant when Mrs. Lawrence retired. Room 31 was also vacant when she retired. Five people came in and four rooms were assigned to them after Mrs. Lawrence retired.

Brown Left at 12:50

Mrs. Lawrence recalled a conversation which she had with Gummer in the morning of the seventh and in the presence of Officer Nelson in which she asked Gummer what time the previous night Andy Brown had left the hotel at ten minutes to one. She further stated that that was the only time that Gummer had made any statement to her as to the time of Brown's departure.

May Melaas had been employed at the hotel for about a year previous to the time of the murder but had left the hotel about the fifteenth of June following the murder. Mrs. Lawrence recalled a conversation she had with Miss Melaas in which she asked her if she had heard any noises during the night and to which Miss Melaas answered that she had not. Alice Kruse was with her at the time this conversation took place in the room of Miss Melaas.

She also recalled a conversation with May Melaas regarding certain blood stains found on the doors of the some of the rooms. Mrs. Lawrence stated that she had seen blood stains on the door of room 31 after her attention had been called to them by Mrs. J. Burgess. Her attention had also been called to blood stains on the door of room 63 and said that she had never noticed the stains there previous to the night of June 6. The window of room 63 leads to the roof of the annex and furnishes a means of exit by way of the roof and fire escape, from the hotel.

Foot Print Found

Mrs. Lawrence saw Mrs. Van Vorst the morning following the murder and Mrs. Van Vorst told her of having heard noises during the night which led her to believe that some man had walked across the roof to the annex at that time. Mrs. Lawrence, accompanied by several others, went out and examined the premises about three o'clock that afternoon and is that examination found one foot print facing to the south away from the ladder which leads from the ground to the fire escape. This foot print was quite plain with the heel mark of impression noticeably deeper and plainer than the toe mark. The second floor hall was covered with paper with a Brussels carpet wide on top.

Mrs. Lawrence stated at at one time the key to room 29 would unlock the door of room 30 but that she was not sure as to whether this condition existed at the time of the murder. The regular key to room 30 was attached to a brass tag similar to the one produced in court.

When Gummer entered the employ of Mrs. Lawrence she had instructed him to leave the electric sign on until about 10:30 in the evening and to then turn it off and to turn out the two front lights in the office at the same time. She had also told him to turn out all of the lights in the office except the light on the switch board and two lights above the desk after No. 4 had left. She stated that under these conditions the office would be very dimly lit. She had also instructed the accused to turn out the balance of the lights in the hall at daylight. To the best of her knowledge her instructions regarding the lights have been followed.

Witness Cross Examined

Under cross examination Mrs. Lawrence reiterated her statement regarding the lights in the building and her instructions to Gummer relative to turning them out.

Mrs. Lawrence stated that the floors in the hall on the second floor were old and might creak some when being walked on but that she was certain that ordinary walking in the hall would not be heard by her if she were in the office owing to the manner in which floor was covered.

Regarding the foot print near the fire escape the witness said that there had been a great many people around the hotel and premises during the day and that she had not seen this foot print until 3 o'clock that afternoon, although she had not looked for anything previous to that time.

When asked if she had ever told the officers regarding the blood stains on the doors of room 31 and 63 she stated that she had not done so as she had been requested by a certain party not to say anything about it as he had been 'pestered enough about it'. She had never noticed any other stains on other doors or walls and did not think there were any as she had just completed house cleaning.

Mrs. Lawrence said that she was not particularly friendly toward the defendant but that she had nothing against him.

Brown Quite Dapper

Andy Brown was placed on the stand by the defense. He appeared in court clean shaved, quite neatly dressed and dapper in appearance. He said that he had been held by the state in the Cass and Barnes county jails since September 24, 1921. He had met the defendant at the Addison flats about the first of January 1921. He had only seen Gummer about three times in January and three or four times in February as Mr. Brown was at that time canvassing in the Neighborhood of Mayville and did not get into Fargo more than once a week. During March he and Gummer occupied a room together at the Addison flats. At that time Gummer had left the Prescott Hotel and was writing accident insurance. Gummer returned to his home in Mayville the last of March or the first part of April and Brown saw a great deal of him at his home, stopped at the Gummer home a great many times for the day or to stay over night.

Andy Brown was in the Prescott hotel on the night of June 6 arriving there about 12:25 that night. The witness fixed the time of his arrival by saying that he had gone to a show that night with a young lady who roomed at the Addison and had come back to the rooming house about 11 o'clock. He had been in her room until midnight, when he went to his room and wrote a six page letter, walked to the postoffice and mailed it and walked back to the Prescott. He estimated that would take about 25 minutes. He was shown a letter three pages in length and identified it as the letter he had written at that time and said that he had been mistaken in the length of the letter.

He left the Prescott at ten minutes to one according to the clock in the Prescott hotel lobby. This statement substantiated Mrs. Lawrence's testimony as to Gummer's statement regarding the time of Brown's departure. He went from the Prescott to the Grand pool room where he ordered a malted milk. He was waited on by Steve Gorman and there were two other men in the pool room at that time, one of whom he knew as the secretary of the baseball club and the other being a traveling salesman whom he did not know. He was in the pool room from 1 o'clock until 1:15. He then went directly to his room at the Addison flats, undressed and went to bed where he remained until 7 o'clock the following morning. The witness was very emphatic in denying that he was outside his room at 6:30 that morning. When leaving his room he went to Madison's restaurant had breakfast, and continued on to his work at a house at 618 eighth avenue north. Mr. Brown stated that he kept his working clothes in a grip where ever he was working and that he went to work wearing his good clothes, changing clothes on the job.

Brown Still On Stand at Noon

While confined in the Cass county jail Andy Brown occupied a cell in the extreme northwest corner of the jail. Mr. Brown stated that he had had no conversation with Gummer from the time of Gummer's arrest on June 14 until some time in January this year. Brown had been called to get a pair of shoes which Attorney Brickner brought him and there saw Gummer and talked to him for the first time after Gummer's arrest. During this conservation Jailer Jim Maloney was present as were Attorney Brickner, a man who came with Brickner, and trustee Roy Murphy. When Brown stepped up to the group Gummer gave him a part of a box of candy which he had received and Brown sat down on the bottom step of the stairway to try on his new shoes. While trying on these shoes Gummer leaned over the stair rail at the left of Brown, Murphy was by the right rail and Attorneys Brickner and Maloney were in front of him. Mr. Brown state that Mr. Maloney was not out of sight or hearing at any time while he and Gummer were together and that he thought that if their positions had been reversed he, Brown, would have been able to hear everything that was said.

At this point court was adjourned for the noon recess.

Brown is still on the stand this afternoon. When asked to tell of his conversation with Gummer in the Cass county jail he said 'After Gummer gave the candy I sat down on the steps and Gummer leaned against the stair rail and I said to him, "Bill, are you locked up all the time?" He replied: "Not all the time. I get out in the corridor once in a while." He asked me "Where are you? And I said "in No. 2 upstairs." Gummer said "I am in No. 6 on the first floor." Then Murphy went upstairs or out doors or some place and when he came back Maloney said "Come on, Bill, and I'll lock you up." Bill leaned over the stair rail and shook hand and I said "So long, old man, until I see you again," and that is all the conversation there was.'

Attorney Murphy read a transcript of a part of Murphy's testimony to the witness and asked him if the conversation as related by Murphy had ever taken place at any time, to which Brown replied, 'No sir, it did not, and nothing of that kind ever took place.' Brown stated that he entered the hotel the night of the murder and stepped four or five paces into the lobby and Gummer was not visible when he opened the door but when he stepped into the lobby Gummer raised his head above the cigar case and leaned over and talked to Gummer. Gummer stretched and arose and came around the counter and went to the center of the lobby and sat down on a settee and Brown walked over and sat down beside him. Witness was instructed to tell of his conversation with Gummer at the time and he said: 'I asked Bill if he had written to his mother lately and he replied that he had not but expected to that night, and I told him that I received a letter from Morris, meaning Gummer's father, in which asked me to to see if I could get him a harness and see about some barbed wire. I told Bill I could not get them at that time and asked him to tell his father so when he wrote home. Bill asked about my girl and asked if there was anything doing with her and I told him 'Hell no, Bill, she's a good girl" and I got up to leave but Bill called me back said "what's the hurry". I said "How's business" and Bill said "well, there's a man and his son checked in, a couple of women and some kids, a man with his wife, and there's a good looking girl in 30." I then got up and told him not to forget to tell Morris about the harness and left. That was absolutely every word that was said about the girl.' The witness stated that he was not in the Prescott after 10 minutes to 1 that night. When asked 'Did you write any name at that time or any time on the hotel register,' Brown said 'No sir, I did not'. 'Were you ever requested by Gummer or any other person to write the name of James Farrell on the register which Brown replied emphatically 'No, sir'. Brown denied ever having been on the second floor at any time on the night of June 6 or the morning of June 7, and stated that he was never in room 40. He did not leave the lobby of the hotel between 12:25 and 12:5$[sic] of that evening. He also stated that no person had entered the lobby while he was there. Under cross examination Brown stated that Andy Brown was not his true name but his name was Leslie Locke and that he had assumed the name Andy Brown ever since his mother died nine years ago. He said that he had been estranged from his father for the past eight or nine years, and had adopted the name of Andy Brown in Texas. He was divorced in Oklahoma 8 years ago and had some children living in Oklahoma at the present time. Brown objected to that line of questioning but was ordered to answer the questions as put to him. Brown stated that he had never been confined for any crime anywhere. When asked as to his occupation he stated that he was a painter by trade but had sold stock in the equity cooperative exchange and had sold a few rabbits for that Fargo rabbit concern.

The witness denied that he had ever questioned Gummer concerning a girl of a 'a swell looking jane' in room 30. He also denied that he came in the rear door of the Addison flats at about 6:30 the morning of the seventh, called a number and asked, 'Is everything all right?' or something to that effect. In regard to this testimony given earlier in the trial by a roomer at the Addison flats Gummer stated that the man who testified he saw him come in at 6:30 on the morning of the seventh was a man to whom he had given a worthless check at some time or other.

The cross examination of Brown did not shake his previous testimony in any particular. He maintained when Murphy testified as to his conversation with Gummer, Murphy lied. He was asked as to statements he had made to a couple of other persons in the Cass county jail which he denied. Brown was excused at 3:15 and court recessed. Owing to a slight indisposition of one of the jurors court was recessed at 3:30 until 10 o'clock tomorrow morning.

Gummer will be placed on the witness stand tomorrow morning to relate this movements on the night of the murder."

DAILY TIMES—RECORD [Valley City, ND], Vol. XVI—No.
230, Tues., Feb. 14, 1922, at pp.1,3. Print.

Willam Gummer is On Stand Today

D AILY TIMES—RECORD [Valley City, ND], Vol. XVI—No. 231, Wed., Feb. 15, 1922, at p.1. Print.

WILLIAM GUMMER IS ON STAND TODAY

Describes Arrival Of James Farrell At Hotel Prescott On The Night Of The Murder.

Claims Admissions Obtained From Him By Officers By Unfair Tactics

"When court convened this morning the court room was jammed with spectators who had come to see the defendant, Gummer.

The first witness called was Mrs. Lawrence who was returned to the stand by the defense to clear the record as regards the changing of Marie Wicks call from 6:30 a.m. to six. She was only on the stand a few minutes.

Gummer Slightly Pale

When Gummer was placed on the stand he was slightly pale and appeared more nervous than at any time during the trial, evidently dreading the ordeal to which he was about to be subjected. In spite of any slight nervousness which he might feel he makes a good witness, not hesitating much in replying to the questions asked.

William Gummer said that he was 23 years old last December, had been born and raised at Mayville, N.D. And that the first time he had ever been in Fargo was in the spring of 1917 when he had attended a basketball tournament there. He had gone to Fargo again in the spring of 1920 and had first begun to work in the Prescott Hotel in June, 1920. He worked there until January 15, 1921, when he [was] laid off, went home for a few days visit, returned to Fargo and roomed at the Addison flats and sold accident insurance for about two weeks. While he remained in Fargo for some time he was not working after the first of February and he returned home about the first of April and worked for two months on the farm with his father. During this time he also assisted Brown a little in the sale of equity stock. He returned to Fargo on the twenty-seventh of May at the request of Mrs. Lawrence who called him up by the telephone and asked him to come back and go to work.

Gummer was questioned as to the time of arrival of all guests registered in the hotel after the supper hour and substantiated previous testimony on this point. Marie Wick was the fifth guest to register that night and was registered and assigned to room 30 by Mrs. Lawrence. Marie Wick came into the hotel while Gummer was showing W.H. Flaugher and son to their room and was standing at the desk when Gummer returned to the office. Gummer showed her to her room at the request of Mrs. Lawrence.

Hesitates Mentioning Name

The first time that it became necessary for the accused to mention the name of Marie Wick he hesitated, colored, and seemingly was embarrassed.

When taking Marie Wick up the stairs to her room the murdered girl asked Gummer as to the leaving time of her train in the morning and he told her that it left at 7:45. Gummer asked her if she wasn't going to stick around the city for awhile and she said 'no'. After reaching room 30 Gummer tossed the key to the room on the dresser and in response to a reaction by her as to where she should leave the key when she left the room Gummer told her that, since she had two suit cases to kick the door and leave the key at the office. The accused was shown two keys which are numbered 15 and 21 and he stated that the key to room 30 was very much similar to these keys but not one of them.

Gummer related the movements of the murdered girl when coming to the office, going out, and when she returned for the night, saying that she was confused as to what door led to the stairway but that she went to her room alone. Gummer said 'That was the last I saw of her until she was found dead in her room the next morning'.

31 Only Room for Hagan

H.J. Hagan came in about 1 o'clock and was put in room 31 by Gummer. At the time Hagan came in there were six unassigned rooms on the second floor of the hotel. Of these room 21 was an inside room and was never used unless the hotel was extremely crowded. Room No. 23 was a double room with two beds in it and would not be suitable for one guest. No. 25 had just been vacated and was not made up. The lock on room 27 would not operate. No. 26 was a room with a bath carrying a rate of $2. Room No. 35 was connected with a bath and was not used unless a guest wanted a room and bath and the rooms of that description were taken. No. 31 was the only vacant room which could be used and which carried a rate of $1.25.

When Hagan came in her inquired as to whether they had any vacant rooms or not and as to their rates for rooms. After being informed as to the rates he said 'give me a $1.25 room'. As 31 was the only $1.25 room that could be used Gummer assigned him to it.

Gummer took Hagan to his room. The key to 31 was not in the key rack and Gummer took a pass key with him. When he got to the room he found that the door was open and swung back against the wall with the key to the room in the lock on the inside of the door. This is contrary to the testimony as given by Mr. Hagan in which he stated that Gummer was very nervous and fumbled badly when unlocking the door. Gummer told Hagan there was a bath room with plenty of water across the hall. He then returned to the office.

Ed. Smith and wife were the next guest assigned to a room and were placed in room 26.

Farrell Enter Hotel

The next guest to arrive was James Farrell whom Gummer said came in the hotel about 2 o'clock that morning. Farrell asked the price of a room and Gummer told him that he could have a room for $1 but that it would be $1.50 if occupied by two persons. Farrell told him that he had a buddy and would go out and find him. Farrell went out and returned in a few minutes saying that he could not find his buddy but that he would take the room. He paid the dollar for the room out of a $10 bill. As there was less than $8 in the till in change Gummer took $2 in paper bills out of his pocket to make change. The following day Gummer called the attention of Fred Lawrence as to the $2 discrepancy in the case and Fred gave him back the $2.

Did Not Write Name

Barrett—'Did you write the name "James Farrell" on that hotel register?'

Q. 'Did Andy Brown write the name "James Farrell" on that hotel register?'

A—'No sir, Andy Brown did not write the name of "James Farrell" on the register?'

Q—'Did you see the man write the name of "James Farrell" on the register?'

A—'Yes sir, I did.'

Gummer stated that he was not out of the lobby from the time Marie Wick went to her room at 11:15 until he took H.J. Hagan to his room shortly after 1 o'clock.

Gummer stated that he was not out of the lobby from the time Marie Wick went to her room at 11:15 until he took H.J. Hagan to his room shortly after 1 o'clock.

Gummer changed Marie Wick's call from 6:30 a.m. to six o'clock himself. This was done after talking to her over the phone. While he was talking to her Mrs. Van Vorst was standing at the desk about ten or 12 feet from Gummer and according to Gummer was not talking herself and could have heard his part of the conversation. When asked to give his version of the conversation Gummer said: 'I asked her what time she wanted to be called and she said that she had left a call for 6:30 a.m. But she wanted it changed to six o'clock. I then asked her if she was still up or if she had gone to bed. She said that she was still up and asked me to be sure and call her at 6 o'clock and I said, 'all right, I will.' That was all there was to my conversation with her.'

Gummer stated that when Hagan came in about 1 o'clock he was seated behind the desk in a rocking chair and did not hear Hagan come in the lobby and was not aware of his presence until Hagan was nearly across the lobby. Gummer did not know whether the double light above the desk was turned off or one at that time but said it was customary to turn the light off late in the evening when there were not many people around.

Substantiates Brown's Testimony

He substantiated Brown's testimony as to coming to the hotel and as to their sitting on the settee. He did not recall their conversation any more than he had been reminded of it by Brown's testimony. He stated however that in the admissions regarding the conversation which the state had read into the record were not entirely according to his recollection of the conversation. He said that the officers had told him that Brown had said that Gummer made certain statements during his conversation and Gummer had told them that, while he did not remember saying those things, if Andy Brown said he had said them, it must be so.

When Barnett asked the defendant how the questions were put to him at time the admissions by Gummer were made Gummer said that they did not ask him to state what happened or what had been said, but rather had asked him if such and such conversations had taken place, getting the admission in that way.

Gummer Assisted Police

During the eight days following the murder Gummer spent at least six hours a day with the officers giving them all the information he could and assisting them in the investigation of the mystery. He was with them every afternoon and often during the evening or night. On the night of the seventh Gummer was in his room at the Addison flats when two policemen came and told him he was wanted at the police station.

He got up and dressed and went with them to the station without asking any questions. When they arrived at the police station the officers took his finger prints and Bertillon measurements, and although

Gummer knew why they were taking these measurements he made no objection, feeling that he was willing they should have his finger prints.

Gummer told about going into room 30 with Officer Pickering, the morning after the murder and said that Pickering made the statement that it was suicide, then changed it to murder and asked Gummer what he thought. Gummer denied ever having made the statement that it looked like a case of suicide. When asked if he had changed any article of clothing during the night he said that he had not, and also said that he had worn the same clothing all the week following the murder that he had worn the night of the murder. He also said that he had worn the same shirt and all other articles of clothing when being measured for the police records that he had worn on the night of the murder. He stated that he did not know that his rights as an American citizen would permit him to refuse to answer any questions put to him by the States Attorney and police officers, but that he had answered all questions to the best of his knowledge and had corrected his three statements voluntarily without the police having had any knowledge of the fact that they were misstatements. Questioned as to his entering room 30 that he had called her on the phone at 6 o'clock and received no reply. He called again at 6:10 and rang 2 or 3 times after that. Receiving no reply he then went upstairs and knocked on the door; went back to the office, swept out the lobby, called again, went up and knocked and receiving no reply, opened the door with a pass key and walked in 2 or 3 steps, retaining his hold on the doorknob. When he saw the condition in the room he immediately backed out, closed and locked the door, and returned to the office. He explained this action by the fact that he was scared and did not want it to be known that he had discovered the body while alone, being afraid that it would then throw suspicion on him. Although thinking it over later in the week he decided that it was better for him to correct his misstatement. He told of calling Fred Lawrence and in this particular merely substantiated previous testimony.

Gummer substantiated previous testimony concerning the movements of Mrs. Lawrence during the night in question and also substantiated Andy Brown's testimony regrading any conversations.

When questioned regarding the testimony of Mr. Murphy, another prisoner in the jail who testified that he had heard Brown and Gummer warn each other to 'stand pat' Gummer declared that this testimony was absolutely untrue. He stated that a Mr. Monohan who had come to the jail with Attorney Brickner was much closer to him when he was talking to Brown than Murphy was and that it would have been much easier for him to hear what they were saying. It was expected that Mr. Monohan would be called to the stand this afternoon to substantiate Gummer's testimony.

When asked to describe 'James Farrell,' Gummer said:

'He was a man about five feet, 8 inches in height and appeared to be about 25 to 30 years of age. He was very tan and wore a dark suit of clothes with a cap on his head. He appeared to be a laborer or a man just knocking around, which you may call a bum.'

Owing to a slight illness of Att. Swenson for the defense court was adjourned at 3:30 p.m. Until 10 o'clock tomorrow morning."

DAILY TIMES—RECORD [Valley City, ND], Vol. XVI—No. 231, Wed., Feb. 15, 1922, at p.1. Print.

Gummer Cross Examined By State

DAILY TIMES—RECORD [Valley City, ND], Vol. XVI—No. 232, Thurs., Feb. 16, 1922, at p.1. Print.

GUMMER CROSS EXAMINED BY STATE

STATE'S ATTORNEY GREEN GETS ANGRY WITH WITNESS THIS MORNING AND DEMANDS THAT GUM-MER "QUIT GRINNING."

Gummer Slept From Three A.M. To Court A.M. On Night of Murder.

Illness of R.R. Kane, Juryman, Causes Adjournment at Noon Today Until 10 A.M. Tomorrow.

"When court convened this morning all the seats in the court room were filled but there were very few standing as Judge Cooley had ordered that the doors be closed when the seats were taken owing to the fact that the air in the court room became so foul when spectators were allowed to stand in front of the windows.

It is evidence that the Gummer trial will not be concluded, or rather than the case will not be given to the jury for consideration until Saturday eve and possibly not until the first of the week. It is reported that the state will call approximately fifteen witnesses to the stand in rebuttal. The cross examination of Gummer will take up the entire day today and probably a part of tomorrow morning.

Gummer Still on Stand

When court convened this morning the defendant was still on the stand under direct examination. After being questioned as to the manner in which the officers removed the electric light bulb from room 30 on the morning of the seventh, and to which the witness replied that they had wrapped it in cotton baton so that the finger prints would not be disturbed they had placed it in a paper sack and taken it with them.

Judge Barnett and States Att. Green discussed a question of permissible evidence before Judge Cooley and Gummer was also called into the conference. When they concluded the attorneys for the defense, Barnett, Swenson and Brickner, retired to the Judge's chamber for a few minutes to discuss a matter of procedure.

Gummer said that to the best of his recollection he had turned off the light in the hall on the second floor at daylight but was not certain as to whether he had turned off the light in front of room 30 or not, not being sure whether it had been turned on or not. Gummer also said that he had had no occasion to pass room 30 at any time during the night and that he had not passed room 30 when taking Hagan to room 31. He also stated that he had not been in room 30 between the hours of 11 on the night of June 6 and the hour of six the following morning. When asked by Barnett, 'Did you in any wise[sic] assault this young lady who occupied room 30'? Gummer replied, 'No sir. I did not'.

Q—Did you tie the hands of Marie Wick in any way?

A—No, sir. I did not.

Q—Did you assist in tying the hands of Marie Wick's?

A—No, sir.

Q—Did you assault this young lady in any manner, either by choking, tying her hands, or beating her with this nozzle or any other instrument?

A—No sir, absolutely not.

Gummer stated that he did not remember whether the nozzle had been attached to the fire hose previous to the night of the murder or not and that he had known that the hose and nozzle were there but never had an occasion to use them and knew nothing about them. He further denied having had anything to do with the nozzle on the night in question.

When Gummer was shown the bent hat pin he denied ever having seen pin until it was shown to him by the officers and denied ever having used the pin for the purpose of unlocking any door.

He stated that the first time he had ever seen the pants which are produced in evidence was in the sheriff's office on June 12. Gummer described the plan of the basement and the location of the lights in the basement and that that he had been with Milligan when he inspected the basement the day following the murder, that Milligan had a flash light which he used and that they inspected the windows and all possible exits from the basement. This took about fifteen minutes. Gummer was turned over to the state for cross examination at 10:30. His education, as brot out by the cross examination, had extended to three years in high school and a business course in the Mayville Normal.

Gummer's hours of duty at the Prescott hotel were from seven p.m. until seven a.m. and after midnight he had sole charge of the hotel and was the only employee on duty. On the night of the murder he was not outside of the hotel from ten o'clock in the evening until the officers came in the next morning. He did not go out for lunch that night.

Green Gets Angry

States Attorney Green propounded a lengthy question as to whether Meyer had been in the lobby when Gummer returned to the hotel after meeting the train at 10 o'clock, and demanded that the question be answered by yes or no. Barnett objected to this as it could not be answered in that manner and the objection was sustained.. When Green asked Gummer if he had not positively stated to Green and Kraemer in the sheriff's residence that Meyer had been there in the lobby when Marie Wick came in Gummer stated that it had been his impression that Meyer had been there but that he was not certain to that. Green demanded an answer of yes or no which Gummer refused for some time to give, qualifying his answer with the statement that he was not certain but wanted some other person's opinion on the matter. Green asked him if he had not made this statement and that when he had made it Green had called up Mrs. Lawrence, who informed him that Meyer was in the lobby when Marie Wick came in. Gummer answered by saying, 'you called Mrs. Lawrence at my request'. Green tried to get a positive answer without Gummer's statement that Mrs. Lawrence had been called at his request and had difficulty getting it. Attorney Green after much questioning got angry and said, 'stop your grinning and answer my questions!'

Gummer finally said that he had found out that Meyer had not been in the lobby when Marie Wick came in from what he had been told, not from his personal knowledge. When asked by States Att.

Green 'these pants (meaning the pants produced in the court) were found Monday morning were they not?'

Gummer replied—'You say they were'.

Tells of Smith and 'Wife'.

Gummer was not certain that he had taken a pass key with him when taking Hagan to his room although he had stated yesterday that he had taken a pass key. He was quite certain that the door to room 31 was unlocked, that he did not have to put the key in the door from the outside, that he did not have any difficulty in opening the door and that Hagan was mistaken when he so testified.

A taxi driver had reserved a room for Ed. Smith and 'wife' about twenty minutes before they appeared at the hotel. Gummer had told Ed. Smith the next morning that he had better leave the hotel before he, Gummer went off duty. When asked why he had told him this Gummer said that Smith had come in without any baggage and that Smith had tipped him off that they were not a married couple when Gummer took him to he room.

Gummer had met train No. 4 practically every night to mail a letter for Fred Lawrence but he did not meet No. 4 the night of the murder claiming that he had forgotten about the train until Hagan had come in for a room. Green referred to the transcript of admissions made by Gummer in the presence of Green and Kraemer and read 'why didn't you meet train No. 4 that night?' 'And didn't you say that you didn't meet the train because O'Brien had mailed the letter for you?'

Gummer replied, 'If you have all of my statement there, as you claim you have, you'll see more to it than that.'

Gummer stated that he had corrected this misstatement himself and that the misstatement was merely a mistake and no attempt at deceit. Questioned as to his statement that he is supposed to have made to Officer Milligan and which Milligan had testified to, that he,

Gummer, had a friend with him most of the night, Gummer said that this testimony was untrue. The same thing applied to the testimony of Mr. Kincaid which had substantiated Milligan's testimony. He said that Mr. Leimbacher was mistaken when he said that Gummer had told him that he was not asleep during the night.

Slept from 3 to 4

Gummer stated, 'I was dozing from about 3 o'clock until 4 o'clock in the morning and had been dozing a part of the time during the evening when no one was around as I was very tired that night.' When his alarm clock woke him up about 4 o'clock in the morning. Gummer went upstairs and turned off all the lights in the hall. Questioned as to whether he turned off the lights in front of room 30 or not Gummer said that he did not remember whether that light had been turned on or not but that if it had he turned it off. Questioned as to his statement to Kraemer, according to Kraemer's testimony, Gummer said, 'I did not state that I met Brown at the station at any time and if Kraemer so testified he was mistaken.'

When calling recess for the noon hour Judge Cooley informed the jurors that, inasmuch as the case was drawing to a close they should be particularly careful not to discuss the case with any one nor to permit any one to discuss it in their presence. Judge Cooley stated that he had been informed that the case had been discussed before some of the jurors and asked that if any one spoke to any of the jurymen about the case that they tell him who it was that they might be dealt with accordingly.

When court convened at the noon hour the courtroom was packed and there was a large crowd in the hall who were not permitted to enter the courtroom.

Court Again Adjourned

R.R. Kane, of Spiritwood, had been feeling poorly the past two days and called a doctor at noon. It was found that he had a temperature of 101 and his pulse was very irregular and the doctor ordered him to his bed for the balance of the day. Owing to this court was again recessed until 10:00 tomorrow morning with a possible adjournment until the end of the week in sight."

DAILY TIMES—RECORD [Valley City, ND], Vol. XVI—No. 232, Thurs., Feb. 16, 1922, at p.1. Print.

Gummer Trial Is Again Postponed Illness of Juror

DAILY TIMES—RECORD [Valley City, ND], Vol. XVI—No. 233, Fri., Feb. 17, 1922, at p.1. Print.

GUMMER'S TRIAL IS AGAIN POSTPONED

Serious Illness Of R.R. Kane, Juror, Necessitates Adjournment Until 10 A.M. Monday.

"The Gummer trial is again postponed due to the serious illness of one of the jurors, R.R. Kane of Spiritwood. The jury serving on the case were called to the court room this morning at 9:00 o'clock and dismissed until Monday morning at 10:00 o'clock, when it is hoped that Mr. Kane's condition will permit the resumption of the case.

There seems to a jinx in this case as the frequent illness of different court attaches has required four adjournments so far. They all seem to be taken in about the same way, seemingly an attack of influenza, and is thought that this is a result of the crowded condition of the courtroom during the trial. The air becomes stifling and it seems almost impossible to get good ventilation. For this reason Judge Cooley order the doors closed yesterday morning as soon as the seats were filled.

It is reported that Mr. Kane is very ill and will be forced to remain in his room for three or four days at least. He has a high temperature and a severe cold."

DAILY TIMES—RECORD [Valley City, ND], Vol. XVI—No. 233, Fri., Feb. 17, 1922, at p.1. Print.

Gummer's Cross Examination Ended

DAILY TIMES—RECORD [Valley City, ND], Vol. XVI—No. 235, Mon., Feb. 20, 1922, at pp.1,4. Print.

GUMMER'S CROSS EXAMINATION ENDED

GUMMER NERVOUS DURING CROSS EXAMINATION AND CONTRADICTS MUCH OF PREVIOUS TESTIMONY.

NOTORIOUS CASE DRAWING TO A CLOSE AND TO-MORROW MAY SEE END OF TESTIMONY.

DEFENSE RESTS AT 3:40

"When court convened this morning Gummer was still on the stand under cross examination. The defendant seemed to have lost some of his self-confidence during the adjournment and was somewhat paler than usual. During the cross examination it was apparent that he was endeavoring to answer the questions, not truthfully, but in a manner that would best suit his conception of the defense. He hesitated frequently in answering of questions and continually licked his lips, appearing nervous. He hedged considerably in answering questions regarding the admissions he had made to the officers and repeatedly said that the admissions, as set down by the officers, were not complete, and were incorrect in most of the details, claiming that he had not made definite answers to the questions that the officers had asked him. When asked whether he had made certain statements to the officers Gummer invariably said that he had not—to the best of his recollection, but refused to state positively that he had not made the statements.

When States Attorney Green asked Gummer if he had told Andy Brown, when Brown had been in the hotel on the night of the murder, that there was a swell looking girl checked into room 30, Gummer stated that he had not told Brown that. Green than read from the transcript of admissions made to the officers in which Gummer said that he had told Brown there was a swell looking girl in room 30 in answer to Brown's question as to whether there were any 'wild women' in the hotel. Gummer said that he had never made any such statements.

By Green—Do you want to say that his statement as I have read it to you here is not correct?

A—Not in the order in which you have given it there.

Gummer insisted that the officers had done a lot of questioning about 'Wild Women' before he had made the statement regarding his conversation with Brown and also insisted that there were a lot of questions asked about the conversation that are not down in the transcript.

Green asked Gummer why, in the direct examination, when questioned about this conversation, he had said 'there's a swell looking girl in room 30' and then hesitated. Gummer was unable to explain this hesitation but after hedging a great deal in answering Mr. Green's questions he indicated that he had not mentioned the room number to Brown.

Whenever States Attorney Green asked Gummer if he wanted to swear that the record of the admissions made by him was incorrect Gummer replied: 'To the best memory they are not.'

During further questioning regarding this conversation with Brown Green asked, 'Did Brown ask if you had dated her up?'

A—'He might of'

Q—'Do you want to say that he didn't?'

A—'He might of.'

When asked as to his admissions which the transcript show Gummer told that Brown had said, 'There is something for your list bill.' Gummer said, 'I think that's your own making.'

Green asked several questions as to the authenticity of the transcript and had considerable difficulty in getting definite answers from Gummer. During the questioning Gummer started off on quite a speech in which he said that the time these admissions were gained from him the officers all asked him questions at once at the rate of about four hundred a minute, pushing him around the room while they were asking them. When he stopped Green said, 'Is there anything else you want to say before you answer my questions?' Gummer made no direct reply.

Gummer said that he had told Andy Brown about being in room 30 before informing 'Fritz' Lawrence, and that he had told Brown this before he had told the officers but didn't know why he had not told the officers sooner except that he was afraid that he would be suspected if they knew it.

Gummer claimed that he did not say, in direct examination, that he had told Brown about calling Marie Wick up on the night of the murder. When the spot of the direct evidence was read to him by Green he stated that this statement by him was not true, even though he had made the statement last Wednesday. When asked why he had lied last Wednesday he said that he did not know. Gummer insisted that he had not told Brown about calling Marie Wick up that night before he told the officials about it.

His Story Not Consistent

Asked as to the condition of room 30 when he went in at 6 o'clock in the morning after the murder Gummer said that he knew something was wrong although he did not see that the girl's hands were tied, did not see the bloody rags on her face, did not see the blood marks on the wall and did not notice that the bed clothing were misplaced. He also said that he knew something was wrong in the room although he didn't see anything to indicate to him that the girl was dead or had been murdered.

Q—Then why were you afraid to tell Fred Lawrence about being in the room?

A—I didn't want to be the person to find her in that position.

Q—But you didn't know she had been killed, what do you mean by 'that condition?'

A—I just felt that something was wrong although I didn't stop to examine the room.

Q—Then what was you scared of?

Gummer could not explain his reasons for being scared.

Q—Didn't you tell Sheriff Kraemer that you knew she was dead when you went in the room?

Gummer tried to hedge in answering this question but finally admitted making the statement to Kraemer.

Q—Why did you wait five minutes before calling Fred Lawrence up?

Gummer was unable to explain this.

Gummer stated that when Pickering came in on the morning following the murder he did not tell Mr. Pickering that he had seen that the girl was covered with blood. He was quite positive on this score although Officer Pickering has testified that Gummer did tell him that the girl was covered with blood.

Gummer admitted that the officers had intimated that they did not believe he was telling the truth about the phone episode before he, Gummer had admitted that he lied. Gummer denied that he corrected this misstatement because he knew that Kraemer had talked to Brown and was afraid that Kraemer would find out from Brown that he had lied.

Gummer was asked why he was so positive as to the movements of Murphy on the day that Murphy claims Gummer and Brown had their conversation in the hall of the Cass county jail in which Murphy claims they admonished each other to 'stand pat.' Gummer said that he called Marie Wick up that night to find out what time she wanted to be called in the morning.

Q—You had a call sheet, didn't you?

A—Yes, but I didn't look at it.

Q—Was that your only reason for calling her up?

A—Yes, sir.

Q—Didn't you call her up to find out if she was sporty?

A—I (hesitation) no sir.

Q—Did you call anybody else up to the hotel that night to ask them about their call?

A—No.

Gummer made these statements regardless of the fact that the evidence shows that the call had been changed on the call sheet by Mrs. Lawrence and that it would have been easier for Gummer to have looked at the call sheet then to have called her.

Gummer Denies Desire

Gummer denied having made statements to Green and Kraemer in which he expressed his desire for intimate relations with the murdered girl when taking her to her room the previous night.

Q—Did you ask her, when calling her up, if she needed any help, or if you could put her to bed?

A—I. . . . I. . . . No sir!

The statement in which Gummer had said that he did not think such a question was too much to ask any girl was read to him and Gummer said that he had never made any such statement or least did not remember having made it.

Q—Do you think now that that question isn't too much to ask any girl?

A—What I think now and what I thought then hasn't anything to do with this case.

Denies Trying Out Girls

Gummer denied that he had 'tried out' all good looking single women who came to the hotel but admitted that he had made that statement to the officials. Questioned as to statements he had made to the officers regarding his relations with two other women in the hotel during the week previous to the murder Gummer said 'if you want to rehearse all that you had better read it to the jury.' On being told by Barnett to answer the questions Gummer admitted the statement he had made to the officers. Green asked Gummer if he wanted to swear that the admissions he had made, and which have been read in court by the state, to the officers, were correct and Gummer replied that to the best of his recollections they were not, but refused to swear positively that such admissions had not been made.

Green indicated that he was thru with the cross examination and the noon recess was called.

When court convened this afternoon Gummer was still on the stand under redirect examination. He stated that the suicide theory was first advanced by Officer Pickering who later changed his theory to that of murder. Gummer said he did not remember of ever having made the statement that it couldn't be murder as the girl was alone and the door was locked. He reiterated his statements as to the questioning by the officials at the Cass county jail on January 14. Gummer also denied that Sheriff Kraemer had intimated that he, Gummer had not told the truth regarding the telephone call with Marie Wick. This is contradictory of his evidence under cross examination this morning in which the questions asked at the time was read from his transcript and show that the officials had doubted his word in this respect.

Reiterates Previous Testimony

Gummer reiterated his previous testimony regarding the movements of Ray Murphy during the conversation with Gummer and Brown in the Cass county jail describing the position of everyone present during the conversation very minutely.

Gummer was undressed and in bed on the night of June 14 when Sheriff Kraemer came to the door of his room about 2 o'clock. Green, Kraemer, Sydness, Brandies and Milligan came in and closed the door. The lights were snapped on and off twice at least during the time he was being questioned, chairs were pushed back and forth across the floor and loud, profane and abusive language was used with him Milligan told him that if he lied to him he would choke the wind out of him and Milligan said 'Don't lie to me G___ d____ you.' Kraemer told him they were going to take him to Bismarck before daylight because if the citizens of Fargo knew he was there the jail wouldn't be stout enough to hold them, or something to that effect. Gummer said the questions were put to him very fast at times. He also said that when the lights were turned out, Kraemer would push him from behind and say 'tell them, tell them, you know you murdered her, you know you're gone.'

Gummer said he didn't mean to charge the other witnesses with having lied but his answers were made to seem that way by the way the questions had been asked.

Under cross examination Gummer reiterated his statements as to the light being turned off but admitted that there was no profane language used until after the admissions were made Green asked Gummer if it wasn't a fact that Milligan had not touched him until after the admissions were made. Green asked Gummer if it wasn't a fact that Milligan had not touched him until after the admissions had been made but Gummer insisted that he had.

Gummer Excused from Stand

Gummer was excused from the witness stand at 2:50 this afternoon after being under direct examination almost three days.

James Monahan was called to the stand by the defense.

Monohan stated that during the conversation in the Cass county jail between Brown and Gummer he was standing about five feet from Brown and Murphy was seated on the steps beside Brown and between Brown and Gummer. Monahan heard all of the conversation and absolutely refutes the testimony of Murphy.

Under cross examination which was conducted by Att. C.C. Wattam, it was developed that Monahan is a law student in the office of Att. Brickner who is one of the attorneys for the defense. Monahan stated that he paid attention to the conversation between Brown and

Gummer as he thot it was funny that those two should be allowed to talk together.

John Sporlie, a private detective was in the hotel on the seventh of June conducting a investigation as to the murder and said that he had tried to open the door to room 40 but couldn't find a key that fit. He found a hat pin, bent it, and picked the lock with it throwing it away when he was through.

He identified the pin which was produced in court as being similar to the one he had used.

Under cross examination he stated that he had formerly been deputy of Pierce county for four years which was the extent of his experience in running down criminals.

At this point a recess was taken.

After recess Brown was placed on the stand and stated that he had never known any one by the name of James Farrell. He was excused and Gummer returned to the stand. He also stated that he had never known a man by the name of James Farrell and had never seen the name written until the man wrote his name on the register that night. He was excused and the defense rested with this provision:

They are in communication with an another witness who may be here tomorrow morning and they reserve the right to place this witness on the stand if he appears.

Officer Pickering was the first witness called to the stand by the state in rebuttal."

DAILY TIMES—RECORD [Valley City, ND], Vol. XVI—No. 235, Mon., Feb. 20, 1922, at pp.1,4. Print.

Defense Introduces Evidence to Show There was a James Farrell at Willmar, Minn.

DAILY TIMES—RECORD [Valley City, ND], Vol. XVI—No. 236, Tues., Feb. 21, 1922, at p.1. Print.

ALL EVIDENCE IN AT 10:40 THIS MORNING

Court Again Adjourned Until Thursday Morning Owing to Illness of State's Attorney Green.

Defense Introduces Evidence to Show That There Was a James Farrell at Willmar, Minnesota.

"As the Gummer trial draws to a close the interest in the ultimate result is becoming more keen. It is the consensus of opinion that the defendant damaged his own cause during the cross examination yesterday morning, and the effect of his replies to questions asked him during the cross examination, on the jury was noticeable to everyone in the courtroom. It is not expected that the case will be given to the jury today but they will probably be charged on Thursday. Tomorrow being Washington's birthday there will be no court and if the case is not completed today it cannot be continued until Thursday.

Officer Pickering was the first witness called to the stand by the state in rebuttal yesterday afternoon. He was on the stand for several minutes but was not allowed to answer was 'did you ever say that it "it looked like a case of suicide to you" to which he replied 'No'.

Did Not Call Brown

Minnie Thompson, proprietress of the Addison Flats in Fargo said that she did not call Andy Brown on the morning of the 7th. Andy Brown's testimony was to the effect that she did call him at 6:00 o'clock. She further stated that she did not see Brown that morning, that her room was adjoining the room occupied by Brown and that she heard him go out about midnight but that she never heard him return. Cross examination failed to shake her direct testimony.

E.G. Charlson was placed on the stand and asked as to the conversation which it is alleged that Brown had over the telephone at the time he returned to the Addison Flats on the morning following the murder. This was objected to by the defense and the objections were sustained. The witness was excused.

[?]S. Knight, telegraph operator of Fargo, for whom Andy Brown was working at the time of the murder, was not allowed to answer the questions put to him by the state and was excused without giving any evidence of material value to the case.

T.J. Collins stated that Andy Brown had told him that he had gone from the Grand pool hall to the Prescott hotel on the night of the murder. This is contrary to Brown's testimony in which he stated that he had gone directly to his room after leaving the pool hall.

'Tell Bill Not to Squawk'

Myrle Schultz, a prisoner in the Cass county jail who is held for the [?]ing of a check was next placed on the stand and said that he and Hendrickson had a conversation with Brown on New Year's Eve in which he told Brown 'not to talk too much as there are a lot of "stools" around here'. He also said that Brown had told him to 'tell Bill not to squawk until the last minute' and also that Brown had said 'and don't let anyone hear you tell him'.

The cross examination was aimed at the discrediting of the testimony of the witness and was partly successful.

F.M. Hendrickson, another prisoner, substantiated the testimony of Schultz regarding the statement as to Brown asking him to 'tell Bill not to squawk until the last minute.'

Under cross examination several were asked of the witness tending to bring out the fact that he had been promised a quick release from custody for his testimony. The witness evidently did not understand the questions and seemed bewildered, finally saying, 'I just know I didn't kill the girl anyway'. He was excused.

Court Convened at 9:30

Court convened at 9:30 this morning to complete the case before the adjournment for the holiday. This was a vain effort as State's Attorney Green had been taken ill with the prevailing epidemic yesterday afternoon and the attending physician would not permit his appearance in court this morning. Several witnesses were examined with Assistant States Attorney C.C. Wattam conducted the case for the state. Both sides rests at 10:40 and Judge Cooley, in view of the fact that Mr. Green would be unable to appear in court, today, adjourned court until 10:00 o'clock Thursday morning.

As both sides have rested the pleas to the jury will start when court reconvenes. This will probably take the greater part of the day but is confidently expected that the jury will be given the charge by the court late that day and the defendant William Gummer, may expect to know his fate within a short time after the case is resumed.

Mrs. Minnie Thompson was recalled to the stand by Judge Barnett, for the defense, and questioned as to certain statements she is called to have made to Attorney Brickner, in which she is alleged to have stated that she was unable to recall whether she had called Andy Brown on the morning of June 7 or not. However, she stoutly, and most emphatically maintained that she had not called him that morning and was certain that her memory was correct in this particular.

Deny That Storlie Opened Room

Capt. Welsh denied that John Storlie had opened the door to room 40 on the 7 of June with a bent hair pin. This testimony was directly opposed to the testimony as given by Mr. Storlie yesterday afternoon. Officer Al. McDonald corroborated the testimony of Capt. Welsh.

Sheriff Kraemer was return to the stand and asked some perfunctory questions regarding the meeting in the Cass county jail at the time Gummer is alleged to have made the admissions which have been read in court.

James Milligan was returned to the stand and questioned regarding the meeting at the Cass county jail. He stated that he had not said 'Don't lie to me, G____d___ you' but had lost his temper when Gummer persisted in lying to them and had called him a 'G___d___ liar'. Under cross examination Milligan said that this incident did not take place until after the completion of the taking of admissions by Gummer and after Green and Kraemer had left the room. He denied that he had gotten angry because he was disappointed that they had not gotten more out of Gummer and was trying to force further admissions from him, but said that it made him sore to think that Gummer would lie to them the way he had. He also stated that there was no moving of chairs during the time of taking the admissions and that the lights were not switched on and off until after the taking of admissions was completed.

Green's Notes Complete

It was agreed between opposing counsel that testimony which Green would give, were he able to appear in court, should be read to the jury and Attorney Wattam read the statement that the shorthand notes were taken at the time the admissions were made that they were taken as to the questions were asked and the answers given, that the notes were continuous and complete, that no part of the conversation had been omitted and that the lights had not been turned off during the time the questions were being asked.

At this point the state recessed.

There Is a James Farrell, Willmar

A.P. Bergeson, former chief of police of Willmar, Minn., was called to the stand by the defense and stated that he had been chief of police there in 1918, that while he was on the police force there, there was a man in Willmar, who was employed by the Great Northern as brakeman, and who name was James Farrell. James Farrell had been around Willmar during the summer and fall of 1918 but had left there and the witness had not seen him since.

Under cross examination the witness said that he did not know whether James Farrell had gone by the name of R.F. Farrell or not. He described James Farrell as being a man about 5 feet, 7 inches in height, weight about 150 pounds, medium built, round faced, dark complexioned and about 27 to 30 years of age.

Judge Barnett showed the witness a photograph of R.F. Farrell and asked him if that was a likeness of James Farrell. The witness said that it was not. This was objected to by the state and the objection was sustained,—but Judge Barnett had gotten the matter before the jury.

Clair Brickner was placed on the stand by the defense and said that Mrs. Minnie Thompson had told him, less than ten days ago, that her mind was a perfect blank as to whether she had called Andy Brown on the morning of June 7 or not. He also said that, in a conversation which he had with her in September, she had stated that she was not sure whether she had called Brown or not. At this point both sides announced that they rested and Judge Cooley adjourned court at 10:40."

DAILY TIMES—RECORD [Valley City, ND], Vol. XVI—No. 236, Tues., Feb. 21, 1922, at p.1. Print.

Attorneys To Plead Case Tomorrow

DAILY TIMES—RECORD [Valley City, ND], Vol. XVI—No. 237, Wed., Feb. 22, 1922, at p.1. Print.

ATTORNEYS TO PLEAD CASE TOMORROW

"William Gummer will be again brought to the courtroom tomorrow morning to face what is expected to be the final day of his trial for the murder of Marie Wick.

The evidence has all been presented both the prosecution and the defense resting before the adjournment yesterday morning, and the attorneys will begin their pleas to the jury when court reconvenes in the morning. States Attorney Green will address the jury first, reviewing the evidence as presented by the state, and present the state's reason for claiming that the defendant committed the crime which resulted in the death of Marie Wick, and attempting to show that it would have been impossible for anyone, other than William Gummer, to have committed the act.

Judge Barnett will address the jury for the defense and will review such evidence as has been presented by the defense tending to prove the innocence of the accused.

After the final address by Green the court will instruct the jury and they will receive the case for consideration in the jury room.

Speculation is rife as to the final verdict of the jury but it is evident that the accused man will know his fate sometime Friday."

DAILY TIMES—RECORD [Valley City, ND], Vol. XVI—No. 237, Wed., Feb. 22, 1922, at p.1. Print.

Green Addresses Jury Entire Day

DAILY TIMES—RECORD [Valley City, ND], Vol. XVI—No. 238, Thurs., Feb. 23, 1922, at p.1. Print.

GREEN ADDRESSES JURY ENTIRE DAY

The Gummer Case Will Not Be Given To The Jury Until Some Time Tomorrow.

"The final stages of the Gummer trial were begun when court reconvened this morning. States Attorney Green began his address to the jury at the opening of court.

In his opening remarks he drew attention to the value of evidence, which is purely circumstantial in the fixing of the identity of the perpetrator of any crime, but more especially the crime of murder. He drew attention to the fact that the majority of murders are committed without there being any eye witnesses and more particularly, such heinous crimes as that for which William Gummer is now on trial.

He reviewed the evidence as presented by the state in their contention that the defendant is guilty of the crime of murdering pretty
Marie Wick at the Prescott hotel on the evening of June 6, 1921.

The various guests of the hotel on the night of the murder have all
been accounted for with the single exception of one James Farrell, who
registered, according to the defendant, between two and three o'clock
on the night of the murder, as being from Willmar, Minn. No such
person has been found residing at Willmar, and the attention of the
officials was drawn to the signature, and lead them to believe that the
signature was false by the fact that the name, Willmar, was incorrectly
spelled, only one 'l' being used. The various guests have told of their
movements on the night in question and have shown that they could
have had nothing to do with the crime, according to Mr. Green. It has
been shown that the perpetrator has been shown that the perpetrator
of the crime had intimate knowledge of the plans of the hotel as he
knew of the location of the hose nozzle with which the girl was killed,
and also knew the location of the bathroom, where he went to remove
the traces of the crime from the house nozzle. It has been shown that
there was no logical means of exit from the hotel except through the
lobby, of which the office was a part.

The fact that the defendant is devoid of moral scruples in his relations toward unaccompanied women who registered at the hotel while
he was night clerk there were shown by the admissions which he had
made to the officials and by the testimony of a pretty Glyndon, Minn,
19 year old girl who testified that he had made improper advances to
her when she stayed at the hotel in 1921.

The state contends that the name of James Farrell was signed to the
hotel register by Andy Brown, the chum of Gummer. They base their
contention on the testimony given by T.J. Caton, the Minneapolis
handwriting expert, who stated that, in his opinion, there was no

question but that Brown wrote the signature. Their belief is further strengthened by the fact that Brown writes the name of the town, Willmar, with only one 'l' the same as it is written in the signature of the register, and which is incorrect.

The state has shown that the defendant has made many misstatements when questioned by the officials. While he had corrected these misstatement himself, the state contends that he did not correct them until he became afraid that the officials knew that he had lied.

The state has contended that the door to room 30, occupied by the murdered girl, was opened by the use of a hat pin which was bent at the end and could have been used in turning the key on the inside of the door. This pin was found on the second floor hall several days after the murder.

The state contends that the accused and his chum, Andy Brown had an understanding that they were to 'keep mum' regarding their knowledge of the crime. This was shown by the testimony of two other inmates of the Cass county jail who claimed that Andy Brown had asked them to tell the defendant not to 'squawk' until the last minute.

The state contends that the crime could not have been committed by anyone other than the accused without the knowledge of Gummer, owing to the fact that he was the only person around the hotel during the night who was awake and on duty. They maintain that it would have been impossible for anyone to leave the hotel without Gummer seeing or hearing him. As Gummer has sworn that he did not see or hear anyone, other than those who have been accounted for, and James Farrell, around the hotel, the possibility of there being an unknown person on the premises that night is eliminated. This narrows the commission of the crime down to two people, James Farrell and the accused, and the state contends that James Farrell is a fictitious person whose signature was placed on the register to throw suspicion away from the accused.

States Attorney Green had not completed his address to the jury at the time of the 3:30 recess and it is evident that he will occupy the time of the court the entire day in reviewing the evidence as presented by the state.

Judge Barnett will address the jury tomorrow morning and will review the evidence as presented by the defense, contending that the charge against the accused has not been proven, that no evidence tending to show his connection with the crime has been presented and that the contention of the accused that he is innocent of any connection with the murder of Marie Wick is shown to be a fact.

The case will probably be given to the jury, with the instructions of the court, late tomorrow.

At the opening of court this morning the state entered a stipulation in evidence made by the foreman of the J.I. Case Co., in Fargo. The statement sets forth that the foreman would, if able to be present, testify that John Storlie, who testified that he was at the Prescott hotel on the afternoon of June 7, was not at the hotel that afternoon, but was at work for the J.I. Case Co. from 1 p.m. to 6 p.m. of that day.

Mr. Storlie had testified that he opened the door to room 40 that afternoon with a hat pin which he bent and used in picking the lock. Captain Welsh and Officer McDonald both refuted his testimony, saying that he did not open the door but that they had opened it themselves with a key furnished by Mrs. Lawrence."

DAILY TIMES—RECORD [Valley City, ND], Vol. XVI—No. 238, Thurs., Feb. 23, 1922, at p.1. Print.

Defense Attorneys Address Jury

DAILY TIMES-RECORD [Valley City, ND], Vol. XVI—No. 239, Fri., Feb. 24, 1922, at p.1. Print.

DEFENSE ATTORNEYS ADDRESS JURY [H.W. Swenson & W.H. Barnett]

Judge H.W. Swenson Opens Argument For The Defense and Talks For One Hour.

Judge Barnett Makes Strong Plea And Decries Value of Circumstantial Evidence.

"States Attorney Green completed his initial address to the jury at 5:00 o'clock yesterday afternoon.

When court convened at 10 o'clock this morning Judge H.W. Swenson opened the plea for the defense, stating that there were certain points of the case with which he was more familiar than Judge

Barnett and for the reason Judge Barnett has asked him to cover those points before the Judge began his address. Judge Swenson talked to the jury for one hour, completing at 11:00 when Barnett began his address. Judge Barnett had not completed his address when recess was taken for the noon hour and it is hardly probable that the case will go to the jury before tomorrow.

Judge Swenson Addresses Jury

Judge Swenson began his address by stating that testimony which has been introduced shows that the defendant, Gummer, was at his place at the desk at all times whenever anyone came to the hotel on the night of the murder. He said that great stress had been laid, by the state, upon the fact that the murdered girl had been assaulted between 12 and 1 o'clock. Testimony has shown that Mrs. Lawrence had not retired until about 12 o'clock, nor had Mrs. Van Vorst left her downstairs apartment until midnight. Testimony has also shown that J.J. Meyers had come into the hotel and seen Fred Lawrence about 12 o'clock and did not leave until a few minutes after that hour. Andy Brown came in at 12:25 and stayed in the lobby until 12:50. About 10 or 15 minutes after Brown left the hotel H.J. Hagan came in and found the defendant apparently dozing behind the desk. No witness have been produced to refute Brown's testimony as to the time he was at the hotel or the time he left, although his leaving time could have been easily checked up the proprietor of the Grand pool room, where Brown claims to have been about 1:00 o'clock.

Judge Swenson said that the testimony does not show that Gummer had tried to throw suspicion on J.J. Meyers, although the state had argued that this had thrown suspicion toward Gummer.

Judge Swenson stated that all the guest arriving at the hotel between midnight and three o'clock had found the accused at his place behind the desk with the single possible exception of James Farrell, and, since there is no refuting testimony, the conclusion might be drawn that he also found Gummer behind the desk.

Refers to Expert Testimony

In referring to the handwriting testimony Judge Swenson stated that the state had first gone to F.L. Watkins with the disputed signature and the undisputed specimens of Brown's handwriting but that Mr. Watkin's opinion evidently did not coincide with the theory of the state and they then went to Minneapolis to find an expert who agreed with them, getting T.J. Caton. Mr. Caton's own testimony is that he has testified in 12 to 15 cases of disputed handwriting during the 20 years he had been engaged in that field. Mr. Swenson drew attention to the fact that Mr. Watkins had testified in 75 to 100 cases while he has been in that business. Mr. Swenson claims that Caton overlooked several characteristics in Brown's handwriting when comparing it with the disputed signature. He also said that Mr. Caton had drawn particular attention to certain peculiarities in the signature which he claimed to be unusual and characteristic of Brown's handwriting which were later shown to be quite common. When Caton had been shown that these were not unusual he had hedged by saying that they were characteristic of Brown when taken into consideration with the multiplicity of other things.

Judge Swenson drew attention to the fact that the two experts who testified for the defense, F.L. Watkins and George Dangum, are both residents of the state and are property owners in the state and would be more interested in the upholding of the laws of the state than would be an outsider.

James Farrell Actually Exists

He said that the testimony of Mr. Bergeson, chief of police of Willmar, Minn., shows there actually did exist a man by the name who resided at Willmar in 1918 and the description of this man coincided with the description as given by the accused.

Judge Swenson said that the defense did not know who committed the murder, any more than did the state, and that they were not attempting to prove that the murder had been committed by James Farrell but merely wanted to show that there was a person in that hotel on the night in question who had not been accounted for.

He also drew the attention of the jury to the fact that the bloody and gruesome exhibits had been brought into court by the state to inflame the minds of the jury against someone, presumably the defendant.

Judge Swenson completed his address at 11:00 o'clock and Judge Barnett began his plea to the twelve men who will decide the fate of his client.

Judge Barnett began his address to the jury in a rather sarcastic vein, saying that the state had always referred to the defendant as a man when he was merely a boy of 22 years inexperienced and not familiar with the ways of the world. He referred to the inalienable right of every man, given to him by the constitution which entitled him to life, liberty and the pursuit of happiness and asked the jury if they were convinced, beyond a reasonable doubt, by the evidence presented, that the defendant was guilty of the crime as charged. He then brought up the question of the method of elimination as used by the state in disposing of the various guests at the hotel that night. He said, 'If you ask every man in this room, "Did you murder Marie Wick" it is likely they would be unanimous answering "No", yet that is the way the state had eliminated many of the guests of the hotel that night'.

Evidence of No Value

In illustrating the fact that circumstantial evidence may often be very misleading, Judge Barnett advanced two or three suppositious cases. The first one concerned Fred Lawrence. He said that the state was basing their claim to Gummer's guilt on the fact that he was the only man in the hotel that night who had the opportunity of committing the crime without detection. In view of the evidence would it not be as reasonable to suppose that Fred Lawrence had an usual opportunity. Fred Lawrence retired shortly before midnight and his movements between that time and 7 o'clock the next morning have not been checked in any way other than his own testimony. Fred Lawrence had lived in the hotel for some time, was thoroughly familiar with everything in the hotel, knew the location of the different guests for the night, and knew that Marie Wick had been checked into room 30. He had the additional advantage of having some authority around the hotel and if he had attempted the crime and been discovered in the act by Gummer, could have ordered Gummer back to his place at the desk. Why should Fred Lawrence be eliminated on his own testimony any more than Gummer?

Case Base On Morality

The state has based a large part of their claim against Gummer on the fact that his morals, sexually, are not of the best. The state has claimed that nothing could be proven against J.J. Hagan but Judge Barnett asked, if Hagan were on trial, the circumstances, in this respect would not point toward the guilt of Hagan as much as towards Gummer.

Judge Barnett said that assuming that Andy Brown is in the reality the 'James Farrell' and that he signed 'James Farrell' on the hotel register, that he occupied room 40 the night of the murder and that he was seen going into the Addison flats at 6:30 the following morning, all of which the state claims to be true, would not the evidence point to Brown as the guilty man as much as Gummer. Would not the fact that Brown appeared on the stand very nervous with a blanched face lead one to believe that his demeanor was more consistent with guilt than the attitude of the accused.

Judge Barnett said that the state was perfectly satisfied with, and vouched for the truthfulness of Andy Brown when they put him on the stand but that they claim that Brown testimony was absolutely untrue which he gave when on the stand for the defendant. He asked asked why the truthfulness of Andy Brown when they put him on the stand but that they claim that Brown testimony was absolutely untrue which he gave when on the stand for the defense. He asked why the truthfulness of a witness should be vouched for when his testimony suited their theory but should be impeached when contrary to their own views.

Judge Barnett paid a sincere tribute to States Attorney Green when he said that 'Green was the greatest little prosecutor in the state at this time and that he did not know of anyone who could have built up a stronger case with the material which he had'. However he drew attention to the fact that Green was undoubtedly prejudiced in the matter owing to the work and enthusiasm he had put into the case."

DAILY TIMES-RECORD [Valley City, ND], Vol. XVI—No. 239, Fri., Feb. 24, 1922, at p.1. Print.

Gummer Guilty Of Murder In First Degree

D AILY TIMES-RECORD [Valley City, ND], Vol. XVI—No. 240, Sat., Feb. 25, 1922, at pp.1,2. Print.

GUMMER GUILTY OF MURDER IN FIRST DEGREE

Jury of Twelve Good Men Convict Gummer of First Degree Murder. Jury Out Seven Hours. Verdict Gives General Satisfaction in This Community

---

Andy Brown Arrested For Complicity and Will Have To Face Jury. Taken To Fargo This Morning and Will Be arraigned in District Court, Cass County, Monday.

There Was One Witness Present At This Trial Who Did Not Testify In The Case', said State's Attorney Green, In Closing His Appeal For

Conviction To the Jury, 'It Was The True Soul of William Gummer
Bared To The Jury, Monday Morning Coming Out In the Real Gum-
mer. This Spirit of Gummer Coming Out As a Silent Witness Convicted
Him As The Murderer and [?]raducer of Marie Wick That Fateful
June Night.'

"William Gummer spent a sleepless night in the Barnes county jail,
following the reading of the jurors verdict which will result, in his imprisonment for life at the state penitentiary at Bismarck. He displayed
no emotion when the verdict was read and smiled when he left the
courtroom but evidently realized the predicament he was in, as the
result of murdering Marie Wick, after he was returned to his cell. He
paced the floor of his cell continuously throughout the night, cursing
the jurymen who have decided that he raped and brutally murdered
Marie Wick in the commission of the most brutal and beastial crime
in the history of the state.

He has made no statement regarding the verdict or his part in the
crime.

At 12:20 this morning, after having had the evidence under consideration for seven hours, the Barnes county jury, of which Henry
Helmers of Wimbledon was the foreman, returned the verdict of
guilty of first degree murder against William Gummer. This verdict
carries with it the penalty of life imprisonment in the penitentiary at
Bismarck.

Gummer Unmoved

The defendant was brought into the courtroom when the jury announced that a verdict had been reached. He appeared as nonchalant
as usual and displayed but very little interest in the proceedings. He
received the verdict with no sign of emotion, sitting in his place quite

calmly and not changing color. When he was led from the courtroom he smiled at the spectators assembled there. He did not speak on his way from the courtroom to his cell in the county jail but, after being locked in his cell by Sheriff Larson, he shouted to W.A. Jarvis, who is confined across the hall, and, with an oath, said, 'The G___d___ dirty bunch of _____ found me guilty'.

The court officials were notified by Sheriff Larson as soon as the jury was ready to return their verdict and they arrived at the courtroom within a few minutes. States Attorney Green and his assistant, Charles Pollock, were in their places to receive the verdict. Clair Brickner appeared for the defense. The verdict was read and Judge Cooley complimented the jurymen on the good judgment they had shown in arriving at that verdict, stating that the evidence showed their verdict to be the correct one. He then told them that, inasmuch as they had served for a little over five weeks on this case they would be excused from further duty during the present term of court and were free to return to their homes.

Thirty Day Stay Denied

Attorney Clair Brickner moved for a stay of sentence. Judge Cooley denied the motion, saying that commitment seemed advisable. Attorney Brickner then demanded his legal right of a two day stay and asked that the court consider the thirty day request. Judge Cooley granted that he would pronounce sentence at 10:00 o'clock Monday morning.

It is understood that the jury was unanimous in their verdict, only one ballot being taken. Before putting the question to a vote they reviewed the evidence to be certain they they were making no mistake and the first ballot taken resulted in a verdict of guilty in the first degree, with no dissenting vote. Henry Helmers of Wimbledon, was selected as foreman of the jury.

The local feeling has been running high the past few days and speculation has been rife as to the probable verdict of the jury. Since the verdict was announced the general feeling is that justice was meted out properly and in accordance with the evidence produced, the great majority of citizens expressing satisfaction that the accused man was not to be released from confinement.

Hans Hoff, a cousin of the murdered girl was in the courtroom when the verdict was read, and expressed the satisfaction of the family at the outcome of the trial. He said that, while the verdict would not return Marie Wick to the family, there was a certain amount of comfort to be derived from the fact that William Gummer would not be permitted to practice depredations on any other innocent young girls.

There were none of William Gummer's family in the courtroom when the verdict was read.

Yesterday Afternoon's Session

In yesterday afternoon's session Judge Barnett resumed his plea to the jury. He contended that, as the state had contended that the assault was committed between 12 and 1 o'clock, and that all of the time between these two hours was accounted for by the presence of Andy Brown, with the possible exception of 10 or 12 minutes, it would have been impossible for the accused to have committed the assault and been dozing in the chair behind the desk when H.J. Hagan arrived.

Judge Barnett characterized the crime as worse than murder, it was the assault and rape of an innocent girl who had no means of protection, and could have only been committed by the most bestial of men. He drew attention to the defendant and asked the jury if they thought it possible that that young boy could have been guilty of such a crime.

Judge Barnett said that the state staked their case on the fact that two separate crimes had been committed and at two separate times. He contended that the testimony of witnesses, when first interviewed, did not coincide with the state's theory in that the only two people who heard noises during the night heard those noises at two separate times. Taking this into consideration the state had been obliged to reconstruct their case to agree with the statement of these witnesses.

He suggested that the experiments had been conducted in such a way that the witness, Mrs. Van Vorst, would be sure to bolster up their case. He contended that May Melaas could not have heard the noise of anyone jumping on the floor above as the floor was covered with three thicknesses of paper, a carpet and a rug, which would have deadened the sound. He also gained that the defendant would not have walked down the hall with sufficient noise to have been heard by Miss Melaas after committing such a heinous crime.

Judge Barnett contended that the light in room 30 would have shown thru the crack between the door and door jamb, of the door connecting the two rooms, directly in the face of Mr. Hagan and would have awakened him. This was based on the supposition that Mr. Hagan slept on his right side.

Judge Barnett attempted to prove, by the use of the bedstead produced in court, that it would have been impossible for the accused to have struck the wall with the hose nozzle from across the bed, claiming that the distance was too great. He also contended that the dent in the wall was not caused by the nozzle as the crescent mark produced by the nozzle would have been opposite to the dent which the photograph showed. The crescent in the photograph is inverted.

Judge Barnett placed great stress on the fact that the evidence had shown that the accused was apparently dozing when H.J. Hagan came in and questioned whether it would have been possible for him to have committed the assault and been so composed within the time which had been unaccounted for.

Judge Barnett completed his address at 3:45 and States Attorney Green immediately began his closing rebuttal argument.

Green Begins Rebuttal At 3:45

Attorney Green claimed that some of the statements made by Judge Barnett and Judge Swenson in their addresses to the jury were wrong and stated that he would correct the impression that they had left.

He said that counsel for the defense had stated that the evidence did not show that Gummer had attempted to throw suspicion on John Myers by reading from the admissions made by Gummer on the night of June 14. Mr. Green contended that the reason this feature of the case did not show in the admissions was because the attempt had been made on the afternoon of June 14, at which no shorthand notes had been taken, but that the testimony given by other witnesses had shown that such an attempt had been made.

He also claimed that the defense had argued that the state had made it appear that Andy Brown was not in the hotel after one-clock but Mr. Green maintained most emphatically that Brown was there and that his fact would be proven later.

He stated that he would not argue the matter of the handwriting expert testimony, feeling that the jurors had already made up their minds as to who wrote the signature and that anything he would say would be superfluous.

He took strenuous object to Judge Swenson's testimony and evidence. He claimed that the officials had searched Willmar and vicinity for a possible James Farrell but had been unable to find any such person. That there had been such a person there in 1918 was merely a coincidence. He drew attention to the fact that the evidence produced had shown that this James Farrell had been a brakemen on the Great

Northern railway. He said that it was necessary for brakemen to make out reports and sign orders that if this James Farrell had been a brakeman a sample of his signature could have been easily obtained. If this was obtained and shown to coincide with the signature on the hotel register it would have been conclusive proof of the innocence of the accused. Why did the defense not produce this proof?

Swenson Made Green Angry

States Attorney Green admitted that the charge made by Judge Swenson, that the officials were attempting to convict an innocent man merely that their records as prosecutors would not be damaged, had made him angry and he insisted that no possible recompence could repay an official for the lifelong knowledge that he was responsible for the life imprisonment of an innocent man.

States Attorney Green, in speaking of the handwriting testimony, said that Judge Swenson had been cross examined for three hours in his, Caton's, attempt to teach Swenson something about the science of writing.

Green contended that Mr. Sydness had opened the door to room 30 with a bent hat pin but insisted that Storlie had not used a pin in opening the door to room 40. He insisted that it was his personal opinion that it would have been impossible for any man to have picked the lock with such a pin as the construction of the lock would not permit its opening in this manner.

Elimination Not Absurd

States Attorney Green asked why, if their process of elimination and been so absurd, the defense had not pointed out some error in their reasoning instead of making the bare statement that it was absurd.

Green claimed that the defense had shown no point of error in the states theory that two separate crimes had been committed at two separate times but had spent their time in arguing over minor, unimportant matters.

Green showed another photograph of the steam pipe in the room 30 which showed it to be directly on the floor, the photograph which the defense had shown was the photo of the air pipe.

Green stated that the state had vouched for the truthfulness of Brown only in respect to his identification of the handwriting specimens which were used in court. The defense had couched for his truthfulness in all other particulars.

Green stated that the officials had not brought H.J. Hagan 1600 miles to testify to insignificant details but had brought him here because the name of James Farrell would have been an insignificant detail in the case if Hagan had not appeared on the stand. In other words, they had brought Hagan to eliminate some of the stories being circulated and to prevent Hagan being made the goat in the case.

Green said that there was no reason for Andy Brown and Gummer telling several different stories regarding the same things which had happened in the presence of both, unless they had been attempting to lie out of their predicament.

Defense Tried to Raise Doubt

Green contended that the defense had merely tried to raise a doubt in the minds of the jurymen to overcome the preponderance of evidence presented by the state.

He corrected a slight misstatement of the defense in which they said that the state claimed that May Melaas was awakened by the noises in the room above. May Melaas was awakened a moment or two before she heard any noise.

Green said that the officials had used low, obscene language in their questioning of Gummer during the time he had made the admissions to them in order to get down to his level, and that they had couched their questions in a language that he could understand.

Green insisted that any man capable of committing such a cold blooded murder in the manner in which it had been committed, staying in the room until the blood had dried on her arm so that he could place the body back in bed without getting any blood on himself, was capable of apparently dozing within a minute after committing the crime.

Gummer Convicted Himself

States Attorney Green, in closing his rebuttal argument, said that Gummer was the best witness that the state had when he was on the stand under cross examination Monday. He said that there was a strong witness for the state that had not testified from the stand and that this witness was the soul of Gummer himself. That his soul, as exhibited, under cross examination, showed the real Gummer who did not hesitate to do anything to enforce his own desire, either in petty things or in satisfying his bestial passions. He characterized the defendant as being unfit, morally, to associate with respectable persons, and asked that the jury see that he be confined that he might not have any further opportunity of assaulting unaccompanied, innocent young girls.

States Attorney Green completed his address at 4:40 and Judge Cooley immediately charged the jury, saying that it was possible for them to bring in one of three verdicts, and that they were compelled by law to set the penalty if they found him guilty. They could acquit, convict of murder in the first degree, which carries the penalty of life imprisonment, or bring in a verdict of murder in the second degree. Under the latter verdict they would be required to set the penalty as imprisonment for a term of years. Their latitude in the number extends from the minimum of 10 years to the maximum of 30 years.

The jury was sent to the jury room at 5:20 and they deliberated for six hours. They did not return the verdict until 12:20, but one hour was spent in the election of a foreman and in serving supper."

DAILY TIMES-RECORD [Valley City, ND], Vol. XVI—No. 240, Sat., Feb. 25, 1922, at pp.1,2. Print.

Andy Brown Charged Also As Murderer

DAILY TIMES-RECORD [Valley City, ND], Vol. XVI—No. 240, Sat., Feb. 25, 1922, at p.1. Print.

ANDY BROWN CHARGED ALSO AS MURDERER

"Andy Brown, who has been held in the Cass county and Barnes county jails since September 24, 1921, as a material witness for the state, and during the trial of William Gummer appeared as a witness for the defense, was released as a witness at 5:30 in the morning.

He was immediately placed under arrest on a warrant charging him with murder in the first degree in connection with the death of Marie Wick on June 6(, 1921) at the Prescott hotel in Fargo. This is the same charge under which William Gummer has been found guilty by a Barnes county jury, and under which Gummer will be sentenced to life imprisonment in the state penitentiary at Bismarck.

Andy Brown was taken to Fargo on Northern Pacific train No. 136 at 6:20 this morning. Deputy Sheriff James Milligan served the warrant, which has been in readiness for two weeks, and took the prisoner in custody. He had him in charge in his removal to Fargo.

Andy Brown will be arraigned in Fargo this afternoon under the charge and a date set for his preliminary hearing, providing he does not waive preliminary examination. His trial will be held in the near future in Fargo, providing he does not ask for a change of venue.

Mr. Brown was decidedly surprised when told the verdict in the Gummer case but made little comment. When served with the warrant charging him with murder he exhibited considerable emotion but refrained from making any statement.

This is the sequel to the Gummer case which has been confidently expected for some time.

The Cass county officials feel that they have a strong case against Andy Brown as they had against Gummer, with the added intent to kill rather than that of rape. This case will be watched with interest equal to the trial just completed."

DAILY TIMES-RECORD [Valley City, ND], Vol. XVI—No. 240, Sat., Feb. 25, 1922, at p.1. Print.

William Gummer Receives Life Sentence

D AILY TIMES-RECORD [Valley City, ND], Vol. XVI—No. 241, Mon, Feb. 27, 1922, at p.1. Print.

WILLIAM GUMMER RECEIVES LIFE SENTENCE

GUMMER SENTENCED TO LIFE IN PRISON

Convicted Man Shows Very Little Evidence of Emotion When Sentenced to Life Imprisonment

---

"William Gummer, who has been convicted of having murdered Marie Wick on the night of June 6, 1921, was sentenced at 11 o'clock this morning to serve the balance of his natural life within the walls of the state penitentiary at Bismarck.

The sentence was to have been passed at 10:00 o'clock but, owing to the fact that Judge Barnett, his attorney was unable to be present at that time, he did not receive his sentence until 11:00.

When brought to the courtroom just before 10:00 o'clock, Gummer seemed his usual self with the exception that he was slightly paler than at any time since he had been confined in the Barnes county jail and his countenance showed the strain he had been under since the verdict was read to him at 12:20 Saturday night.

When brought into the courthouse he stopped and shook hands with his father and brother who'd been awaiting his appearance at the foot of the stairs. His mother and sister had been visiting him in his cell at the county jail and came in just after him. He merely said 'good morning' when shaking hands with his father and brother.

After waiting for some time it became evident that Judge Barnett would be delayed in arriving and the prisoner was returned to his cell. He was brought back at 10:50 and sentence was passed at 11:00 o'clock.

Judge Chas. M. Cooley made no remarks in sentencing Gummer other than the usual formula in telling him that he had been tried and found guilty by twelve men who had rendered a verdict of guilty of murder in in the first degree, which verdict carried the sentence of life imprisonment, and that, therefore, he sentenced him to serve the balance of his natural life within the walls of the state penitentiary at Bismarck.

The convicted man showed very little sign of emotion when sentence had been pronounced.

Judge Barnett announces the intention of the defense to appeal the case to the supreme court with the request that the convicted man be granted a new trial. He will base his appeal on the admission of the evidence relating to Gummer's relations to other women, and on certain decisions of Judge Cooley's admitting this evidence.

Andy Brown, Gummer's chum, is to be arraigned on the same charge, in Fargo, tomorrow. Assistant States Attorney Wattam said this morning that Brown would not be tried until the appeal of Gummer's case had been decided by the supreme court, as that case would be based on practically the same evidence as that which convicted Gummer.

At the request of Judge Barnett, for the relatives of the convicted man William Gummer will remain in the Barnes county jail for a few days, no definite time for his removal being set as yet.

Gummer's father, mother, sisters and brothers were in the court room when sentence was pronounced. The sentence effected them to a greater degree than it did the convicted man. They were not in court at the time the jury returned their verdict as they were not informed that a verdict had been reached."

DAILY TIMES-RECORD [Valley City, ND], Vol. XVI—No. 241, Mon, Feb. 27, 1922, at p.1. Print.

Brown Measured By Police

DAILY TIMES-RECORD [Valley City, ND], Vol. XVI—No. 241, Mon., Feb. 27, 1922, at p.1. Print.

BROWN MEASURED BY POLICE

"Fargo, Feb. 27—At Fargo this morning Andy Brown, pal of William Gummer also under arrest as co-partner of the convicted man in the horrible crime, was measured for the criminal records at the police station this morning. His finger prints were taken and the bertillion measurements recorded. His arraignment is set for 10 o'clock tomorrow morning."

DAILY TIMES-RECORD [Valley City, ND], Vol. XVI—No. 241, Mon., Feb. 27, 1922, at p.1. Print.

———————

DAILY TIMES-RECORD [Valley City, ND], Vol. XVI—No. 242, Tues., Feb. 28, 1922, at p.1. Print.

HEARING OF BROWN POSTPONED TODAY

Brown Will Have Hearing March 7, Declared Through His Attorneys He will Demand Hearing Now.

"Fargo, Feb. 28—Preliminary hearing of Andy Brown, charged with first degree murder in connection the death of Marie Wick of Grygla, Minn., was postponed until March 9 (,1922) on application of the state when the case was called in justice court.

Mr. Brown, according to his attorney, Claire Brickner, will demand a hearing immediately.

Chum Of Gummer

The defendant was a chum of William Gummer who last week was convicted of first degree murder in connection with the death of Marie Wick on June 7 in the Prescott Hotel in Fargo where Gummer was night clerk. Brown was arrested on the same charge immediately after his release as a state witness for which he had been held since last September. Although it was rumored that Gummer's case would be appealed, Judge Barnett declared no steps had been taken as yet. The defense has a year in which to ask for a new trial."

DAILY TIMES-RECORD [Valley City, ND], Vol. XVI—No. 241, Mon., Feb. 27, 1922, at p.1. Print.

Gummer Sentenced To State Prison For Life

THE PEOPLES OPINION [Valley City, ND], Vol. VI—No. 34, Thurs., March 2, 1922, p.1. Print.

GUMMER SENTENCED TO
STATE PRISON FOR LIFE

"Monday morning at about eleven o'clock William Gummer, the convicted murderer of Marie Wick, was brought before Judge Cooley and was formally sentenced to imprisonment in the North Dakota state penitentiary for the remainder of his natural life.

Judge Charles M. Cooley, in pronouncing sentence, informed the defendant, who stood before him, that he had been informed against in the Cass county district court as the man responsible for the murder of Miss Marie Wick in the Prescott hotel in Fargo on June 7 last.

The case had been transferred to Barnes county, and now a jury of his peers had declared him guilty as he had been informed against.

'Is there any legal reason why sentence shall not be imposed this time?' the defendant was asked.

Judge W.H. Barnett, representing the defendant, stated that there was no reason.

And so Judge Cooley formally pronounced the sentence that had been fixed by the jury—that of life imprisonment —the only sentence provided in the case of persons convicted of first degree murder.

For 20 years no state board of pardons, or no state parole board, will have the power to either pardon or parole Gummer from the prison.

Under the law enacted by the legislature a year ago, it is provided that no pardon or no parole shall be granted to any lifer until he shall have served at least half of his expectancy, as it existed at the time he was sentenced.

Gummer is 23 years old. His life expectancy is 39.39 years.

Gummer will be the 19th lifer in the state penitentiary. Seventeen of the lifers are in for murder, and one for assault with a dangerous weapon.

Gummer came into court today lacking something of the confidence and assurance that he has evinced throughout this trial. Somewhat paler than usual, he heard the sentence pronounced while his mother, father, brother and sister sat near by.

His parents heard the sentence in silence.

His brother and sister cried.

A few moments later, Gummer, hat in hand, quit the courtroom —back to his cell in the county jail.

On the request of Judge Barnett, Judge Cooley stated this afternoon that he would enter an order permitting the retention of Gummer in the county jail here several days before ordering his removal to Bismarck.

This was requested to permit Judge Barnett an opportunity to confer with the prisoner on plans for the indeed appeal of the case to the state supreme court, his counsel intending to see a retrial on the theory that Judge Cooley permitted the introduction of certain inadmissible evidence. In particular, the evidence challenged is that relating to Gummer's conduct toward women guests in the hotel other than Miss Wick.

The Cass county state's attorney, W.C. Green, was not present in court today, C.C. Wattam representing the prosecutor's office.

A prisoner in the cell next to Gummer's, informed Sheriff Larson of Barnes county Saturday afternoon that two or three times during Friday night—after the jury had returned its verdict—he heard Gummer crying in his cell. Officials had supposed that he slept all night.

Sheriff Larson says the verdict has had the effect of breaking down some of the confident air the prisoner had assumed during most of his trial.

When he was told that Brown had been charged with murder, Gummer said: 'They got another innocent man mixed up in it.'

In a few conversations he had had with Sheriff Larson since the verdict of guilty was returned, Gummer has maintained innocence. Gummer's mother called on the convicted man in the jail Saturday, and she was with him again this morning prior to his sentence, and also she was with him afterwards.

Gummer's father did not come to the jail until Saturday night, when he came alone. He was with his wife both times she was at the jail today.

His parents both broke down and cried as they were with him this morning—as they did when they called on him Saturday.

Andy Brown, alias Leslie Locke, charged with first degree murder in connection with the Marie Wick case was arraigned at 10 a.m. Tuesday before Justice H.F. Miller of Fargo. If he demands a hearing, it is likely the case will be delayed two or three weeks, or until State's Attorney W.C. Green returns from Stephen, Minn., where he has gone to rest at the farm home of his parents.

Estimates today of the cost of the trial of William Gummer ranged up to $10,000.

Barnes county has financed the trial so far as the payment of witness fees, jurors' fees and other costs is concerned.

Shortly that county will bill Cass county for the amount it has expended. The bill probably will be nearly $8,000.

Other expense incident to the case will add from $1,500 to $2,000."

THE PEOPLES OPINION [Valley City, ND], Vol. VI—No. 34, Thurs., March 2, 1922, p.1. Print.

Commendation For Jurymen

Daily Times-Record or Peoples Opinion. March 1, 1922.

COMMENDATON FOR JURYMEN

Former Citizen Of The County And Former Chief of Police Of Fargo - Expresses Satisfaction at Gummer Verdict.

"Chief of Police E.H. Swanson received a letter from Con Keefe yesterday in which Mr. Keefe expresses the satisfaction felt by the people of Fargo and Cass County at the verdict returned the Gummer trial.

Mr. Keefe is a former resident in the county and is well known to many of the older residents here. He was also Chief of Police of Fargo for number of years.

We print his letter below:

Fargo, N.D., 2-27-22.

Mr. Editor:

As a citizen of North Dakota and Fargo for the past 41 years I feel as though I would like to express a few words on behalf of the justice done in regard to the murder trial that has just been finished in your wonderful little city and I am sure that our people, as well as myself, appreciate the many good things our people got while there, both in kindness as well as in justice. If there is any reward we are sure that you will get it as it is coming to you all, and especially the jurors who so loyally defended our states attorney, Wm. C. Green, and all others who were interested in this awful murder case.

I am sure that the people of Fargo and Cass county will always be under obligations for the good and loyal service we got at their hands, and I for one will always be ready to reward them for it.

The counsel for Gummer was afraid to have this case tried here, where it ought to be, on account of this past record in a great many of the criminal cases that have been tried here. He was afraid that he wouldn't get a jury to suit him. Thank God that the good citizens of Barnes county who were drawn as jurors did not know anything about the case except to see that justice was done. They relieved the people of Cass county, to whom it rightfully belonged, of the awful deal, and decided what that awful murderer, Gummer, was to do for the reminder of his dirty life. It is too bad that it could not be solitary confinement. We all hope that the other fellow with him will soon follow. It is hard to say bad things about anyone but words can't be used that would place this man where he ought to be. When a man will so mercilessly murder an innocent girl as he did, nothing can be done that would be bad enough for him.

The mother and father, and all others that knew her, have been deprived of her company just to satisfy a dirty brute. The change of venue was taken to bulldoze the people of Fargo and Cass county, but thank God the people of Barnes county were too loyal to be bulldozed by such a change and the noble jurors brought in a verdict of guilty without a dissenting vote. While they won't get any reward in this world I hope they will in the next.

It is a small thing for a mother and father to get for the life of a daughter who was so kind and good as Marie was, but it is a great comfort for others to know that such a brute is where he won't do the like to others, and it can be hoped that he will be kept there and eat in confinement all of his time. Bread and water is a swell dish for him, with very little light.

I hope that the fathers and mothers of North Dakota will give this case thought, and you will in the near future get such a legislature as will make all such criminals as this one suffer solitary confinement for life,—and that means life.

Now just another word for the great and valuable service that each of you gave in this long and tiresome trial. I, as one of the North Dakota's eldest citizens, want to thank you from the bottom of my heart for the good and valuable service you gave to our attorney, W.C. Green and all others who so kindly assisted in bring this ordered to justice. Again thank you, I am,

CON KEEFE, 207 4 St., No., Fargo, N.D."

Daily Times-Record or Peoples Opinion, March 1, 1922.

———

State v. Gummer, 200 N.W. 20 (N.D. 1924) (Appeal for new trial - Denied)

tant case, stay up to date with new opinions as they are filed, or do deep analysis using our raw data."

"Free Law Project seeks to provide free access to primary legal materials, develop legal research tools and support academic research on legal corpora. We work diligently with volunteers to expand our efforts at building an open source, open access, legal research ecosystem. Currently Free Law Project sponsors the development of CourtListener, Juriscraper, and RECAP."

State v. Gummer, 200 N.W. 20 (N.D. 1924)

North Dakota Supreme Court

Filed: February 16th, 1924

Precedential Status: Precedential

Citations: 200 N.W. 20, 51 N.D. 445

Docket Number: Unknown

Judges: PER CURIAM.

[EDITORS' NOTE: THIS PAGE CONTAINS HEADNOTES. HEADNOTES ARE NOT AN OFFICIAL PRODUCT OF THE COURT, THEREFORE THEY ARE NOT DISPLAYED.] *Page 447

Statement of facts.

The defendant was convicted of murder in the first degree. He has appealed from the judgment of conviction and an order denying a new trial. The record is voluminous. The facts necessary to be stated are as follows: In June, 1921, Marie Wick was a strong, healthy, good-looking, unmarried, and virtuous girl of eighteen years, living at Grygla, Minn., a small inland town about 100 miles north of Fargo, N.D.; she was steady and industrious; she possessed an ordinary education, supplemented by a business course had in a college at Warren, a small town not far distant from Grygla, Minn. She had never been in any town larger than Warren, Minn. Her parents were farmers living near

Grygla. For some eight months prior to June 4th, 1921, she had been working for a co-operative company at Grygla. She desired and intended to visit her aunt at Pettibone, N.D., another small town some 150 miles west of Fargo, on a branch of *Page 454 the Northern Pacific Railway. Thus, for her visit, she with her father went from Grygla to Thief River Falls on June 5th, 1921. She had then $20.00 in currency and a cashier's check for $20.00. The next morning she proceeded alone on the train (Soo Line) to Warren; thence, she proceeded, again alone, on another train (G.N. Ry.) to Crookston; thence, on a train (G.N. Ry.) from Crookston to Fargo, riding with some women and children whom she had met at Crookston. She neither talked nor paid any attention to other passengers on this train. Previously, she had written to one Rasmussen, a boy whom she had known since her childhood days at home, requesting him to meet her at Fargo, because never had she been in a town as large as Fargo. At Moorhead, a town across the river from Fargo, Rasmussen met her and rode with her on the train to Fargo. Together they walked from the G.N. depot in Fargo to the N.P. depot to ascertain when the N.P. train left the next morning for the trip to Pettibone. The parties with whom she rode on the train to Fargo, talked about going to the Prescott Hotel in Fargo. In fact, they did stop at this hotel. Mrs. Lawrence was the proprietress of this hotel. So, from the N.P. depot, they went to the Prescott Hotel. There they arrived about 10:15 or 10:20 P.M. There she was registered by the landlady, Mrs. Lawrence, assigned room 30, given a key to the room, and dated on the call sheet for a call at 6:30 A.M. Defendant Gummer was the night clerk at this hotel. He had shown to their rooms the parties with whom Miss Wick had ridden on the train from Crookston to Fargo. As he came downstairs, the landlady requested him to conduct Miss Wick to her room. This he did. She remained in her room for a few minutes, came downstairs, left her key at the desk, and, with Rasmussen, went to an ice cream parlor. In a short time she returned. Rasmussen left her and went to Moorhead. She procured her key at the desk, requested the landlady to change her call to 6 A.M. and proceeded to her room for the second time at about 11 P.M. Mrs. Lawrence and her son Fred retired about 11:40 P.M. All of the guests at the hotel had retired at or about midnight with the exceptions hereinafter noted. One Hagen arrived in Fargo on the N.P. train, No. 4, due there at 12:55 A.M. He went to another hotel, found it filled, then came to the Prescott; defendant assigned to him room 31, adjoining the room of Miss Wick. One Smith and wife came to this hotel after Hagen and *Page 455 before 2 A.M. One McKenzie registered as a guest about 3 A.M. One Van Vorst, a guest, left at 11 P.M. and did not return until about 5 A.M. Another guest Myers, left the hotel about 11:30 P.M. and returned about 2 A.M. Pursuant to defendant's statements, a man, having the appearance of a laboring man, came to the hotel about 2 A.M., registered as James Farrell and was assigned room 40. About midnight Andy Brown, defendant's room mate, called at the hotel and visited with defendant. Pursuant to defendant's testimony, at 6 A.M. he called her room by phone; no response was given; again he called two or three times; then he rapped on the door; then he swept out the office; then he called on the phone again; then he got the keys, unlocked the door, walked in a few steps, backed out, went down into the lobby, stayed there a few minutes and then called Fred Lawrence, the son of the landlady. This was about 6:45 A.M. Lawrence went to the room; the door was locked; he looked over the transom; he directed a maid to open the door; a call was sent for the police and a doctor. The first officer to arrive was a police officer in Fargo. At the hotel he found Lawrence and defendant standing behind the desk. Defendant stated to the officer that a girl in room 30 was covered with blood and he thought it was suicide. Defendant then took the officer to room 30 and unlocked the door with a key having a brass slab attached to it. There they found Marie Wick in the room on the bed, stretched out, tied, gagged and bound, raped and murdered. Her arms were tied to the bed post above her head; pillow slips had been removed from the pillows; she had been gagged by inserting the major portion of a pillow slip in her mouth, slipping the balance over her face and bandaging it. In tying the girl, strips of a sheet had been used, torn from a sheet on the west side of the bed. The portion of the pillow slip in her mouth was not bloody; the portion outside, was soaked in blood. The bandages did not cover her eyes; they were wide open. There were four distinct finger marks on the left side of her throat and one on the right side, black and blue marks which had not broken the skin. Her head had been badly battered; at least four cuts appeared outside the hair line; and on top of the head, she had been struck seven or eight times by some heavy instrumentality; it required about 167 to 170 stitches to close these wounds; her skull had been fractured; her face showed signs of suffocation; the right arm had been securely tied with *Page 456 seven or eight knots between the arm and the bed; the left arm had not been so tightly tied; the right arm and bandages thereon were free from blood excepting a few smears; the left hand and wrist were entirely covered with blood; the bandages around the left hand wrist were free from blood; an examination of her genital organs revealed that the hymen was partially ruptured and the vagina full of blood; it was apparent that previous to that time she had been a virgin; otherwise, there were no marks or bruises on her below the throat excepting a slight abrasion on the right elbow. Between the bed and west wall of the room there was a space of about 18 inches; there were smears of blood on the wall paper of this west wall; certain finger prints appeared on this west wall but they could not be read excepting that three finger prints appeared to be similar to those of the girl's left hand. There was an indentation in this west wall and also in a round at the head of the bed (as if made by a heavy bludgeon). On the carpet between this west wall and the bed there was a heavy deposit of blood; also, of white hair-like substance, which likewise appeared on the left hand and some of the bandages. The bed clothes were neatly pulled over her body; at the head of the bed, alongside the body, and underneath the bed clothes, towels were found; these towels showed traces of blood and verdigris, also mucous such as would come from the genito-urinary tract. In the opinion of a doctor, the girl when examined about 9 A.M., had been dead four to six hours, possibly longer. Her clothes, hat, shoes, hose and toilet articles were arranged about the room; her two suit cases had not been disturbed; the only money found was a few pennies in her pocketbook.

Thus was Marie Wick found on the morning of June 7th, 1921. The state's attorney and police authorities immediately began a diligent investigation. All of the guests and persons associated or connected with the hotel were investigated and their possible connections with the affair ascertained. The situation of the room, the construction of the building in relation thereto, the manner and means through which the crime and crimes had been initiated, carried on and consummated, all produced evidence, now in this record before the court, which tended to establish that the crime had been committed by no one without, but by some one within and familiar with the hotel. By processes of elimination, unnecessary to relate in a detailed statement of facts herein, all *Page 457 persons, guests in, associated or connected with, the hotel were absolved, through such testimony with probative effect, from any direct connection with the affair excepting James Farrell, the mysterious stranger, unknown and unfound, the defendant, and his room mate, Andy Brown. The defendant became an important personage concerning the affair, either as a witness or a principal. He advised and consulted with the authorities; he was questioned by them time and again. As the investigation proceeded, many conflicts and misstatements appeared in his stories. Finally, on June 14th, 1921, he was arrested, charged with the commission of the crime. After his arrest and while in custody, defendant talked freely about the affair with the authorities. The state's attorney had been theretofore a court reporter. He recorded in shorthand many of the questions to and answers by defendant in these talks by him had with the authorities. As a witness at the trial he verified in evidence defendant's talks and statements so made. Thus, with these statements of defendant, his evidence at the trial and other evidence adduced, there is evidence in the record to the following effect:

Defendant, a single man aged 22 years at the time of the trial, was born and reared near Mayville, a town distant from Fargo some 50 miles. From June, 1920 to about March 1st, 1921, he was employed as night clerk at this Prescott Hotel. This was his first experience in hotel work. Then he ceased this employment and for a time solicited insurance and later worked on his father's farm near Mayville. On May 27th, 1921, he resumed his employment as night clerk in this hotel and continued as such until his arrest on June 14th, 1921. The defendant previously never had been arrested nor charged with crime. Defendant's hours of service as night clerk were from 7 P.M. to 7 A.M. As defendant expressed it, he had full swing of the hotel all night from 12:30 A.M. Defendant roomed at the Addison apartments, a few blocks distant from the hotel, with his room mate, Andy Brown, a painter by trade, aged 28 years. Sometimes, defendant, after his hours of service at the hotel, slept at the hotel because it was more quiet there. Between June 7th and June 14th, 1921, pursuant to the testimony of the state's attorney, defendant had several conversations with the authorities but no stenographic verbatim report of these conversations, only notes thereof, were taken. In the afternoon of June 14th, 1921, *Page 458 before defendant's arrest, another conversation was had at the sheriff's office between the authorities, namely, the sheriff, a detective and the state's attorney, and the defendant. A stenographic report was taken of the greater portion of this conversation and it is in the evidence here. In the course of this conversation, defendant told about Brown coming to the hotel about midnight; how he mentioned to him about the swell looking girl in room 30; how Brown mentioned that he, Brown, needed a sexual affair; that Brown stayed there five or ten minutes; then he detailed an affair he had with a girl named Florence, the night of June 4th, 1921; this girl was getting a divorce; he took her up to her room, No. 50; he got into a conversation with her; later he went back to the room; and again to the room and had a sexual affair with her; then he mentioned about a girl whom he designated as a kid, Elvira, a kind of green girl but she had been married and had a divorce; he got into conversation with her; made remarks to her about putting her to bed; he did have a sexual affair with her that night, on June 1st, 1921, in room 50 of the hotel which he called the jazz room, meaning a room for sexual affairs; then, further, he stated in his previous experience at the hotel, he averaged about two a week (meaning sexual affairs with women); that he could average three or four a week if he was real industrious. Later, about 8 P.M. on June 14th, 1921, and before defendant's arrest, the sheriff had a conversation with defendant in which defendant stated that when he took Marie Wick up to her room he had a desire for sexual intercourse with her; that he called her up on the telephone that night and tried to "josh" with her but she cut him short and did not care to carry on a conversation; that then he further told the sheriff that he was at the hotel all night and did not go to meet a train as he had previously stated; that he might have dozed during the night although previously he had stated that he was awake all night. After this conversation with the sheriff defendant went back to the hotel office and in a short time he was arrested. Then about 2:00 A.M. on June 15th, 1921, after defendant had been arrested and after the state's attorney had talked with defendant in the jail, at about 10:30 P.M. without taking any shorthand notes of the conversation, another conversation was had in the county jail with defendant. Then the defendant was in custody, under arrest, but no warrant had been issued. The state's attorney, the sheriff, the *Page 459 detective and others were there. The defendant was asleep when they came in. He was aroused. The state's attorney testified that some one said "Wake up, Bill" or "Get up" as they came in and he took the first question that was asked him, after they came into the room, in shorthand and that, from the time these questions and answers commenced until they closed, as disclosed by the stenographic record, every question and answer which was asked him during that space of time was taken down in shorthand. Defendant stated that he called Marie Wick at 6:00 A.M. She did not answer; he called her again in probably ten minutes; he called her three times on the phone; then he went up and rapped on the door and heard nothing; then he rapped on the door again; he took the keys along, two keys on a safetypin; he unlocked the door, opened it and looked in to see her and there she lay, just as she was found in the morning; he did not take more than three steps inside; then he locked the door; then went downstairs and called Fred Lawrence; Lawrence said he was tired and wanted defendant to call him in about twenty minutes; defendant said that the girl had either got sleeping sickness, or was dead, or something; that Lawrence suggested that he get a glass of water and throw it over the transom and told him to look over the transom and see if anybody was in there; that the defendant went down and pulled a table up to the door and looked over the transom. That he was afraid to tell that she was dead: After he was in the room the first time he locked the door again: The keys he had were skeleton keys: He knew that if the key to the door was in the door his skeleton key would not open it. Then defendant stated that he called her up about 11:30; he asked her if she had gone to bed; She said that she was just about ready to go to bed: Defendant said, "So early?" Immediately she said "Call me at 6:00." He called her up because if she had wanted to carry on a conversation and started kidding along, if she had let on that she was a "sporty girl" and he thought there was "anything doing," he naturally would have gone up there. In this telephone conversation he might have asked her if she needed any help to go to bed or something like that but she chopped off, did not want to talk about it, and said "Call me at 6:00." Then, further, defendant stated that there were two girls who were steady roomers at the hotel with whom he never tried to have any sexual affairs; that the longest he ever talked to any girl before he had a *Page 460 sexual affair with her was with this kid Elvira. Then he said that, generally, as a matter of fact, when a single woman came to that hotel who was goodlooking at all and did not seem to have some fellow of her own, he would try her out in some way to find out if she was sporty: He would kid her along that line like a d___ fool: Further, that the girls usually fell for him quickly; that he did not fall down on many whom he tried there at the hotel; that when he took Marie Wick up to the room he thought of having a sexual affair with her; it kind of entered his mind; he was kidding her along: If she had been a girl that wanted a sexual affair he would have had it: When she did not want to talk to him, he rather thought that she was kind of innocent and never had had a sexual affair.

As previously mentioned, defendant, in some of his admissions made to the officers, stated, concerning this James Farrell whose name was written on the hotel register and to whom he assigned room 40 in the hotel, that about 2:00 A.M. this party appeared, dressed somewhat like a laboring man, registered and was assigned to room 40; that he went to his room and some time thereafter came down, left the hotel, and did not return.

Andy Brown, the roommate of defendant, was used by the state as a witness. He identified numerous exhibits, some of them postcards, some written in the office of the state's attorney when Gummer was present and some in the Cass County jail, all as being in his handwriting. Later, the state, through experts on handwriting, adduced evidence to the effect that the signature of James Farrell on the register was in the same handwriting as that upon the exhibits as written by Brown. Upon cross-examination of Brown, the defendant sought to inquire whether, in fact, he had written the signature of James Farrell upon the register. An objection of the state to this question was sustained.

Further testimony was adduced on the part of the state, through the witness Charlson, that at about 6:30 A.M. June 7th, 1921, Andy Brown was seen by the witness to come in the back door at the Addison apartments, hurriedly and in an apparent excited condition, and to go to a telephone booth and engage in a telephonic conversation. The defendant objected to this testimony and the overruling of his objection is again specified as error by the trial court. Andy Brown testified as a *Page 461 witness for the defendant. He stated that on the night of June 6th, he arrived at the hotel at 12:20; that previously that evening he had been to a show with a young lady whom he had taken to her room and left at midnight; that he was a painter; that he was dressed in his street clothes; that he always wore his street clothes until he went to work, his working clothes being at the place of his job; that he found defendant that night at the desk, sitting in a chair back of the cigar case or counter; that their conversation concerned Brown's girl, about business at the hotel, and about a good-looking girl having checked in there; that he was not in that hotel after 12:50 A.M. that night and did not return to the hotel after he left; that, after he left the Prescott Hotel, he went to a pool room for a drink; that he left the pool room about 1:10 A.M., went directly to his room and retired; that there he was in his room from a few minutes after 1:10 A.M. until 7:00 A.M. when he was called by Mrs. Thompson (the proprietress of the Addison apartments); that he did not write any name upon the register of the Prescott Hotel or the name of James Farrell thereon; that, with the exception of just one second, defendant was in his presence all the time he was there; and that no person entered the lobby while he was there. Upon cross-examination, the state sought to show that this witness Brown had made contradictory statements inconsistent with his testimony as given upon direct examination. On rebuttal, the state introduced the testimony of Mrs. Thompson, the proprietress of the Addison apartments. She testified that Brown occupied the room next to her room, with a partition between the two rooms; that, on the night of the crime, he came to his room about 11:55 P.M. and went out again in a few minutes; that she did not call him on the morning of June 7th, the morning of the crime; that she did not see him again until about noon of that day. Further, on rebuttal, the state introduced some evidence, through the witness Schultz, that while defendant was a prisoner in the Cass County jail, being held there as a witness, he, Brown, told the witness Schultz to tell defendant "not to squawk until the last minute" and also told such witness "don't let anybody hear you tell him." The defendant objected to such testimony and it is made the basis of error by the trial court.

In the record there is the testimony of the witness Osman introduced by the state to the effect that in the latter part of October, 1920, *Page 462 having arrived in Fargo on N.P. Train No. 4 at about 2:30 A.M., she went to the Prescott Hotel and registered there October 23rd, 1920. She was 21 years old and was a stenographer. The defendant started a conversation with her. She did not notice much what he was saying. She requested him to show her to the room. In the room he turned on the light. She walked in and stood in front of the door. He stood opposite to her and again started to talk to her. He took hold of the handbag and said, "Got any jack?" She said "No" and jerked it away. She asked him to leave the room. He said "Shall I take off your shoes?" She said "No." Then he said "Oh, don't they come off?" and then left the room.

The Hotel Prescott was a 3 1/2 story building with a two-story annex at the rear. The lobby of the hotel, where the clerk's desk was, is in the front of the building on the ground floor. Room 30, to which Marie Wick was assigned, is located on the second floor. On this second floor there are 16 rooms in the main part of the building and, in the second story of the annex, three rooms which were occupied by the Van Vorsts, husband and wife. Room 30 was located at the rear of the main building and next to the annex. Fred Lawrence, the son of the proprietress, occupied room 20 in the front of the building. Room 31, adjacent to room 30, was occupied by Mr. Hagen after he came off the train on the night of the crime. Room 9, adjacent to room 30 but in the annex, was occupied by Mrs. Van Vorst on the night of the crime. The room directly beneath room 30 was occupied by a chambermaid at the hotel. Room 46 on the floor above was occupied on the night of the crime by one Christianson, a steady guest at the hotel. Between rooms 30 and 31 there was a communicating door. When the crime was discovered by the authorities the door between rooms 30 and 31 was found locked. The keyhole was plugged from the side of room 31. The door was also nailed. Further observation disclosed that the door was dusty on the side of room 31 and had no appearance of having been touched so far as the keyhole was concerned. On the door to room 30, going into the hall, there was a Yale lock, which, from the hall, appeared to be, though in fact it was not, in working order. The door leading into this room 30 could be locked or unlocked by a plain key for an ordinary door lock. Further, there is testimony in the record to the effect that the only possible points of *Page 463 ingress and egress to and from the hotel and this room 30 were the main door leading into the lobby, a window in the hall of the so-called annex, a window in the dining room on the first floor immediately off the office and a few feet from the lobby, and a window from a room on the fourth floor. With respect to these ways of entrance or departure, testimony was introduced by the state to the effect that they were either locked or in such condition that they could not be opened, or had not in any manner been used, excepting a way leading into the lobby and to the main door of the hotel. In the record there is evidence of two witnesses who heard noises during the night of the crime. Mrs. Van Vorst, who occupied the room in the annex adjacent to room 30, testified that between 12:30 A.M. and 2:00 A.M. she heard noises such as thumps or thuds or like one throwing a baseball against the wall of the hotel. She went to sleep and awoke again about 2:00 A.M. The chambermaid who roomed in the room beneath room 30 testified that at about 4:00 A.M., she suddenly heard someone jump out of the bed in room 30 and strike the bed a few times. She heard somebody there walking about and heard a door open and close and someone walked down the hall the front way. Mr. Hagen, who had a room adjacent to room 30, being very tired and sleeping soundly, heard no noises or disturbances. Mr. Christianson, who roomed above room 30 on the next floor, was the foreman of a construction company. He went to bed about midnight. He was pretty tired. He got up about 5:45 A.M. He heard no noises below him during the night.

At the end of the hall on the second floor and some distance from room 30, was located a fire hose with a metal nozzle. In the forenoon following the discovery of the crime, this nozzle was found lying on top of the hose rack, but not screwed upon the hose. It was so bent out of shape that it would not screw upon this hose. Upon this nozzle were found pieces of flesh, blood and hair. This nozzle fitted into an indentation existing in the west wall of room 30.

This is a brief narrative of the circumstances of the crime as gleaned from the voluminous record of a trial which consumed the major part of a month.

Pursuant to the theory of the state, Marie Wick was killed by one who entered her room, in the first instance, for the purpose of having sexual intercourse with her; that, in order to accomplish this purpose, *Page 464 it was necessary by force to choke and gag her; that she was thus choked into unconsciousness immediately and before she had an opportunity to awaken; that this crime in its larger aspect was committed through two separate crimes; the first between about midnight and 1 A.M.; and, the second, about 4:00 A.M.; that the person who committed the crime knew that Miss Wick was in room 30 and knew that he could act without detection; that the choking, gagging and rape took place between 12:00 and 1:00 A.M., and the blows about 4:00 A.M.; that the motive which finally prompted the killing was a fear of discovery and that the only person who needed to fear recognition was some person known to Marie Wick and who had been exposed so as to be known to her; that the crime was committed by some person within the hotel since there was no means of ingress or egress as disclosed by the evidence excepting the door leading into the hotel lobby; that the bandages which had fastened the gag into her mouth did not cover her eyes; that she became conscious because she struggled and threw herself off of the bed, with her head hanging between the bed and the wall, and made a mark with her left hand upon the wall; that the murder was not necessary to accomplish the rape because the choking, gagging and tying was sufficient to permit the accomplishment of such act; that the hose nozzle was procured and she was beaten about the head; that some of the blows missed when her head was moving about and hit the round at the head of the bed and the wall; that then her body was arranged upon the bed and the bed clothes upon her; that nearly a dozen times she was struck and her blood flowed copiously upon the carpet, while her head was between the bed and the wall; that the nozzle was wiped off and put back in its place; that the key which locked, from the inside, the door to room 30 was dislocated and then the key of the hotel used to unlock the door; that the name James Farrell was placed upon the hotel register through the procurement of defendant to aid in concealing the crime of rape. Thus does the state conclude upon the record and the evidence from the physical facts and all the surrounding circumstances that the defendant committed this crime; that he had the desire, purpose and opportunity for sexual intercourse and to commit rape in so doing, and that the murder followed, as a result of the accomplishment of such purpose and of the necessity of forever sealing the lips of the one person who could identify the perpetrator of *Page 465 the crime; that even her money was stolen for the purpose of making it appear that the motive was robbery rather than rape.

Decision.

The record reveals the evidence to be wholly circumstantial. With the law concerning circumstantial evidence, and its effect, there is no disagreement. It is conceded that the trial court submitted the cause to the jury with proper instructions in that regard along well settled and well recognized legal principles.

Defendant's First Contention. Upon general perspective the first broad contention is made that the evidence is not absolutely consistent with guilt and inconsistent with innocence; that the cause of the state in its general aspects rests upon suspicion and not proof; that the circumstantial evidence, viewed as a whole, is, as a matter of law, insufficient to support or warrant the verdict for the reason that it does not exclude every reasonable hypothesis of innocence; and further, too, because upon such circumstantial evidence the defendant can just as consistently be found to be innocent as to be guilty.

Circumstantial evidence, of course, is evidence. As Wigmore in his monumental work on evidence has stated, there are two kinds of evidentiary facts: (a) The assertion of human beings, i.e. testimonial or direct evidence; (b) Any other fact, i.e. circumstantial or indirect evidence. 1 Wigm. Ev. 2d ed. § 24. Circumstantial evidence may just as unerringly prove or establish a fact, within the realms of logic and reason, for human minds, as evidence perceived and related through the senses. In the case at bar, the fact of the crime, in its general essentials, being admitted, the paramount question arose, — Who committed this crime? Man, woman, or beast? Assuredly, upon this record, it may be said that it was neither woman nor beast but man. Next, followed the query, — Was this man one from without, or one from within, the hotel? This query is answered by circumstantial evidence in the record, sufficient for the jury's consideration, to the effect that only some man from the vantage position of being within the hotel, had the available opportunity to commit, and did commit the crime. Then follows the logic and reason of the situation to human minds, — namely, if a man and woman be locked within a sealed compartment *Page 466 and the woman is raped and murdered, the survivor is the rapist and the murderer. Again, elaborating, if instead, five persons are in such sealed compartment, but each in a separate subcompartment therein, and one of such persons is raped and murdered, some one, or all, of the persons surviving are rapists and murderers; or, if three establish an alibi or non-connection, then the fourth is the rapist and the murderer. The legal inquiry is ascertainment or identity and the legal evidence that proves ascertainment or identity.

There is evidence in the record, if within legal rules, sufficient for the jury's consideration that no person within the hotel had connection with the crime, excepting possibly the mysterious James Farrell and the defendant. Who was James Farrell? The state answered by proof that James Farrell was a fictitious person whose name had been written upon the hotel register by one Brown, the roommate of the defendant, in defendant's presence. So, defendant did commit this crime unless some other, or any other reasonable hypothesis of innocence can be gleaned from the evidence. The law, of course, presumes defendant to be innocent. He must be proved guilty beyond a reasonable doubt. Defendant says any one of a dozen men might have committed the crime. But this is not a case of speculation but of proof; not of suspicions, as defendant suggests, but of facts proven. Hence, follows the chain of circumstances to establish the fact of guilt beyond a reasonable doubt and to eliminate any other reasonable hypothesis of innocence. The state asserts, and the evidence is sufficient to support, as a finding of fact, that the person who raped Marie Wick murdered her. Consequently, the motive of the murderer is involved and it is to be found associated or identified with the motive and intent of the rapist.

Directly, already upon logical grounds of reasoning, the finger of guilt has been pointed towards the defendant. But to the rational mind of ordinary men of ordinary understanding the law requires, lest any innocent man might suffer, proof beyond a reasonable doubt. The reason for his guilt must appear; otherwise, the reasonable mind and the mind of reason might point to some other hypothesis to explain his innocence, such as defects in eliminating other possible participants, impossibility or improbability of performance for any proper reason. Thus, comes within the comprehension of the reasonable mind the *Page 467 necessity of identifying the guilty perpetrator to a moral certainty. Thus are concerned the elements of primary motive and intent. Within these may be considered desire, willingness and intent to accomplish that desire, personal ability to accomplish the ends of that desire, the personal and peculiar plan always or generally adopted or followed to accomplish that desire, the opportunity afforded for the consummation of the desire, and the general primary motive and intent all pervading the affair. What desire had defendant? The state answers, in the evidence, a desire sexually that predominated his thoughts and personal activities to the extent that he might be classed as a pervert; sexed strongly, the lascivious thought and the sexual impulse to him in his desire was ever uppermost for access and approach to a woman pleasing to his fancy. Towards Marie Wick this very desire was expressed in his mind when first he saw her and it continued by his actions towards her until and after she retired to her room. It was again evidenced in his communing with Andy Brown about or after midnight: The continuity and domination of this desire was further shown by his expressions concerning womanhood generally, by his expressed desires and actions towards other women who had been guests at this hotel.

What willingness and intent to accomplish his desire did defendant express, generally or particularly, as concerns Marie Wick? The state answers in the evidence: — As a general proposition defendant could, by his easy mode of approach, accomplish his desire with the woman of his choice; when he wished and willed it was simply a matter of a little activity along the lines of his knowing how to act. His method of approach and accomplishment was evidenced by his own acts towards other women who had stayed or been guests at the hotel. Toward Marie Wick the same method of approach was used up to the time when she retired. His methods of approach and accomplishment were impliedly continued when he was talking with Andy Brown at or about midnight concerning the possibilities of an affair with the girl in room 30, namely, Marie Wick.

What personal ability to accomplish the ends of his desire did defendant possess? The state answers in the evidence; — his own expressed ability, repeatedly stated; his own acts with other women in the hotel.

What personal and peculiar plan did defendant always or generally *Page 468 adopt or follow to accomplish his desire? The state answers in the evidence; — a plan of solicitation, which, as artfully applied by him, brought the results he sought.

What opportunity was afforded defendant for the consummation of his desire? The state answers in the evidence; — defendant came in direct contact with Marie Wick; the desire possessed him; it was with him from the time he first met her and until after she retired to her room; it still possessed him when he was talking with Andy Brown about midnight, or after; he had charge of the hotel after midnight and as such owed some duty of protection to the guests; the guests were within his keeping. He was familiar with the entire hotel and its surroundings; he knew how to gain access to room 30; he knew that although this room had the appearance of being locked by a Yale lock, that the Yale lock was not functioning; that the door thereto could be opened by an ordinary key; he had a key in his charge and under his supervision that would open this door; he knew that there was no means provided for locking this door on the inside except by the key which would lock it from without; he knew the probability or improbability of detection during the time when he would be accomplishing his desire; he had accomplished his desire before in this very hotel when he was on duty and had not been detected; he knew that to him was presented the opportunity of acting when the opportune time came, because it was his duty to be awake, upon guard, and possessed of all his active faculties, while others within the hotel slept.

What was defendant's general primary motive? The answer upon the whole record is an impelling sexual desire. What was defendant's intent? The answer is, again upon the whole record, to accomplish this sexual desire, first, perhaps without thought of force; then, followed by force which became necessary to overcome resistance; then, detection being forecast, artfulness came to create a fictitious guest, Farrell, to conceal the identity of the performer; then, force resulting in murder and theft to escape detection and to provide concealment. Defendant's contention that always heretofore in the sexual desires and their accomplishment by defendant the element of force was ever absent is answered by the observation that theretofore always the force of persuasion had been sufficient; with Marie Wick the force of brute strength was required. And, so upon the record, we are satisfied, as a *Page 469 matter of law, that the verdict of the jury finds support in the evidence and should not be disturbed in the absence of prejudicial error otherwise existing in the record.

Defendant's Second Contention. This is based upon the general complaint that the state was permitted, over defendant's objection to practically associate the witness Brown as a co-defendant with defendant in the trial of the case and to place all of the inference and suspicions which the state had against Brown, as a part of the case against defendant; that this resulted in practically requiring defendant to acquit Brown in order to acquit himself, although Brown was neither arrested nor prosecuted for the crime but was simply held as a witness; that Brown was considered by the state in the same light as defendant, namely, as one of the perpetrators of the crime; that no conspiracy between them was charged in the information; yet, the whole theory of the state was based on the existence of a conspiracy.

As supplemental to this general complaint, the defendant further specifies that the trial court erred in sustaining the state's objection when defendant, on the cross-examination of Brown, as the state's witness, sought to show that Brown did not write the name Farrell on the hotel register. (Later, as a witness for defendant, Brown did thus testify); further, that the trial court erred in permitting the witness Charlson to testify that Brown came to the Addison apartments on the morning of June 7th, 1921, about 6:30, apparently much excited, and hurriedly went to a booth and engaged in a telephonic conversation; further, that the trial court erred in permitting the witness Schultse to testify that Brown told the witness to tell defendant "not to squawk until the last minute" and "don't let anybody hear you tell him."

Brown's connection with defendant so far as the state's case was concerned was disclosed through defendant's statements made to the authorities before and after his arrest; these statements were introduced into the evidence by the state. They simply showed that Brown was the roommate and intimate associate of defendant; that Brown, on the night of the crime and about midnight called at the hotel to see and visit with defendant; that there in the lobby of the hotel in defendant's presence during all of a period of time not exceeding about 30 minutes Brown and defendant talked about girls and the girl in room 30; that then Brown left to go to the Addison apartments. The *Page 470 state used Brown as its witness for the sole purpose of procuring his identification of his own handwriting. Brown made such identification concerning numerous exhibits. Then the state, through experts, introduced evidence to show that the writing on the exhibits was in the same handwriting as the name, "James Farrell" on the hotel register.

In the task of establishing the proposition to be proved, namely, that defendant committed the crime, it was necessary for the state, through relevant evidence, to adduce much so-termed negative testimony. In the process of elimination, many persons were concerned who were within the hotel during the night of the crime. For instance, Lawrence, Hagan, Myers and others might be mentioned. These, under the circumstances of the state's evidence, the state must first identify and then eliminate as possible or probable perpetrators. So it was necessary for the state to eliminate the possibility or probability of an outside perpetrator. Accordingly, testimony of the acts and conduct of these men during the night of the crime or of their surroundings, including the possibility of ingress to the hotel from without, was competent and relevant whether occurring in or without the presence of defendant. So, it was necessary and proper for the state to first identify the mysterious "James Farrell" and then eliminate him as a perpetrator. If Brown wrote the name "James Farrell" on the hotel register, then the acceptance of this as a fact through proper testimony both identified and eliminated James Farrell as being a fictitious person. This fact, if so established, served further as a corroborative circumstance that the name was so written in defendant's presence or with his procurement for some purpose of concealment. It was proper for the state to show that Brown wrote the name "Farrell." It would have been proper for the state to show that Brown wrote the name "Farrell" on the register out of the presence or without the knowledge of defendant; all for the purpose of eliminating Farrell as a person or as a person concerned with the crime. The fact that his name, "Farrell," was written by Brown in the presence of defendant or even with his procurement did not make Brown necessarily a co-conspirator with defendant; for a multitude of reasons, Brown, through defendant's procurement, might have written such name. The sole purpose of the state was to show that the name "Farrell" was fictitious and that Brown wrote his name; then, it was proper for the state to show through some *Page 471 testimony that Brown had the opportunity to write such name. This it did through the testimony of the witness Charlson that Brown came in the back door of the Addison apartments at 6:30 A.M. on the morning of the crime, and also, as a concomitant part of the act of so writing the name, and of the opportunity therefor, that Brown appeared then, dressed in his street clothes, in an apparently excited condition, and hurriedly went to a telephone booth. His arrival at a certain time, his physical expression, whether he was dressed for work or not, whether he was excited and hurried or not — not his mental expression — was a circumstance as an observed fact, concerning the act of writing the name on the register and the opportunity therefor. Thus considered, it might be treated as a concomitant part of the act connected with the making of the signature. 1 Wigmore, Ev. 2d ed. p. 466.

Whatever Brown's participation in the whole affair was, the proof of the state did not proceed further than to show that Brown wrote the name "Farrell" on the hotel register with defendant's knowledge or consent, and that whatever Brown did at the hotel on the night of the crime, as revealed by the defendant's admissions, was in the presence of the defendant. This falls far short of showing that the state either asserted or sought to prove that Brown was a conspirator in the commission of the crime charged. Defendant's statements, his evidence later, as well as that of Brown, eliminated Brown as a conspirator in the crime so far as this record is concerned. The trial court properly rejected the attempt of defendant to show on Brown's cross-examination that the signature "James Farrell" was not written by Brown. Jones, Ev. 2d ed. 1038. Further, the defendant objected to the admissibility of the testimony of the witness, Schultz, wherein he stated that the witness Brown said to him: "Tell Gummer not to squawk until the last minute," and, "don't let anybody hear you tell him." If the state could prove that Brown was in some way connected with the case, or showed unusual interest in the matter, it would affect his credibility, and, therefore, on cross-examination, it was proper to ask him whether he had made such statements. He denied making them, and to impeach him the defendant Schultz was placed on the stand and these questions, objected to, were propounded to him. It is the claim of the defendant that this impeachment was highly prejudicial to him as *Page 472 being part of an attempt by the state to prove a conspiracy between Brown and the defendant. The trial court specifically limited this testimony to the question of the "interest" of Brown in the case. It is clear the testimony was admitted to show the bias, or prejudice of Brown, in favor of the defendant. Brown was the defendant's witness. Foundation had been laid for the reception of this testimony. The state was not bound by the answers of Brown and had a right to show statements inconsistent with his testimony. It does not fall within the rule prohibiting impeachment on a collateral matter and therefore was admissible. State v. Malmberg, 14 N.D. 523, 105 N.W. 614.

Defendant's Third Contention. This relates to restrictions imposed upon the cross-examination of the state's attorney as a witness.

Upon cross-examination of the state's attorney, defendant's counsel inquired if it was not a fact that during that conversation the lights in the room were snapped off and on. To this question the state objected unless it related to a time prior to the conclusion of the admissions which were testified to. This objection was sustained by the court. The court suggested that defendant's counsel should ask the question and let them state when it did take place, if it did take place. Then the questions were asked, viz.

Q. Now, Mr. Green, is it not a fact that some time during the visit to the jail and to the cell in which Mr. Gummer was locked, that these lights, the electric lights, were snapped off and on at different times?

A. I will answer that in this way. At no time prior to the conclusion of the admissions which we testified to yesterday were the lights snapped off or on.

Q. I will ask the question again. Now, Mr. Green, will you kindly answer my questions, were the lights snapped off and on during that conversation?

Objection was made for the reason that the question did not fix the time. This objection was overruled. The court indicated that if it transpired after the admissions took place the testimony would not be competent. Then the defendant made an offer of proof that, at the time referred to by the state's attorney in his testimony, some of the persons present used violence and threats towards the defendant and that the lights were snapped off and on and that chairs were slid and pushed about on the floor, and light and indecent talk was indulged *Page 473 in and defendant told he would be removed to Bismarck before morning; that, if the people knew, they would mob him, and that defendant was not permitted to dress or clothe himself during that period. Then the state stated that it had no objection to the showing of any such matters, providing they were confined to a time prior to the conclusion of the admissions testified to as having been made by the defendant, but, if such offer referred to any time subsequent, it objected to the offer as immaterial, incompetent and irrelevant. The court sustained the objection, if it related to matters or conduct had after the conclusion of the admissions which were testified to by the state's attorney, but, indicated that evidence of such conduct would be admitted, if it related to a time, prior to the beginning of such admissions. Then defendant propounded the question to the state's attorney. "If any of these matters or things occurred which we referred to and did not take place until after the confessions were made —." The state objected to this question upon the ground that it was an indirect way of getting into the record that which defendant could not get in directly. The court indicated that the question could be asked in another way. Then defendant's counsel suggested that the court ask the proper question. Then the court propounded this question:

"The Court: Did any matters, or things, or conduct, such as has been mentioned in the offer of proof, did any such thing take place before the admissions were made?

A. Before the conclusion of the admission, no."

It must first be observed that the witness' testimony, as refreshed from his stenographic transcript, related to and covered every question propounded to and every answer made by defendant during the time of the examination on the morning of June 8th. Defendant on cross-examination sought to elicit the answer that threats and force were used upon defendant during the time of this examination. The state objected unless the time was fixed. The trial court indicated that anterior to or during such examination and until the end of the questions and answers, questions concerning the use of threats and force would be proper. Defendant's counsel requested the court to propound the question and in response to the court's question, the witness answered that during and up to the time of the conclusion of the answers nothing occurred as the offer of proof indicated. Defendant's counsel *Page 474 did not then renew his offer of proof so as to fix the time of the occurrences anterior or during the time of such examination; nor did he offer to prove that such occurrence happened at such a time or so adjacent in point of time and sequence as to be part and parcel of such examination. No attempt was made by defendant's counsel to show that such occurrences which he offered to prove occurred during the same interview when the questions and answers were made. We are satisfied that the trial court did not err in this regard upon the record as made by defendant's counsel.

Defendant's Fourth Contention. There are assignments of error challenging the correctness of the rulings of the trial court with reference to the admission in evidence of certain statements made by the defendant soon after the crimes were committed and also the admission of testimony on the part of a girl, who had visited the hotel some eight months prior to the crimes, as to certain acts of the defendant at that time. The principal interview with the defendant, at which the statements were made, was had at about two o'clock A.M. on June 15th in the jail in Fargo. This interview was taken down in shorthand by the state's attorney and, upon the trial, the transcript was read to the jury. It seems that prior to its being read and in the absence of the jury, the defendant's objections to the contemplated procedure were made to the court and all objections were overruled. The objections were directed not only to the answers given by the defendant, but to the form of some of the questions as well, and were sufficient to direct the attention of the trial court to the vice, if any, in their admission. The principal argument in the briefs under this head is devoted first, to the admission by the defendant that on at least two other occasions between May 27th and June 6th he had had immoral relations with two women of easy virtue in the hotel; second, to the salacious character of the questions put to the defendant at the time the admissions were obtained, it being claimed that they were so phrased as to give the jury the impression that the defendant was abnormal in sex matters;

and, third, to the testimony of a girl concerning advances made by the defendant upon the occasion of her stopping at the hotel some eight months before the crimes in question.

It is the contention of the state that the evidence of other acts of the defendant at other times and concerning other women is admissible *Page 475 upon at least one of the following grounds: That in view of the whole case, it tends to prove one or more of the elements making up the case and is consequently relevant; that it tends to prove that the defendant possessed the motive that actuated the crime charged and proved by the other evidence; or, that it shows a plan of action pursued by the defendant on former occasions which is so far similar to the plan pursued in the instant case as to have characteristics in common with it; and that it has a legitimate tendency to establish the identity of the defendant as the perpetrator of the crimes. As against this contention the appellant asserts that all of this evidence is of a highly prejudicial character; that it constitutes a direct assault upon the character of the defendant; that the obvious effect of its introduction was to create in the minds of the jury the impression that the defendant was sexually degraded; and that he possessed an abnormal desire for promiscuous sexual intercourse which was thus made to appear to be so strong as to readily lead the jury to infer guilt in the particular case. It is said in short that the law does not allow another crime to be proved for the purpose of establishing thereby the commission of the crime for which the defendant is on trial, particularly where the crimes are not so related as to involve the same parties or so connected that proof of one may be said to be a part of the res gestæ of the crime under investigation.

This evidence is not to be considered as a detached part of the case but must be viewed in the light of the circumstances which are otherwise disclosed in the state's case. For, obviously, evidence which under given facts might be wholly improper and prejudicial would, under other facts, fall within the legitimate range of inquiry and be admissible regardless of its prejudicial character. If the other circumstances be such as to point to the logical and legal relevancy, the evidence objected to may be none the less proper, notwithstanding admissions made by the defendant concerning his lascivious thoughts towards the victim. It cannot be argued that, as the defendant was shown to have admitted a desire to gratify his sexual passions with her, it was not necessary for the state to prove such passion by showing his conduct towards others in a similar situation. At the time this evidence was offered, the state was justified in assuming that the defendant might deny the truth of the statements previously made by him, or some of *Page 476 them, and it was the duty of the prosecutor to present all the evidence he had which would tend to connect the defendant with the crime charged. If it is a matter of any importance, it must be borne in mind that this suddenly aroused passion for Marie Wick is not an admitted fact in the case. It is only a fact for purposes of this trial if the state has proved it, and the defendant's admission is only evidence of the fact for what it is worth. On the trial he sought to destroy the effect of the admission entirely.

Is this evidence properly in the case for any purpose? While the circumstances of the crime have been somewhat fully stated heretofore, it is proper here to again summarize what is shown, both by the evidence objected to and by that which is not subject to the particular objection. It is only in this way that its significance and bearing can be properly ascertained. It is shown that the defendant was in the vicinity of the crimes in question (the rape and the murder) when they were committed; that he was in a superior position to know the facilities afforded for accomplishing acts of sexual intercourse and for concealment afterwards; that on different occasions in the past he had used the vantage ground afforded by his position to gain admission to the rooms of other guests, and, while there, to make indecent proposals which in some instances were assented to; that in the instant case there was a like opportunity open to him; that somebody had entered the room of the victim actuated by a desire for sexual gratification; that the defendant generally took measures to ascertain whether attractive female guests were susceptible to his advances and that they generally "fell for him;" that such measures were taken by him in the case of this victim; that he was attracted by her to the extent that his passion was aroused and that if she had shown a "sporty" inclination he would have gone to her room; and that the desirability of the victim for his lustful gratification was under discussion between him and his intimate associate, Andy Brown, with whom he was prone to discuss such matters, a very short time prior to the crime.

The evidence objected to shows how the defendant acted on other occasions towards women with whom he sustained the same relation as with Marie Wick (that of hotel clerk and guest) on the night in question. His actions on those occasions were the manifestations of desires then experienced and, according to his admissions, such desires were *Page 477 prone to manifest themselves in a similar manner towards all women who were attractive to him and who were so situated as to afford him opportunity of access in the hotel. If these acts, so connected with the defendant in his surroundings, properly evidence the desire experienced by him when he was situated as he was on the night in question, they are admissible to establish that desire, as an attendant circumstance, notwithstanding the fact that they constitute proof of other offenses or acts involving moral turpitude. It is settled law that the proof of the crime with which the defendant is charged is in no way restricted by the fact that evidence to establish some of the attendant facts will involve proof that the defendant on another

occasion committed a wrong or a public offense. That is, if evidence
of prior acts is relevant as to some element of the crime in question, it
is none the less admissible because of the acts being prohibited by law.

Wigmore, in considering whether facts relevant for some other
purpose should be rejected because they would be inadmissible if
offered to show a bad character, says:

Wigmore, Ev. 2d ed. § 216. "If there is any other material or ev-
idential proposition, for which it is relevant, and if it is offered for
that purpose, it is receivable, and its quality as misconduct or crime
does not stand in the way. The persistency of this fallacy, and its lack
of foundation in law make it worth while to exhibit fully, from the
utterances of the judges, their constant repudiation of the notion that
the criminality of the conduct offered for some relevant purpose is any
objection to its reception."

He then quotes, among others, the following expressions:

Johnson, J., in People v. Wood, 3 Park. Crim. Rep. 681: "The proper inquiry, when the circumstance is offered, is, Does it fairly tend to
raise an inference in favor of the existence of the fact proposed to be
proved? If it does, it is admissible whether such fact or circumstance be
innocent or criminal in its nature. It does not lie with the prisoner to
object that the fact proposed as a circumstance is so heinous in its nature and so prejudicial to his character that it shall not be used against
him, if it bears upon the fact in issue. The atrocity of the act cannot be
used as a shield under such circumstances, or as a bar to its legitimate
use by the prosecution. If it could, many *Page 478 criminals might
escape just and merited punishment solely by means of their hardened
and depraved natures."

Cushing, Ch. J., in State v. Lapage, 57 N.H. 288, 24 Am. Rep. 69,
2 Am. Crim. Rep. 506: "I think we may assume, in the outset, that it is
not the quality of an action, as good or bad, as unlawful or lawful, as

criminal or otherwise, which is to determine its relevancy. I take it to be generally true, that any act of the prisoner may be put in evidence against him, provided it has any logical or legal tendency to prove any matter which is in issue between him and the State, notwithstanding it might have an indirect bearing, which in strictness it ought not to have, upon some other matters in issue."

Brewer, J., in State v. Adams, 20 Kan. 319: "Whatever testimony tends directly to show the defendant guilty of the crime charged is competent, though it also tends to show him guilty of another and distinct offence. A party cannot by multiplying crimes diminish the volume of competent testimony against him."

Allen, J., in Com. v. Robinson, 146 Mass. 571, 16 N.E. 452: "Such preliminary acts are competent because they are relevant to the issue on trial; and the fact that they are criminal does not render them irrelevant. Suppose, for further example, one is charged with breaking a bank, and there is evidence that he had made preliminary examinations from a neighboring room; that his occupation of such room was accomplished by a criminal breaking and entering would not render the evidence incompetent." See also People v. Spaulding, 309 Ill. 292-304, 141 N.E. 196.

It seems to us that every circumstance which goes to characterize the relationship of the defendant with the victim of this crime on the night in question, may be proved as a fact; and that his attitude, customarily assumed towards others similarly situated, is a fact which throws light on the terms of the relationship with Marie Wick. Was he fulfilling the duties of one in the capacity in which he purported to act, or was he wholly neglecting his obligations and affirmatively contemplating or meditating a criminal course of conduct towards this girl? In the case at bar, if the conduct of the defendant on prior occasions, and in circumstances similar to those attending him on the night in question, were such as to reveal a mind given over to lascivious meditation and to show that, as he occupied his station as night *Page 479 clerk in the hotel in solitude, he was in effect lying in wait for a victim to whom he could turn for gratification of his lust, we are of the opinion that the evidence of such conduct is admissible. We think the acts embraced within the defendant's admission concerning his relations with the two women in the hotel within a few days of the alleged offense and the admission concerning his feelings towards attractive women patrons of the hotel in general, do reasonably tend to show the possession by him on the night in question of a strong sexual urge towards the victim, such as would be likely to lead one to go to extreme lengths to gratify his desires if not restrained by moral sensibility; and that they characterize the relationship of the defendant with the victim at the time of the crime because of their bearing to show a course of conduct originating in such a relationship, with little regard for the person who happens to be the guest. Suppose that the defendant has been seen in the halls trying to gain access to rooms occupied by other lady guests, the relevancy of such facts would hardly be disputed, notwithstanding the manifestations were towards other persons. The evidence in question is of the same character — differing only in being somewhat farther removed in point of time, but not in place, relationship or circumstance. The jury should be fully informed as to the exact nature of the relationship of the accused to the victim, and for that purpose the state could properly present all the evidence bearing upon it, the same as it could prove all other circumstances bearing upon guilt or innocence.

We do not regard the evidence as admissible to prove, or as tending to prove, that the defendant was morally deficient; that he possessed a criminal disposition generally, or even that he was particularly disposed to commit sexual offenses. We recognize the full force of the rule that excludes evidence of other acts for such purposes. Furthermore, this rule is too firmly embedded in our trial procedure to be any longer open to question, and it is not justly subject to the criticism that it shows too much mercy to a guilty party. On the contrary, the rule finds ample justification in its clear tendency to protect those who may be innocent of the crime charged against consequences that would naturally follow the showing of an unsavory past record (See Wigmore, Ev. 2d ed. § 194). In this respect the Anglo-American differs from the Continental system of evidence. But we do not understand that *Page 480 this rule precludes the fullest inquiry into the facts entering into the offense charged, and we can see no reason in policy why it should be thus applied. This evidence of former conduct is clearly admissible under the authorities heretofore cited, if it is relevant to prove a fact or circumstance in issue, and, as previously stated, we are of the opinion that it is thus relevant. These crimes of rape and murder were committed in a place which was under the supervision of the defendant, at a time when he was on duty and within the range of ready access to the place. He owed a duty to the deceased of affording protection from harm of all sorts. In what position had he placed himself to discharge that duty? And to what extent did he appreciate the responsibilities of his position? These are, certainly, pertinent inquiries, the answers to which should disclose circumstances of the utmost importance in the deliberations of the jury. We know of no better evidence of his regard for his duties as they existed on the night in question and of the situation in which he had placed himself with respect to this victim than his recent demeanor towards others similarly situated. If this be such as to show that he had virtually set a trap for unsophisticated, as well as for the more experienced, females, why should that fact be barred from the jury? Wherein does such a case differ from a case where one may be shown to have frequented the vicinity of a crime of the same sort as this for some nights or days prior to its commission and to have there evidenced a desire to indulge in the acts that led to a crime which would not have been committed but for that initial desire. Such a case was State v. Lapage, supra.

In that case, the victim of the crime or crimes had been waylaid about nine o'clock in the morning while passing over a certain road on her way to school. She was murdered, the head severed from the body and the body otherwise mutilated. There was no direct evidence that rape had been committed and it seems that the examination of the body, insofar as it was made, did not disclose whether or not such crime had been committed. It was, however, the theory of the state that the victim had been assaulted, raped and murdered. Upon the appeal to the Supreme Court from a judgment of conviction, the admissibility of two classes of evidence was under consideration. Certain witnesses had testified upon the trial to inquiries and remarks made by the accused concerning girls in the neighborhood within *Page 481 two weeks of the murder, which would tend to show that the accused entertained lascivious thoughts regarding such girls. In addition to this, there was evidence of three witnesses to certain acts of the defendant about two weeks prior to the murder upon a highway some three miles distant from the place of the crime and directed towards a Miss Watson (not the murdered girl) who at the time was accompanied by her mother. The acts testified to clearly amounted to an assault although hands were not laid upon the girl. The girl assaulted was placed in such fear that she was not able later to identify the defendant as her assailant, although her mother, and another who was near the scene of the occurrence, did so identify him. The other evidence received, and which was under discussion upon the appeal, was that of a sister-in-law of the defendant who testified to a rape committed by the latter upon her about four years previously and some two hundred miles distant in Canada. Concerning the evidence of the defendant's actions in the vicinity of the crime, including the assault two weeks prior to the alleged crime, Mr. Chief Justice Cushing said it was "properly admitted. It all tended to show that the prisoner, about the time of the murder, was frequenting that neighborhood with a view to the commission of the crime of rape upon the person of some one of the young females whom he knew to have occasion to pass over that road. The obscene and filthy language he is described as using, in connection with his inquiries about one of the young ladies, tends to show what thoughts were in his mind, and what he was meditating. The testimony of the Watsons and Mercy tends to show, not merely an attempt or design to commit the crime on the person of Miss Watson, but also to show generally, in connection with the other testimony, that he was prowling about that place for the purpose of lying in wait for any person whom he might sacrifice to his base and cruel designs. It furnishes an illustration of the doctrine which I shall attempt to illustrate and maintain. The attempt to commit one offence may be put in evidence when attended with circumstances which give it a logical connection with the fact in issue and not otherwise."

While the court held the evidence concerning the rape in Canada to be inadmissible and its reception to have been prejudicial error requiring a reversal of the judgment, it expressly approved, in the *Page 482 above language, that which was so closely connected with the crime under investigation as to prove circumstances attending the crime itself. The court said that the questions in regard to the relevancy of the particular items of testimony (page 288) "always depend upon the peculiar circumstances of the case, and must be solved by the application of sound judgment and common sense. It very often happens, as practical men in the profession well known, that facts which in one state of the evidence and one aspect of the case are entirely irrelevant, suddenly, by a slight change in the conditions, become of great importance." Four propositions were advanced and maintained by the court, all of which, so far as our researches have gone, are abundantly supported by the authorities. They are (page 289): (1) It is not permitted to the prosecution to attack the character of the prisoner, unless he first puts that in issue by offering evidence of his good character. (2) It is not permitted to show the defendant's bad character by showing particular acts. (3) It is not permitted to show in the prisoner a tendency or disposition to commit the crime with which he is charged. (4) It is not permitted to give in evidence other crimes of the prisoner, *unless they are so connected by circumstances with the particular crime in issue as that the proof of one fact with the circumstances has some bearing upon the issue on trial other than such as is expressed in the foregoing three propositions.*

This case, in our judgment, affords the closest parallel to the case at bar that is contained in the books and the reasoning in support of the admissibility of the prior acts of the defendant in the neighborhood and within a short while prior to the crime goes far to sustain the ruling of the trial court. Indeed, in some of its aspects, the case at bar furnishes a stronger basis for the ruling, in the closer connection of the parties through a relationship carrying certain definite obligations and which requires close definition, and in the more restricted circle within which the other acts transpired. We are of the opinion that the evidence objected to is legally relevant as tending to prove the actual facts surrounding the crime and the defendant's relation thereto, and that it is admissible in the circumstances shown in this case for that purpose. We are further of the opinion that, if such evidence had no bearing upon any fact in issue in the instant case, and if its use were confined to its tendency to prove criminal disposition or bad character *Page 483 and as such to furnish a foundation for an inference of guilt in the particular case, it would be inadmissible.

Counsel for the prisoner lay considerable stress in their brief upon the so-called general rule of the law of evidence which excludes proof of other offenses and upon the exceptions to that rule that are so frequently stated in the authorities. The contention is made with great earnestness and ability that the evidence under discussion is not embraced within any of the exceptions and that it is, therefore, inadmissible. The argument in substance is this: That evidence of other acts or offenses is not admissible in a trial charging the defendant with the commission of a particular offense, except (1) to prove motive, (2) intent, (3) to negative mistake or accident, (4) to show plan, scheme or system, or (5) show identity, and that as the evidence under discussion constitutes proof of other offenses, it is inadmissible unless it can be shown to be within one or more of the exceptions. Sufficient has previously been said in this opinion to indicate that in the opinion of the court the admissibility of the evidence in question does not depend upon whether or not it falls within any of the exceptions to the so-called general rule of exclusion and that its admissibility in the instant case depends upon its relevancy to prove facts surrounding the offense. If the evidence be relevant for such purpose, the inquiry as to whether it falls within one or more of the exceptions is beside the question; for, as previously demonstrated, it is not the function of the rule relied upon to exclude any evidence that is legally relevant. We are not required, therefore, to ascertain whether or not it may come within one or the other of such exceptions. It seems to us that these exceptions are only valuable as general guides in determining relevancy in the first instance and if they fail in this it is because of their inadequacy. Their failure to point the way to relevancy leaves that question to be ultimately determined by other considerations.

Counsel stress the doctrine of the leading case of People v. Molineux, 168 N.Y. 264, 62 L.R.A. 193, 61 N.E. 286, in which the rule contended for and the exceptions received elaborate consideration in the Court of Appeals of New York. The appellant had been convicted of the murder of Catherine Adams through the instrumentality of poison claimed to have been sent through the mail, to have been received by *Page 484 one Cornish and administered by him to the deceased without knowledge of the poisonous character. It was shown on the trial that another had likewise been poisoned and died as the result and that the poison in each instance was rare and similar and, hence, indicative of a common origin. The defendant was shown to have had the requisite knowledge of chemistry to enable him to concoct the poison. Premising the inadmissibility, under the general rule, of the evidence to establish the killing of the other person, the majority of the court, by the process of elimination, held that such evidence was not admissible within any of the exceptions. But Chief Justice Parker, in an able opinion, dissented from both the method of reasoning employed to demonstrate inadmissibility and from the result reached under that method, holding that the evidence should have been admitted, even under the exceptions, to establish identity. The case is so far different from the case at bar in its facts that it affords but little assistance as a precedent on the question in hand.

Counsel assert that the apparent initial motive prompting the conduct of the perpetrator of the crime was the desire to commit forcible rape and that the obvious motive for the crime charged was concealment of the rape. From this the argument is made that these prior acts are inadmissible because they do not tend to prove that this defendant had any such motive. They also contend that there is no common peculiarity in the manner of the commission of the prior acts and of the act in question, such as would give the evidence of the prior acts any bearing on the question of identity. Having determined that the evidence under discussion is relevant as tending to prove the circumstances in which the crime was committed and as shedding light on the situation as it existed in the hotel at the time, these arguments do not require further attention. However, we think counsel are mistaken in assuming that the initial motive was the desire for sexual relations through force. The initial motive was simply a desire for sexual intercourse. The argument seems to assume that the defendant must be shown to have had a motive strong enough to lead him to rape the accused, or stated in another manner, that unless the claimed motive be shown to have been proportionate to the heinousness of the offense, the motive is not shown at all so far as the accused is concerned. *Page 485

Wharton says on this subject:

(1 Whart. Crim. Law, 11th ed. § 158). "When a powerful passion seeks gratification, it is no extenuation that the act is illogical; for when passion is once allowed to operate, reason loosens its restraints, and hence when there is a general wrongful intent, no specific commensurate motive need be shown."

Without passing on the question as to whether or not the evidence offered might be properly received to prove that the defendant was actuated by the motive which obviously led to the crime in question, we are of the opinion that it would not be a prerequisite to its reception for such purpose that it should show a disposition to use force. So far as the argument directed to the inadmissibility of the evidence on the question of identity is concerned, we do not hold it to be admissible for this sole purpose. Whatever bearing it has on the question of identity is derived from its connection with the facts generally in issue; as such it bears on identity only in its broad sense, the same as the other evidence.

Hence, it is not necessary that there should be any peculiarity common to the other acts and to those under investigation.

We have not overlooked counsel's contentions concerning the testimony of the girl who visited the hotel some eight months prior to the crime; nor the exceptions to the manner and form of the questions put to the defendant when he was interviewed in the jail, which questions were read to the jury. The evidence of the young lady guest was simply to the effect that when she was taken to her room by the defendant, in circumstances similar to those in which the victim of this crime was accompanied to her room, the defendant displayed a lascivious bent of mind through proposals and suggestive remarks made to the witness. Since this court regards the attitude assumed by the defendant towards unaccompanied female guests in the hotel in general to be a legitimate subject of inquiry for the purpose of determining whether or not he was prone to respect his obligations to the guests and as throwing light upon his attitude towards the victim of this crime on the night in question, we think this evidence can not be said to be so remote in time as to have no legitimate bearing.

As to the form of the questions, it is true they were extremely obscene, but a reading of the entire interview discloses that the questions took the form suggested by the defendant's own vocabulary. If, as *Page 486 a result of this unfortunate vocabulary, the jury gained the impression that the defendant was abnormal in matters relating to sex, it is his own misfortune and he can not complain.

Defendant's Fifth Contention. This is more a specification of error by defendant than a serious contention since defendant has not devoted in his brief any attention to its consideration. Nevertheless, since the ruling of the trial court affects fundamentally the state's case and presents important legal questions, this court has given serious consideration to the specification. It predicates error on the ruling of the trial court which permitted the state, over the objection of the defendant, to introduce into evidence exhibits 55 to 73 inclusive. These exhibits are specimens of the handwriting of the witness Brown and identified as such by Brown when called as a state's witness.

Our statute lays down no rule for guidance in the matter. There is more or less confusion in the American authorities touching the question of whether or not irrelevant papers may be admitted in evidence for the purpose of furnishing a standard of comparison for a writing which is material and in dispute in the controversy. See Smith v. Hanson, 18 L.R.A.(N.S.) 521 and note (34 Utah, 171, 96 P. 1087); University of Illinois v. Spalding, 62 L.R.A. 817 and note (71 N.H. 173, 51 A. 731); Mississippi Lumber Coal Co. v. Kelly, 19 S.D. 577, 104 N.W. 265, 9 Ann. Cas. 449.

The trend of modern authority is to very liberally enlarge and extend the rules with reference to proof and comparison of handwriting. The old common law rule was exceedingly narrow and technical. The reasons that were variously urged in support of that rule may have been well grounded when the rule was first established, but conditions generally have so changed that those reasons no longer apply with any particular force. Nowadays it is only the exceptional individual, whether witness or juror, who cannot both read and write with a greater or less degree of skill. The study of handwriting has become a scientific matter and with modern theories as to individual characteristics as expressed in handwriting and the scientific means for measurement and demonstration that have been devised, the status of handwriting evidence has wholly changed. That being the case, the rules of evidence with respect to handwriting have had to be enlarged accordingly. It is another case of the growth and progress of the law to *Page 487 meet modern requirements. See note to University of Illinois v. Spalding, 62 L.R.A. 817. In the case of Cochrane v. National

Elevator Co. 20 N.D. 169, 127 N.W. 725, this Court, in speaking of the matter there under consideration touching the question, said:

"The rule which we deem the more sound and better rule and the one which we shall adopt is that . . . irrelevant papers are not admissible in evidence for the sole purpose of furnishing a standard of comparison but that to this rule exceptions are made in those cases . . . where the papers offered are conceded by the opposite party to be genuine, or are such as he is estopped to deny, *or where for other reasons no collateral issues can be raised by their introduction.*"

The rule having been thus established, the question raised by appellant's specifications will have to be measured by its terms. The exhibits objected to are wholly irrelevant. The state called the witness Brown to testify that they were his handwriting. Concededly they were offered only for the purpose of establishing a standard for comparison. The defense objects to their introduction. That they are not genuine is not specifically urged as a ground for rejection. Practically, there is no room for denial of their genuineness. The rule stated in the Cochrane Case, supra, is flatly that irrelevant papers are not admissible for the purpose of furnishing a standard for comparison, but this rule is modified by stating the exception thereto. That being the case, do the writings here offered come within any of those stated exceptions? The first exception stated is where the writings offered are conceded by the opposite party to be genuine. Here the defendant by making objection surely negatives any such concession. Such concession must be the concession of the opponent and not of the witness. See Wigmore, Ev. § 2021. Neither is there room to urge that an estoppel can be raised as against his denying their genuineness. So plainly the writings here offered and objected to come under neither the first nor the second exception. That being the case, if they are admissible at all, it must be because of the third exception as stated to the general rule, and that is, "where for other reasons no collateral issues can be raised by their introduction."

In view of what has heretofore been said regarding the modern tendency to enlarge and extend the rules with reference to the matter under consideration, we think that the exhibits in question were admissible *Page 488 under the terms of this third exception. It seems to us that the question of genuineness of the proposed standards is a preliminary question to be determined by the trial court, Wigmore, Ev. § 2020, just as the trial court passes upon the question of competency where a child of tender years is called as a witness, or where a question as to the insanity of a witness is raised, or where objection is made to the admission of a confession on the ground that it was involuntary or where a dying declaration is offered, or where a question of privilege is raised. And, if such evidence is offered and the trial court is thoroughly satisfied, is morally certain, that the proffered writings are genuine, and that it is proper so to do, they may be received for purposes of comparison. That is, in the application of the third exception to the general rule, large discretion must be reposed in the trial court; and except in cases of abuse, the exercise of such discretion should not be disturbed. On the record in this particular case, the evidence objected to could have no tendency, reasonably, to complicate the issues, and there was no error in this respect on the part of the trial court.

Defendant's Sixth Contention. Under this head there may be grouped various specifications of error made by defendant and not deemed well taken by this court. Thus, the trial court did not err in sustaining the objection of the state to the question propounded to Sheriff Kraemer, while a witness, concerning whether defendant in his answers to questions by the authorities usually answered them, yes or no. Upon the record this called for a conclusion of the witness. So the court did not err in receiving testimony of the witness Knight, upon rebuttal, to the effect that Brown had stated to him that he left the Prescott hotel during the night of the crime about 12:30 A.M. since this was proper rebuttal testimony though of slight probative value in view of Brown's testimony as witness for the defendant.

Accordingly, upon full consideration of the entire record and defendant's specifications of error, we are of the opinion that the defendant was afforded a fair trial without the commission of error by the trial court prejudicial to the defendant and that the judgment and order of the trial court must be affirmed. It is so ordered.

BRONSON, Ch. J., and CHRISTIANSON and BIRDZELL, JJ., and BURR, Dist. J., concur. *Page 489

Mr. Justice JOHNSON, being disqualified, did not participate; Honorable A.G. BURR, Judge of the Second Judicial District sitting in his stead.

CourtListener is a project of Free Law Project, a federally-recognized 501(c)(3) non-profit. They rely on donations for financial security. https://www.courtlistener.com/opinion/3933049/state-v-gummer/?

Arthur C. James Extradiction Wyoming to North Dakota

In 1935, Arthur James, an inmate was brought here from Sundance, [Incarcerated in Wyoming Penitentiary, Rawlins, Wyoming] on a murder warrant. James allegedly had made the statement in a conversation with Harry (Blackie) Carter at Denver, that he and Carter killed Marie Wick. Three persons signed affidavits that they heard James make the statement. But subsequently A.R. Bergesen. then states attorney for Cass county, came into court to state that an investigation by his office had convinced him that James was not in Fargo the night of the murder. North Dakota Judge Daniel Holt dismissed the charge against James and sent him back to Wyoming.

The Wyoming State Archives, Suzi Taylor, Reference Archivist, sent me a file in Governor Leslie Miller's records on extradition for Arthur C. James to North Dakota in 1934 (60 pages) and the inmate file for an Arthur Cecil James, inmate #5646, who was incarcerated at the Wyoming State Penitentiary in 1940-1941 forgery (9 pages & 1 mugshot). I will be writing a book on Arthur Cecil James and my visiting in 2017 of the Wyoming Penitentiary, now known as, Wyoming Frontier Prison Museum.

The Wyoming Penitentiary is now a museum, known as the Wyoming Frontier Prison in Rawlins, Wyoming and has guided tours through the Prison. Visiting this Prison reminds me of the prison in the movie, *The Shawshank Redemption*. In December of 1901, the Wyoming Penitentiary opened and consisted of 104 cells, no electricity or running water, and very inadequate heating. After 80 years, the prison closed its door, and abandoned until 1987 when a movie "Prison" was filmed on location. Since 1988, the Wyoming Frontier Prison is listed on the National Registry of Historic Places, and offers tours for numerous visitors. *See* http://www.wyomingfrontierpriso n.org

When Justice Triumphed

L arry D. Haugen, son of Corinne Thompson Haugen, told me the family was concerned about a man going to write about Marie Wick, and invited by Matt Wick (Marie Wick's brother) to stay at his house in Grygla, Minnesota. Corinne's sister, Mildred Thompson Wick' husband is Matt Wick. Family members reported the concern about this man to law enforcement as he may have a connection to the murderer of Marie Wick. However, I am of the opinion, this person may be Peter Levins, a crime writer known for his stories of famous criminal cases, with the *Daily News* of New York and the crime writer of the following article on Marie Wick:

DAILY NEWS, New York, New York, Sun. News, Oct. 6, 1940, at pp.64,65. Print.

WHEN JUSTICE TRIUMPHED

By Peter Levins, Crime Writer [Connecticut-married with 4 children]

"Good Girl's" First Journey from Home Ends in Horror

"One can imagine how thrilled 18-year-old Marie Wick must have been that Sunday in June 1921, as she left her farm home at Grygla, Minn., to visit relatives in North Dakota. For Marie had seen almost nothing of the outside world. She had never been farther away from home than Warren, Minn., where she had attended North Star College. She had never seen a streetcar except in movies.

Marie, quiet, pretty, unsophisticated—a 'good girl' as the saying goes—set forth for Pettibone, N. D., on June 6, with the intention of remaining overnight at Fargo, N. D. At Moorhead, Minn., across the Red River from Fargo, Arnold Rasmussen, a friend from her hometown, boarded the train in search of her, rode across the river to Fargo [to the Great Northern Railway Depot, 425 Broadway] and accompanied her to the [Northern Pacific Railway Depot, 701 Main Ave. to verify the departure time the next morning to Pettibone, N.D. and then they walked to the] Prescott Hotel, where she registered.

Rasmussen, who worked in Moorhead remained in the lobby while Marie followed the night clerk upstairs to Room No. 30. Presently she rejoined Rasmussen, and they went out to a confectionery store for ice cream sodas. The store had an electric piano, something Marie had never heard before.

At about 11 P. M. they returned to the hotel and bade each other good night. Marie got her key at the desk, leaving a call for 6 in the morning—her train was due to leave at 7. She went up to her room.

Rasmussen went [walked] back to Moorhead. He was seen between 11 and 12 o'clock at Pan's Café, where he met his girlfriend, Jenny Halgunseth. He walked to her home with her, both Jenny and her sister said later that he did not leave their home until about 2 o'clock. His roommate at the Scandia Hotel, in Moorhead, said he came in shortly after 2.

The night passed . . .

* * *

According to the story told by Gummer, the night clerk at the Prescott, he made repeated attempts at 6 A. M. to call Marie on the telephone but got no answer. Finally, he went upstairs, he said, and knocked on the door of Room No. 30. Still no sign of life inside.

Return to Find Girl Victim of Brutal Murder.

Gummer took it upon himself to open the door with a pass key. Almost immediately, in the dim light which filtered through the drawn shades, he saw that there was something wrong. Frightened, he stepped back, closed the door, and hastened to tell one of the hotel proprietors, Fritz Lawrence

Together they returned—to discover that Marie Wick had been bludgeoned to death.

Soon policemen were at the scene. At 8 o'clock, Sheriff Kraemer of Cass County arrived with Deputy Sheriff South and State's Attorney William C. Green. The latter's description of what he saw follows:

'Miss Wick's clothing was hung up neatly on a chair near the foot of the bed, her purse was on the dresser, closed. It contained a check book, a few cents in change and a handkerchief. We learned later that a cashier's check for $20 and about $12 in cash had disappeared. The key to the room was not in the room and could not be found.

'Miss Wick was lying on her back, on the bed, the covers were pulled over her neatly from the foot of the bed to her armpits. Both arms were tied, the right arm to the right side of the bed, and the left arm to the left side, both being secured by pieces of sheet. The left arm and wrist were entirely covered with blood. There were thick layers of sheet covering the nose, mouth and chin, which were thoroughly soaked with blood.

Superficial examination showed a large number of head wounds, the worst appearing to be on the left side of the head above the temple.

The upper part of the nightgown was soaked with blood, but the lower part was clean, and the body from the breasts down was free of blood.

At the left side of the head, which was about 18 inches from the wall, there was a large bloody stain on the wall such as would be made by a bloody head of hair. Just below this on the carpet was a large pool of blood. There were bloodstains on the light globe that looked as they were made by fingertips, In the perpendicular rod at the head of the bed there was a dent about as deep as half the thickness of the rod. On the west wall there was a hole in the plaster that had the appearance of having been made with a blunt instrument.

The autopsy showed that the girl had been choked, a large number of finger marks and indentations piercing the skin at the throat, undoubtedly from deeply pressing fingernails. The doctor said that Marie had been a virgin and had been raped.

* * *

That afternoon, a deputy, in the course of an inspection of the hotel, discovered that the brass nozzle of a fire hose had been detached from the hose at the east end of the hall on the second floor. Examination showed that the nozzle had been bent out of shape to such an extent that it could not be screwed onto the hose. Moreover, it had recently been cleaned.

When traces of blood and skin were found on the nozzle, police concluded that this had been used in the murder.

The investigators, reconstructing the crime, decided that Marie's attacker had entered the room sometime during the night, choked her into temporary insensibility, then gagged and bound her, then assaulted her.

But she must have recovered consciousness, the police reasoned, long enough to recognize her visitor—or he may have feared that she recognized him. At any rate, had then gone out into the hall, seized the fire nozzle, and beaten her with it. It appeared that she pulled her left arm loose and ducked the first blow, which hit the rod on the bed, and that as she ducked again the nozzle hit the wall.

Her assailant had struck her repeatedly as her head hung partly off the bed—the officers deduced this from the blood on the floor and wall.

His deed finished, the murderer had replaced the body on the bed, retied the left wrist, then pulled up the covers that to a casual observer it would appear that Marie was asleep.

During the next eight days the movements and alibis of all the guests in the hotel were checked. Then the investigators concentrated upon Gummer, the 22-year-old night clerk.

Police Discover Bloody Clothes.

He admitted talking to a friend, William Brown, at about 10 P. M. on the night of the crime and saying that there was a good-looking girl up in Room 30. He also admitted that he had called Room 30, after she had gone up, to find 'if she was sporty or not.' However, he insisted that, when she rebuffed him, he gave the matter no further thought.

He admitted, further that he had been intimate with two girls who had come to the hotel alone and registered but explained that both these guests had exhibited compliance while he took their baggage upstairs, or in telephone calls to them after they went to their rooms.

The police showed Gummer what seemed an important piece of evidence—a pair of bloody trousers, which they had found at the foot of the basement stairs in the hotel. They had found the trousers on June 13, and since they had not been discovered in previous searches, the police concluded that Gummer had placed them there. He denied ownership.

Gummer, who was the son of a farmer living near Mayville, N.D., was charged with the crime and indicted. He obtained a change of venue and was tried in January 1922, at Valley City, Barnes County.

* * *

The State's case against the defendant followed these lines:

He had the lascivious desire—proven by his own admissions.

He knew Marie was virtuous and would not willingly have relations with him. Proven by his admissions that she tried to cut him off and did not carry on a conversation with him when he tried to talk to her on the phone.

He had the rape motive.

He had the opportunity to commit the crime. He knew he could enter the room between 12:30 and 1 without fear of discovery because he knew, as a matter of custom in the hotel, that there would probably be no guests arriving until the 1 o'clock train came in. Also, he knew there was no one in Room 31, that there was no one directly across the hall, and that if anyone saw him go in or out of the room, it would not arise any comment at that time.

He had exact knowledge as to the location of the fire hose.

He knew at 4 A. M.—and he was the only person who knew this—that there was no danger in having a light on in Room 30.

He was the only person who could go about the hotel at 4 in the morning dressed in underwear and overalls, or in old clothes of any kind, without arousing comment, because he was accustomed to mopping up in old clothes.

He and he alone during the night had the entire run of the hotel and could clean up and dispose of his clothing without fear of observation by anyone, until 7 o'clock.

He was the only man in the hotel who was known to Marie Wick, and who thus need fear positive identification by her. Further, he was the only man in the hotel who, being known by her, knew that is she were alive the next morning, and was discovered before 7 o'clock, she must necessarily see and identify him, as he could not run away without casting suspicion upon himself.

* * *

Assuming that the crimes of rape and murder were committed at two different times, he was the only person who could have made two trips to the room without risk of detection.

He was at the hotel between 10 P. M., June 12, and 10 A. M., June 13; was in the basement toilet by his own admission and had the opportunity of disposing of the bloody trousers without arousing suspicion.

He at all times, until the day of his arrest, concealed the fact that he had called Marie on the telephone.

At all times, until the day before his arrest, he insisted that he had gone to meet Train No. 4 (which arrived in Fargo at 1 o'clock, the time police believed the murder was committed).

He had told police officers that a friend had been with him nearly all night. He had told Sheriff Kraemer that he had met Brown at the Northern Pacific depot. He said first that Brown had been at the depot for five or ten minutes; later he insisted that Brown had been there a much longer time, until 12:50.

He lied when he said Marie had asked him to have her 6 o'clock call changed to an earlier call. (He had 'discovered' the murder before she should have been called.).

Circumstantial Case Enough to Convict.

The prosecution argued that the theft of the girl's money was a stall. This was indicated by the fact that the assailant took the trouble to straighten out the body on the bed, pull down her nightgown and pull up the covers, so that it might appear that she had been slain as part of a robbery and nothing else.

The crime could not be committed by an outsider, the State insisted, if an outsider had done it, he must have known that Marie was in Room 30. Only one outsider knew this, and he was Arnold Rasmussen, who had a perfect alibi.

If an outsider had committed the crime, he must have left the hotel through the front lobby or through the window in the back. All screens on the fire escapes were hooked on the inside and all other doors locked, so there were only two means of ingress and egress. May Malaas, a chambermaid, testified that he did not go out the back way; and if he went out the front, then he would have had to pass clear through the lobby, as the side door was nailed at night.

The State pointed out that an outsider who had choked and gagged his victim would by no conceivable stretch of the imagination take the chances of discovery incident upon the return to the hotel to do what would be for him a wholly unnecessary act—that is, the murder.

It was a circumstantial case that State's Attorney Green presented. But it proved enough for a conviction. Gummer, still protesting his innocence, was sentenced to life imprisonment, the extreme penalty in North Dakota.

* * *

In the ensuing years he never desisted in his fight for freedom, assisted by his brother-in-law and attorney, H. W. Swenson. In 1930 the latter appeared before the State Pardon Board and asked that Gummer be granted his freedom on the basis of new evidence.

He argued that the prosecution had failed to account for two men in the hotel the night of the murder, one of them being James Farrell. The prosecution held that Farrell was a fictitious person whose name Gummer, or a friend, had written on the register in order to send investigators off on a false trail. Swenson asserted that Farrell had been proved to exist.

The other person was A. R. McKenzie, who was registered at the hotel on the fatal night. He had come into the place drunk during the night, had been questioned by officers in the morning and had been released. At the time of the trial, he could not be located.

Swenson said, further, that intense feeling throughout North Dakota had made a fair trial impossible.

The pardon was denied. Three years later another attempt failed.

It has been pointed out that Gummer was the only person who ever saw Farrell, if such a person existed. As for McKenzie, he had not come into the hotel until after 2 A. M., long after the estimated time of the murder.

In April 1934, Arthur James, an ex-convict being held in Sundance, Wyo., on suspicion of robbery and murder there, was turned over to the Cass County authorities after Gummer had declared that fellow prisoner in the penitentiary had told him of hearing one Arthur James boast of the Wick killing. Affidavits from transient workers in Colorado and Texas were produced to back up the claim that James had uttered such admissions.

However, a thorough investigation by the new State's Attorney, A. R. Bergeson, established that James had been employed at Fort Collins, Col., at the time of the Wick murder.

* * *

On June 2, 1939, a third hearing was held before the Pardon Board. As his contribution toward the continued incarceration of Gummer, former State's Attorney Green, now practicing in St. Paul, Minn., wrote the following letter to the board:

'Gentlemen:

I am in receipt of a notice that William Gummer, who was on Feb. 28, 1922, sentenced to imprisonment for life on a charge of first-degree murder committed in Cass County, North Dakota, has made an application for pardon, which will come on for hearing before you on June 2, 1939.

I appeared before the Pardon Board in 1933 and made a full presentation of my views as to this case. After my appearance before the board, I filed a brief, a copy of which I forwarded to Judge Christianson on Jan. 15, 1936.

[Signed by former Cass County State's Attorney, William C. Green].

Excuse for Crime Completely Lacking.

This was not an ordinary crime. It was not even an ordinary murder. It was one of the most heinous crimes and one of the most brutal murders in the history of the State. If there ever be an excuse for murder in the heat of passion, or because of fancied grievances, or even when committed in the perpetration of what might be termed a normal crime, that excuse did not exist here.

Marie Wick was little more than a child. She was a virgin. On the day before she was murdered, she had started out happily on what was the greatest adventure in her life. She was going to take a trip more than 50 miles from home. Within 24 hours all the sacrifice of her parents, all her own work, all her life of decency were wiped out for the gratification of the momentary lust of a man so sex mad that he did not stop at a brutal rape, but to avoid detection, committed a horrible murder.

It is very easy after 18 years to forget the victim in the face of the pleas of the relatives of the defendant. Lest Marie Wick be forgotten, I am enclosing with this letter of protest six copies of a photograph of Marie Wick as she was left by the man who raped and killed her, and I trust that these photographs will be kept in the permanent files of the

Pardon Board so that, so often as this man's application for pardon comes before it, the members of the board may be reminded of the crime which they are asked to condone and of the type of man they are asked to run loose on society.

In this country there is only one way by which the guilt or innocence of a man charged with any crime may be determined, that is a trial before a jury. His rights are further safeguarded by the right of appeal to the [North Dakota] Supreme Court. William Gummer was tried before a jury in a county outside that in which the crime was committed. He was convicted. He appealed to the [North Dakota] Supreme Court and the conviction was affirmed. He was represented on the trial by three able lawyers. In the 18 years which have elapsed since the commission of the crime no new evidence has been produced which is of any value.

In this case there can be no excuse for a pardon unless the innocence of Gummer is established. A man who has committed one crime of this kind is not a normal man, and anyone who would turn him loose on society must do so knowing that there will always exist a possibility that a similar crime will be committed by him when his sex desires are thwarted.

I respectfully submit that the pardon should be denied.'

It was."

[Signed by former Cass County State's Attorney, William C. Green].

DAILY NEWS, New York, New York, Sun. News, Oct. 6, 1940, at pp.64,65. Print.

Paul Welch, aka Blackie Carter

B ISMARCK TRIBUNE, Bismarck, ND. Monday, December 11, 1944, p.3. Print.

PAUL WELCH, AKA 'BLACKIE CARTER,' NOT IN CUSTODY, BUT AVAILABLE

"'Blackie Carter,' The reason 'Carter' is not in custody, [Ralph] Croal [Cass County State's Attorney] said, is that 'he [Paul Welch, aka Blackie Carter] could not be convicted of the crime except on evidence that it is just as circumstantial, or perhaps more so,' than the evidence upon which William Gummer was convicted at Valley City, N.D. in February, 1922."

The state's attorney declared that he is "convinced beyond any shadow of doubt in my own mind" that 'Carter' committed the crime. The name, 'Carter,' said Croal, is an alias and his true name is said to be Paul Welch." (emphasis added). The man has a criminal record, the state's attorney said.

BISMARCK TRIBUNE, Bismarck, ND. Monday, December 11, 1944, p.3. Print.

Man Named 'Blackie' Carter Slew Girl, Charges Croal

B ISMARCK TRIBUNE, Bismarck, ND. Monday, December 11, 1944, p.3. Print.

Man Named 'Blackie' Carter Slew Girl, Charges Croal

First disclosure of investigations and new evidence turned up regarding the 23-year-old slaying of Marie Wick in Fargo is contained In the following statement by Ralph F. Croal, Cass county states attorney, upon which the state pardon board at Bismarck Saturday largely based its action in commuting the life sentence of Miss Wick's convicted slayer, William Gummer.

Pursuant to your request made at the August hearing of the Gummer case, we submit herewith a brief statement of what has transpired and what facts we have assembled since the matter was last fully presented to the board.

In December, 1943, Judge Swenson (H. W. Swenson, Devils Lake) and I went to to St. Paul, Minn., following up on some information that he had received with reference to Blackie Carter for whom a search had been made for several years. This Blackie Carter, it was determined at that time, was the Blackie Carter for whom Judge Swenson had been looking and eliminated the several other Blackie Carters who had been under investigation from time to time over a period of several years. This Blackie Carter was at that time operating a filling station in St. Paul and had been under the observation of the operators of the federal bureau of investigation as a suspect in bank robberies in North and South Dakota and, in fact, was a source of information for the FBI in the apprehension, trial and conviction of some of these robbers.

Through the courtesy of the FBI, Judge Swenson and I together with a man named George Keith, a former convict and an acquaintance of Blackie Carter, were given the privilege of viewing Blackie Carter at his station in St. Paul without his knowing that he was being observed. He was identified by Keith at that time as one of the men who in 1935 had made boasts in a hotel room in Denver, in the presence of several other witnesses, that he had killed a girl in a hotel room in Fargo, N. D., on a date closely coinciding with the killing of Marie Wick.

He also made a statement at that time, before the same witnesses, that a man by the name of William Gummer was serving a life sentence in the North Dakota state penitentiary for the commission of his crime. In addition to Keith other witnesses present in the hotel room at that time were two women, one by the name of Grace Merchant, who later married a man by the name of Sullivan and is now residing near Pampa, Texas, and the other whose last name was Roberts.

Subsequent to our first visit to St. Paul and along in February, 1944, Judge Swenson made a trip to Texas at which time he interviewed Mrs.

Sullivan, formerly Grace Merchant, and George Keith, and a man by the name of Martin, and made arrangements for them to appear in St. Paul at a later date for the purpose of meeting Blackie Carter, who incidentially, went by the name of Paul Welch.

On March 24, Judge Swenson and I and Bill Gummer, in company of Frank McKenzie, the sheriff of this county, proceeded to St. Paul and again met with our Texas witnesses in the FBI office and we confronted Blackie Carter. The conference lasted the better part of two days, during which time we talked with Carter, individually and together, and the witnesses Keith and Mrs. Sullivan both positively identified Carter as the man who had the conversation in the Denver hotel room in 1935 and had made boasts of killing a girl in a hotel room in Fargo, and also made the boast that Bill Gummer was serving life for said crime in the state penitentiary in North Dakota.

Carter, of course, denied that he had killed the girl or that he had made any boasts of so doing and also denied being in Denver at that time or any other time. Later on, however, he admitted that he had been in Denver off and on between 1930 and 1935, and, in fact, had made two trips from Chicago and the Twin Cities to the west coast during that time, stopping off in Denver each time. He also admitted upon being questioned, that he was in Fargo on the night of the murder, which facts bear out a story with which Judge Swenson and I are both familiar, given by a former convict named Robert Campbell, alias, Goldie Benton, who had told Judge Swenson and Mr. Bergesen (A. R. Bergesen, former Cass states attorney) some years ago the facts surrounding Blackie Carter's presence in Fargo on the night of the murder. Blackie Carter also admitted to Judge Swenson and me that he had left Fargo the next morning after the crime and had gone to Minot where fats formerly developed fixed his presence there at that time.

Carter's demeanor while under examination and also his demeanor while conversing with the Texas witnesses indicated clearly to Judge Swenson and to me that he was not telling the truth, except in part and that every indication pointed to his connection with this crime. We felt satisfied in our minds, as did Mr. McKenzie, the sheriff, that Blackie Carter was the Blackie Carter the Texas folks claimed him to be and the one for whom search has been made over a period of years and the one who registered at the Prescott hotel under the name of 'James Farrel' on the night of the murder.

We have also submitted the copy of the register to the federal bureau laboratory at Washington and to F. A. Krupp, handwriting expert named Osborne in New York City. Unfortunately the original register has become lost. It must have been removed from the files in Valley City between the time of the trial and the time the papers had been returned from the supreme court on appeal.

Therefore, it was extremely difficult for the handwriting experts, with only a photostatic copy and with such a meager amount of handwriting for comparison, to commit themselves positively to the fact that the handwriting shown on the register and the handwriting of Blackie Carter were the same, but we did receive an expression from Mr. Krupp and his associate that there was no doubt in their minds but what the handwriting specimens were identical.

A significant thing about the comparison of the handwriting on the register and the comparison of the handwriting given by Blackie Carter in the FBI office, in St. Paul in March, 1944, in addition to the similarity of characters, slant, etc., was the fact that on being asked to write the word Willmar he spelled the same with one 'l' as the same was spelled on the hotel register.

Another interesting feature of our conference was the fact that Mrs. Sullivan had, during the time she knew Blackie Carter, lived with

George Keith as his common-law wife, never having been legally married to him. Subsequently they both married and established homes and have had nothing to do with each other since. In the course of the conversation between Mrs. Sullivan and Carter, in which she accused him of being in the Denver hotel and of saying the things he did, he flared up somewhat and said, 'You have done things too during your lifetime of which you might not be proud.'

Mrs. Sullivan, likewise, flared at this statement and said something to this effect, 'Yes, Blackie Carter, that is right, and you know what they are'; to which he did not reply.

Therefore, I am of the same opinion that I was at the time I appeared before the board in August. I feel that the facts which we have developed in Texas, Denver and St. Paul at this last conference, are sufficient to show that the crime was committed by Blackie Carter and, therefore, that Bill Gummer could not have been the man who committed the crime. My mind has long been open on this question. [emphasis in original] [Statement by Ralph Croal, Cass County State's Attorney to the Parole Board.].

I have had numerous conferences with those who have some knowledge of what happened at the time of the commission of the crime with those who participated in the trial of the action, with Judge Swenson and Mr. Bergesen, my predecessor and while we have not always agreed on some aspects of the case, I have come to the conclusion that my present opinion is well justified and substantiated by the facts and and I have no hesitancy in submitting these facts to the board in support of my opinion.

This opinion has been further borne out by the lie detector test which Gummer submitted to voluntarily and by the many other facts which have been called to the board's attention from time to time prior to my advent into this office and since."

BISMARCK TRIBUNE, Bismarck, ND. Monday, December 11, 1944, p.3. Print.

The author of this book, Eileen Tronnes Nelson states, " I found a Paul J. Welch in the 1940 Federal Census, St. Paul, Ramsey County, Minnesota, Ward 11, Block Nos. 6-7, 41 years old & born in Pennsylvania. Spouse is Marie 32 years old & born in Wisconsin. Paul J. Welch is listed as a part owner of a gas station. No children are listed in the census. Ironically, the spouse has the same first name as Marie Wick, and the next door neighbor is Dallas Carter, born in Wisconsin. Maybe this is the Paul J. Welch, aka Blackie Carter, the suspect in the murder of Marie Wick."

Gummer To Get Freedom On Dec. 28 [1944]

THE BISMARCK TRIBUNE [Bismarck, ND], Monday, Dec. 11, 1944. p.1. Print.

GUMMER TO GET FREEDOM DEC. 28 [1944]

His life sentence in the state penitentiary commuted after serving near 22 years for a murder in which he has steadfastly maintained his innocence, William Gummer quietly went about his routine prison chores Monday.

Prison officials said that Gummer, a model prisoner, expressed natural happiness when he was formally notified Saturday that the state pardon board had commuted his sentence to end Dec. 28.

Decision to release him then was made by the board after Ralph F. Croal, Cass county state's attorney, declared he was convinced that

Gummer did not murder 18-year-old Marie Wick in a Fargo hotel room the night of June 6, 1921.

Thus was written another chapter in the history of the most famous murder case ever chronicled in North Dakota.

At the prison, Gummer has served as a record keeper in the prison twine plant part of the time and as a barber part of the time. Now 44, he was just 22 when he entered the prison, after his conviction in Valley City.

The board met at 10 a.m. Saturday in an adjourned special session to consider the Gummer case on the basis of evidence contained in a statement filed with the board by Ralph F. Croal, Cass county state's attorney.

Mr. Croal's statement was not immediately available.

The board's decision culminated years of effort on the part of Gummer and his brother-in-law, H. W. Swenson, Devils Lake attorney, to gain a pardon or commutation. Gummer throughout has maintained his innocence.

In commuting the sentence, the pardon board said in a formal statement that it had 'reached the conclusion that a grave doubt exists regarding the guilt of William Gummer.

'Investigations have been made from time to time . . . No additional facts have been discovered pointing toward his guilt. However, facts have from time to time been discovered which tend to lessen the circumstances that entered into his conviction. . . .'

It was explained that Gummer was not released immediately in order that he might have a few days to readjust himself mentally to the knowledge that he is to be a free man again after so many years behind bars.

Members of the pardon board are Governor John Moses, Chief
Justice James Morris, Attorney General Alvin C. Stretz and Dr. J. A.
Saathoff, all of Bismarck but Saathoff, who is of Jamestown."

THE BISMARCK TRIBUNE [Bismarck, ND], Monday, Dec.
11, 1944. p.1. Print.

————————————

Marie Wick's Parents Not Fully Convinced Gummer Killed Daughter

B ISMARCK TRIBUNE [Bismarck, ND], Monday, Dec. 11, 1944. p.3. Print.

MARIE WICK'S PARENTS NOT FULLY CONVINCED GUMMER KILLED DAUGHTER, BUT HE [GUMMER] KNEW WHO DID

"On the 200-acre farm just outside the village of Grygla, Minn., about 150 miles northeast of Fargo, life still goes on for an aging couple, Mr. and Mrs. Hans Wick, parents of 18-year-old Marie who was fiendishly raped and murdered in a Fargo hotel nearly 23 years ago.

In those long years Mr. and Mrs. Wick have tilled the land, with the help of their eldest son, Arne, who is now 43 and who has remained at home to share the burden. From time to time the murder case has been revived in the press as hearings have been held and Gummer has renewed his plea to be released from prison appeared in print the old wound has been reopened and the thoughts of Mr. and Mrs. Wick flash back to the day when they received the awful news.

WANT GUMMER RETAINED

Saturday Mr. and Mrs. Wick were reached by telephone and informed that the pardon board was meeting with the intention of freeing the man who was convicted of the brutal murder of their daughter.

'I don't think he should be given his release; they should keep him there,' Mrs. Wick said simply.

Both Mr. and Mrs. Wick said they had never been fully convinced that Gummer was the man who actually committed the murder.

'But he must have known who did it,' Mrs. Wick told The Fargo Forum.

The Wicks have six living children. All but Arne have moved away from home. They are married and are raising their own families. There are four sons and two daughters. [Note by Eileen Tronnes Nelson: My father, Elmer Tronnes' cousins, Mildred Thompson and Beatrice Thompson, are sisters. Mildred and Beatrice married Marie Wick's two brothers, Matt Wick, and Elmer Wick. Mildred Thompson married Matt Wick, and Beatrice Thompson married Elmer Wick.].

CAME TO 'BIG CITY'

Their daughter came to Fargo the night of June 6, 1921, an innocent girl fresh from the country and eager to see the sights. For Fargo, to her, was a 'big city.' She had planned to stay only overnight, then go on to Pettibone, N.D. to visit relatives.

She had no reason to be afraid and, confidently, she went to the hotel, near the N.P. Depot, to get a room for the night.

The man who showed her to her room and engaged her in conversation as he carried her bag upstairs and unlocked the door of room 30, was William Gummer, the night clerk.

Marie came back downstairs a few minutes later and went out to see the sights of the town with Arnold Rasmussen, a youth whom she had known at Grygla and a friend of the family. An hour or so later she returned to the hotel and went upstairs to her room, destined never to leave it alive.

FIND BATTERED BODY

Shortly after 6 a.m. Her battered, mangled, ravished body was found on the bed. Her head and face had been bashed in and mutilated by blows of a fire hose nozzle in the hands of a fiend who had used bed sheets as ropes to tie her hands to the bedposts, attacked her, then—probably for fear she had recognized him and would tell—bludgeoned her to death.

Gummer was arrested and charged with the murder. He stoutly denied it and has maintained continuously since that he did not kill the girl. He was tried in February, 1922, at Valley City, N.D. The case was moved there because of the high pitched anger created in Fargo by the brutality of the crime. The trial lasted more than a month. Then the jury returned its verdict—guilty.

The trial was the most sensational in North Dakota history, with none of the gory details glossed over.

CIRCUMSTANTIAL EVIDENCE

Gummer was convicted wholly on circumstantial evidence. There was no one who saw him commit murder. What evidence there was pointed strongly to him—strongly enough to convince the jury that he was guilty.

Yet there have been many who have doubted that he was the killer. Both his parents, with firm faith in their son, have died while he has been behind prison walls.

One man who has been and remains firmly convinced that Gummer is innocent is his brother-in-law, H.W. Swenson, a Devils Lake attorney.

Mr. Swenson has fought bitterly and unceasingly to gain Gummer's freedom. He has traveled over much of the United States, spent a huge sum of money in tracing down every possible clue that might prove that his brother-in-law could not possibly have committed the act—only to meet up with the disappointment and failure. Swenson's friends say that he has been kept a comparatively poor man because of the money he has spent in Gummer's behalf.

MANY DEVELOPMENTS

There have been some sensational developments—other than Gummer's pleas before the pardon board—that have brought the case back into the headlines in the intervening years.

Andy Brown [aka, Leslie Locke], a painter, friend and roommate of Gummer, also was arrested and charged with murder, but was freed after Gummer's conviction. Brown has since died.

In 1935, Arthur James was brought here from Sundance, Wyo,, on a murder warrant. James allegedly had made the statement in a conversation with Harry (Blackie) Carter at Denver, Colo., that he and Carter killed Marie Wick. Three persons signed affidavits that they heard Arthur James make the statement. But subsequently A.R. Bergesen, then state's attorney for Cass county, came into court to state that an investigation by his office had convinced him that Arthur James was not in Fargo the night of the murder. Judge Daniel B. Holt dismissed the charge against Arthur James.

CARTER HUNTED

A search already had been launched for Carter and it was disclosed Saturday that Ralph F. Croal, present states attorney, had filed a statement with the pardon board in which he related that new evidence had been uncovered in connection with the Denver conversation. What the evidence is, however, was not revealed.

One mystery in connection with the murder of Marie Wick never has been solved. It concerned the whereabouts of a man who had been registered at the hotel but who disappeared the night of the crime and has never been found. The name on the register was James Farrell, Willmar, Minn."

BISMARCK TRIBUNE [Bismarck, ND], Monday, Dec. 11, 1944. p.3. Print.

Gummer Out Of Prison

THE FARGO FORUM [Fargo, ND], Dec. 28, 1944. p.1 Print.

GUMMER OUT OF PRISON

"William Gummer walked out of the state penitentiary at Bismarck today [Dec. 28, 1944]—a free man after nearly 23 years on a charge of first degree murder.

Gummer's life sentence was commuted by the state pardon board December 9, to end today, December 28 [1944].

Now 44, Gummer was convicted in Barnes county district court of the murder of 18-year-old Marie Wick in a hotel room in Fargo the night of June 6, 1921. Through the intervening years he has steadfastly maintained his innocence of the crime.

Gummer told prison officials he was happy to be out and that he 'appreciated the interest' of newsmen but he refused to be interviewed.

He did not reveal any plans for the future but prison officials took him at his request to the Bismarck bus depot where he reportedly boarded a Fargo-bound bus.

In a statement to the pardon board **Ralph F. Croal, Cass County State's Attorney, said 'an investigation had convinced him the crime was committed by Blackie Carter, alias Paul Welch, who was operating a filling station in St. Paul some months ago when he was interviewed by Croal and other officers. Croal said, however, that with the 23 intervening years since the crime, he did not feel that evidence could be obtained to convict Carter."** (emphasis added).

THE FARGO FORUM [Fargo, ND], Dec. 28, 1944. p.1 Print.

"Bill's Barber Shop" in Grand Forks ND

B ill's Barber Shop on DeMers Avenue, Grand Forks ND.

After being convicted of murdering Marie Wick, Gummer was sentenced to life in prison. William Gummer was in the North Dakota State Penitentiary for 23 years. He learned how to be barber and worked as a barber in prison. Upon his commutation release, not a pardon, from prison, Gummer was first a barber in Bottineau ND. He then opened a barbershop on DeMers Avenue in Grand Forks ND. I am guessing it was across the street from the Railroad Depot and the building was later removed during the urban removal project. Gummer was a barber in Grand Forks (beginning from maybe about the late 1940s).

In 1954, William Gummer married Grace McKenzie (Aneta & Grand Forks) (born 15 September 1907). Grace died March 1995 (86). William Gummer died June 23, 1981 (82), both William and

Grace are buried in the Mayville ND cemetery. Source: FindaGrave .com (Pictures are at the website).

Harry "Blackie" Carter

THE FARGO FORUM, Fargo, N.D. Feb. 6, 1950 at p.1. Print.

Tests Clear [this Blackie Carter] Carter in Wick Case.

"The case of Marie Wick, Grygla MN, a farm girl who was murdered in a Fargo hotel 28 years ago, was once more in the news over the weekend.

C.B. Hanscom, professor at the University of Minnesota, revealed that Harry (Blackie) Carter, 54, a Wisconsin farmer, had submitted to the lie detector tests and truth serum sessions in connection with the murder.

Hanscom said that extensive questioning and the detector tests had absolutely cleared Carter.

* * *

H.W. Swenson, a former North Dakota judge now executive secretary of the state's board of administration, brought about the tests.

Swenson is a staunch believer in the innocence of William Gummer, night clerk in the hotel where Miss Wick was murdered, who was given a life sentence after a trial in Valley City.

Gummer was in the state prison at Bismarck until being paroled in 1944. [He first worked as a barber in Bottineau, N.D. and later in Grand Forks, N.D.].

Swenson, who is Gummer's brother-in-law, has spent much of his life trying to clear the former hotel clerk.

In 1938 he employed Leonard Keeler, inventor of the lie detector, to test Gummer. Keeler concluded that Gummer was withholding some information but did not commit the murder. Swenson continued his investigation.

In Fargo today, Ralph Croal, former states attorney, said Carter was located working at a St. Paul filling station in 1944.

'He was given a lie detector test then and though the results were not conclusive he was never arrested,' Croal recalled.

* * *

Disappointed that his years of searching still hadn't cleared Gummer's name, Swenson said in Minneapolis he would continue with his investigation in North Dakota.

[This Harry 'Blackie'] Carter returned to his Wisconsin farm."

THE FARGO FORUM, Fargo, N.D. Feb. 6, 1950, at p.1. Print.

William Gummer
Sketch by Vanessa

When Justice Triumphed, DAILY NEWS, New York,
New York, Sun. News, Oct. 6, 1940, at pp.64,65. Print. (Photograph
of William Gummer).

William Gummer. Sketch by Vanessa. When Justice Triumphed, DAILY NEWS, New York, New York, Sun. News, Oct. 6, 1940, at pp.64,65. Print. (Photograph of William Gummer).

H.W. (Hjalmer) Swenson Sketch by Vanessa

*W*hen *Justice Triumphed*, DAILY NEWS, New York, New York, Sun. News, Oct. 6, 1940, at pp.64,65. Print. (Photograph of H.W. Swenson).

H.W. (Hjalmer) Swenson. Sketch by Vanessa. Swenson Defense Attorney for William Gummer. Theresa Swenson, wife of H.W. Swenson is William Gummer's sister. When Justice Triumphed, DAILY NEWS, New York, New York, Sun. News, Oct. 6, 1940, at pp.64,65. Print. (Photograph of H.W. Swenson).

Ralph F. Croal
Sketch by Vanessa

*W*hen *Justice Triumphed*, DAILY NEWS, New York, New York, Sun. News, Oct. 6, 1940, at pp.64,65. Print. (Photograph of Ralph F. Croal).

Ralph F. Croal, Sketch by Vanessa. Croal, Cass County State's Attorney, investigated & presented evidence to Parole Board for releasing William Gummer from the North Dakota State Penitentiary. When Justice Triumphed, DAILY NEWS, New York, New York, Sun. News, Oct. 6, 1940, at pp.64,65. Print. (Photograph of Ralph F. Croal).

When Justice Triumphed, DAILY NEWS, New York, New York, Sun. News, Oct. 6, 1940, at pp.64,65. Print. (Photograph of Ralph F. Croal).

Peter Levins Sketch by Vanessa

P eter Levins Dies, Obituary, DAILY NEWS, New York, New York, 1950. Print. (Photograph of Peter Levins).

Peter Levins, Crime Writer. Sketch by Vanessa. Peter Levins Dies, Obituary, DAILY NEWS, New York, New York, 1950. Print. (Photograph of Peter Levins).

Peter Levins Dies, Obituary, DAILY NEWS, New York, New York, 1950. Print.

Peter Levins Dies; Famous Crime Writer

Peter Levins, 53, for many years editor, reporter and writer for The News, died at 5:10 A. M. yesterday in Elliott Hospital, Manchester, N. H. While covering the mercy murder trial in Manchester, he was stricken with a stomach ailment and entered the hospital Tuesday.

Fellow newspapermen and Manchester residents jammed the hospital switchboard with offers of blood when it was reported that he needed transfusions. The proffered help was useless, however.

Levins, known for his stories of famous criminal cases, was born in the Bronx Sept. 6, 1896. After graduation from Georgetown University in 1918 he worked on the New York Sun, the Yonkers Herald and the Hudson Dispatch, and joined the Sunday department of The News in 1923. He was Sunday editor for two years, beginning in 1939.

In 1945 he left to write crime features for the American Weekly, returning to The News last September.

Levins, who lived at 2700 Redding Road, Fairfield, Conn., is survived by his widow, Sylvia; four children, Jane, 19; Peter Jr., 17; Michael, 15; and John, 13; his father William J. Levins; a brother, William, and a sister, Mrs. Daniel Lynch.

A private funeral service will be held at 11 A. M. Tuesday at the Fable Funeral Home, Boston Post Road at King's Highway, Westport, Conn. The family has requested that no flowers be sent.

Photo Great Northern Railroad Depot

M arie Wick arrived at the Great Northern Depot in Fargo, from Grygla, Minnesota, on June 6, 1921. She and a friend from Grygla, Arnold Rasmussen walked from the Great Northern Depot, 425 Broadway, about five blocks to the Northern Pacific Railway Depot.

Great Northern Railway Depot, 1909

Great Northern Railway Depot, 1909, 425 Broadway, Fargo, ND. Permission to Publish/NDSU Archives.

Photo Northern Pacific Railroad Depot

M arie Wick and her friend from Grygla stopped at the Northern Pacific Railway Depot to confirm the time of departure the next day, June 7, 1921, to visit her aunt in Pettibone, ND. From the Northern Pacific Railway Depot on Main Avenue, Marie and Arnold Rasmussen walked a short distance to the Prescott Hotel, 15 7th St. South, Fargo, ND, in the line of sight of the Prescott Hotel for Marie to book a room for the night.

Northern Pacific Railway Depot, 701 Main Ave., Fargo, ND. Permission to Publish/NDSU Archives.

Photo Prescott Hotel

Various owners of the Prescott Hotel from 1886-1977:

(1886-1895) Major Alonzo Edwards (The Argus, Fargo Newspaper),

(1895-1901) Terrence Martin, Owner (Name change – Martin Hotel),

(1901-1913) William Prescott, Owner (Name change - Prescott Hotel),

(1913-1922) S.A. & Anna Case, Owners (Prescott Hotel),

(June 7, 1921) Marie Wick Raped & Murdered (Prescott Hotel),

(1922-1942) David Shields, Owner (Name change – Shields Hotel),

(1942-1977) (YWCA, Owner) (Housing for Women),

(1977) YWCA (Building Demolished),

(1978-2023) Parking Lot adjacent to Landmark Building, 17 7th St. South, Fargo, ND.

Prescott Hotel

Prescott Hotel, about 1911

Prescott Hotel, about 1911, 15 7th St. S., Fargo, ND. Permission to Publish/NDSU Archives.

Photo Prescott Hotel Lobby

T he lobby of the Prescott Hotel is on the first floor. Railings in the photograph are on the second floor and the location of the rape and murder of Marie Wick.

Prescott Hotel Lobby, 15 7th St. S., Fargo, ND.
Permission to Publish/NDSU Archives.

Floor Plan of Prescott Hotel Crime Scene

DAILY NEWS, New York, New York, Sun. News, Oct. 6, 1940, at p.64. Print. (Peter Levins, Crime Writer) (Floor Plan of Prescott Hotel Second Floor Crime Scene.).

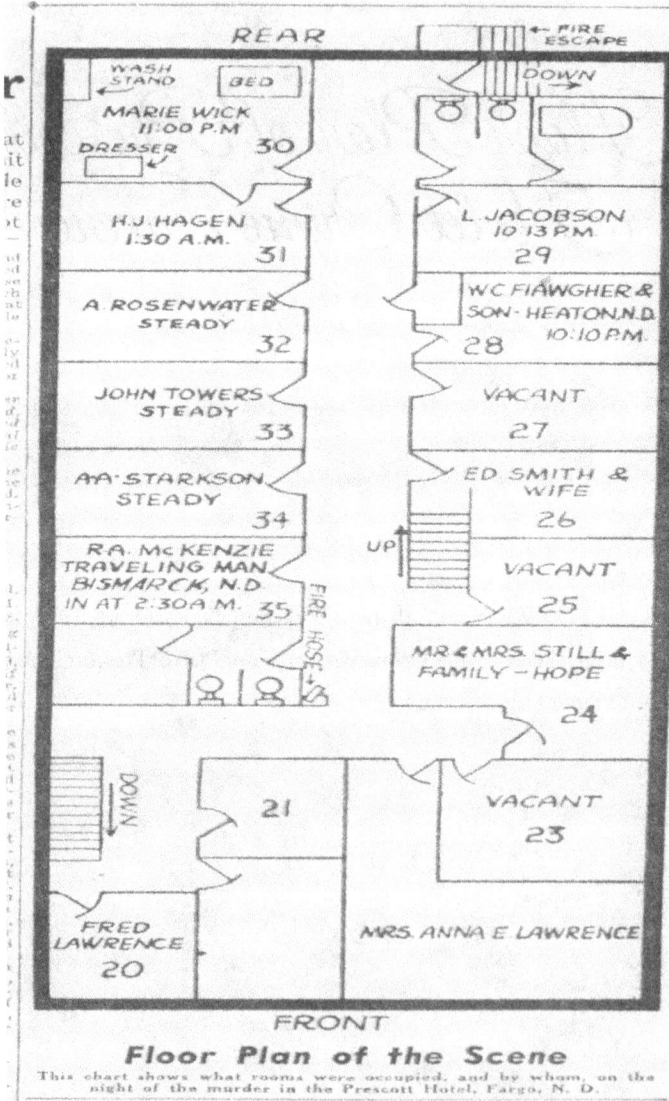

Prescott Hotel, Second Floor Plan of Crime Scene.

Photo Arthur Cecil James Wyoming State Penitentiary Prisoner

Arthur Cecil James, Inmate, Wyoming State Penitentiary, Rawlins, Wyoming. Arthur Cecil James told three people, who contacted the Governor or North Dakota, about Arthur James saying he was with Harry "Blackie" Carter when the girl was killed in the Fargo hotel. James was extradicted to the jurisdiction of Cass County, North Dakota. A hearing before Judge Daniel Holt determined that Arthur Cecil James was not in Fargo on June 7, 1921, and was remanded back to the Wyoming Penitentiary.

Permission to Publish/Wyoming State Archives.

Resources

RESOURCES

Some of my numerous resources of information include:

Ancestry.com

Author Presentations (Numerous)

Barnes County Historical Society & Museum, Wesley Anderson, Director, Valley City ND.

Bonanzaville, West Fargo ND.

Bygdabok. 45 (e) Johanna Marie, født 22/5-1844, gift 12/4-1866 med Tonnes R., Fra Dranga (43). Mogedal, Bygdabok, p.609.

Central Legal Research, University of North Dakota, School of Law, Grand Fork ND.

Chamberlain, Nicole M. Granddaughter, Proofreader, & Podcaster, Texas.

Continuing Legal Education classes for Certified Paralegal requirements for maintaining certification (50 hours within 5 years), Tulsa OK.

Daily Times Record, Valley City ND.

Daughters of Norway, Fargo ND.

Family History Workshops, Heritage Education Commission, Moorhead MN.

Family History Center Library, Church of Jesus Christ of Latter-day Saints (Luana Gilstrap & Karen Vosberg) Fargo ND.

FamilySearch.com

Church of Jesus Christ of Latter-day Saints, Salt Lake City UT.

Fargo Forum, Fargo ND.

Findagrave.com

Fettig, Vanessa. Artist, teacher, Fargo, ND, sketches of Marie Wick and Eleanor Thompson.

Grand Forks County Historical Society, Grand Forks ND.

Hallingdal Lag, Minnesota.

Harvey, Michael. Author, Grand Forks ND.

Hassan, Helin, Canva Assistance, Office Depot, Fargo, ND.

Nord Hedmark og Hedmarken Lag, Minnesota.

Heritage Education Commission's Family History Workshops in Moorhead, MN, PO Box 292, Moorhead MN.

Hillsboro Banner, Hillsboro ND.

Historical & Cultural Society of Clay County (Mark Peihl, Senior Archivist), Hjemkomst Center, Moorhead MN.

Hjemkomst Center, Moorhead MN.

Iseminger, Gordon, Professor, History, University of North Dakota, Grand Forks ND.

James River Valley Genealogical Society, Jamestown ND.

Lela Atwood Peterson, Author, retired elementary school teacher from Reynolds ND. Three Books: *Selma: Swedish Fortitude on the North Dakota Frontier; A House Divided: One Family's Struggle to Survive at the Dawn of the Twentieth Century; Pencil Shavings: Growing Up in a One-Room Country School on the North Dakota Prairie.*

Libraries and librarians in Crookston MN.; Fargo ND; Grand Forks ND; Moorhead MN; UND Chester Fritz Library, Grand Forks ND; West Fargo ND, East Grand Forks MN, NDSU Archives, Fargo ND

Marler, Jackie, Genealogist, Hallinglag & Red River Valley Genealogical Society.

Minnesota Genealogical Society, Mendota Heights MN.

Minnkota Genealogical Society, East Grand Forks MN & Grand Forks ND, for research information shared by members, speakers, and encouragement.

Minnesota State Archives, St. Paul MN.

Moorhead Daily News, Moorhead MN.

Moorhead Friends Writing Group MFWG, Chris Stenson, Founder & Director, meetings every other Tuesday (7-9) (during pandemic met by Skype and then Zoom). Sharing of information, goals, writing suggestions, critiquing, encouragement, support, numerous authors spoke to our group for about an hour about a variety of topics on writing and publishing.

National Association of Legal Assistants, Tulsa OK

Nelson, Jasmine M. Granddaughter.

Nordlands Lag, Minnesota.

North Dakota State Archives, Bismarck ND.

The End is Near For 3.2 Beer, NPR, April 5, 2019. () (accessed July 18, 2021).

Norlie, Olaf Morgan, "Norske Lutherske Menigheter I Amerika" 1843-1916, Augsburg Publishing: Minneapolis MN (1914) (Norwegian).

North Dakota State University Archives (Candy Skauge & John Hallberg), Fargo ND.

North Dakota Historical Society, Bismarck ND.

Norway Archives.

Norway Museums.

Norwegian-American Genealogical Association (N-AGA) Branch of Minnesota Genealogical Society, Mendota Heights MN.

Patterson, Betty, Fargo ND, Norway Genealogy.

Peihl, Mark, Archivist, Historical and Cultural Society of Clay County, Hjemkomst Center, Moorhead MN.

Polk County Courthouse, County Recorder's Office, Crookston MN.

Red River Valley Paralegal Association, Fargo/Grand Forks ND.

Red River Valley Genealogical Society, located in Bonanzaville, West Fargo ND.

Simar, Candace, Author, Pequot Lakes, MN, with a passion for her Scandinavian heritage and a deep love of history. She has 6 historical novels: *Escape to Fort Abercrombie; Shelterbelts; Blooming Prairie; Birdie; Pomme de Terre;* and *Abercrombie Trail.* Her short story collections are *Dear Homefolks; The Glory of Ordinary Time; Farm Girls* is a book of poetry co-written with Angela Foster.

Sons of Norway, Gyda Varden Lodge, Grand Forks ND.

Sons of Norway, Kringen Lodge, Fargo ND.

Sons of Norway, Minneapolis MN.

State v. Gummer, 51 N.D. 445, 200 N.W. 20 (N.D. 1924).

Stor-Elvdal Lag, Minnesota.

Sweden Archives

Sweden Museums

Swedish Cultural & Heritage Society of the Red River Valley, Nels Backman, Fargo ND.

Swedish Genealogical Society of Minnesota (SGSM) Branch of Minnesota Genealogical Society, Mendota Heights MN.

Traill County Courthouse, County Recorder's Office, Tiffany Ambuehl, Assistant County Recorder, currently Assistant County Treasurer, Hillsboro ND.

University of North Dakota, Special Collections (Michael Swanson, Archivist & Curt Hanson, Director), Chester Fritz Library, Grand Forks ND.

Vest-Agder Lag, Minnesota.

Warren Sheaf, Warren MN.

Wyoming State Archives, Suzi Taylor, Reference Archivist, Cheyenne WY 82002

(extradition to North Dakota of Arthur C. James, inmate #5646, who was at the Wyoming State Penitentiary in 1940-41).

Visits, emails, and telephone calls with relatives, acquaintances, and friends entertaining the many questions asked and sharing numerous stories.

Nicole M. Chamberlain,

Doris Teigland Smeby,

Muriel Tronnes Sheridan,

Valerie J. Tronnes,

Vernon L. Tronnes.

Geneva Johnson Anderson,

Wesley Anderson, Director, Barnes County Museum,

Ronald Baker, MGS,

Cindy Dahl, Sons of Norway,

Vanessa Fettig, Art Teacher,

Tiffany J. Fier, MFWG,

Luanna Gilstrap, Family Search Center LDS,

John Hallberg, NDSU Archives,

Larry D. Haugen,

Michael Harvey, MGS,

Tina Holland, MFWG,

Diane Bjerke Johnson,

Kacie Johnson,

Barb Knipe, MGS,

Bob Lind, Fargo Forum,

Jackie Marler, Genealogist, RRVGS,

Minnkota Genealogy Society Members MGS,

Moorhead Friends Writing Group Members MFWG,

Mark Peihl, Archivist, Historical & Cultural Society of Clay County,

Lela Atwood Peterson, MGS,

Charles Rustvold, WWII,

Dr. Casey Ryan MD, Altru,

Candy Skauge, NDSU Archives,

Anna Stenson, MFWG,

Chris Stenson, Director, MFWG,

Michael Swanson, Archivist, UND Special Collections,

Suzi Taylor, Reference Archivist, Wyoming State Archives,

Danielle Teigen, Fargo Forum.

Selected Bibliography

SELECTED BIBLIOGRAPHY

National Association of Legal Assistants, Tulsa, OK.

Red River Valley Legal Assistants, Fargo, ND.

Cohen, Joel and Ethan Cohen. *FARGO*. DVD Video. Universal City, CA: PolyGram Pictures, 1996.

CourtListener From Free Law Project, a 501(c)(3) non-profit. They rely on donations for financial security. https://www.courtlistener.com/opinion/3933049/state-v-gummer/?

Darabont, Frank, Thomas Newman, and Thomas Pasatieri. *The Shawshank Redemption*. DVD Video. Beverly Hills, CA: Castle Rock Entertainment, 1994.

Bygdabøk. 45)(e) Johanna Marie, født 22/5-1844, gift 12/4-1866 med Tonnes R., Fra Dranga (43). Møgedal, Bygdabøk, p.609.

Affield, Wendell. *Pawns: The Farm, Nebish, Minnesota, 1950s*. Chickenhouse Chronicles, Book II. Bemidji, MN: Whispering Petals Press, LLC, 2018.

Affield, Wendell. *Herman: 1940s Lonely Hearts Search*. Chicken-house Chronicles, Book 1. Bemidji, MN: Whispering Petals Press, LLC, 2017.

Affield, Wendell. *Muddy Jungle Rivers: A River Assault Boat Cox'n's Memory Journey of His War in Vietnam and Return Home*. Bemidji, MN: Hawthorn Petal Press, LLC, Amazon Create Space Independent Publishing Platform, 2012.

Anderson, Gerald D. *Prairie Voices An Oral History of Scandinavian Americans in the Upper Midwest*. Moorhead, MN: Northwest Minnesota Regional History Center, affiliated with Minnesota Historical Society, Create Space Independent Publishing Platform, 2014.

Bergeson, Eric. *A True Story: Pirates on the Prairie*. West Des Moines, Iowa: Myers House LLC, 2008.

Calof, Rachel. *Rachel Calof's Story: Jewish Homesteader on the Northern Plains*. Edited by Sanford Rikoon. Bloomington: Indiana University Press, 1995.

Carmon, Irin and Shana Knizhnik. *Notorious RG: The Life and Times of Ruth Bader Ginsburg*. New York, NY: HarperCollins Publishers, 2015.

Daily Times Record, Valley City, ND.

Darabont, Frank and Stephen King. *Shawshank Redemption: The Shooting Script Illustrated*. Newmarket Press Shooting Script ed., 2004.

Fargo Forum, Fargo, ND.

Hampsten, Elizabeth. *Read This Only to Yourself: The Private Writings of Midwestern Farm Women*, 1880-1910. Bloomington: Indiana University Press, 1982.

Hampsten, Elizabeth, comp. *To All Inquiring Friends: Letters, Diaries and Essays in North Dakota* 1880-1910. Grand Forks: University of North Dakota. Department of English, 1980.

Handy-Marchello, Barbara. *Woman of the Northern Plains: gender and settlement on the homestead frontier, 1970-1930*. St. Paul: Minnesota Historical Society Press, 2005.

Harvey, Michael. Vietnam Book & Children's Book.

Haugen, Larry D. *Chuck's [Charles Rustvold's] Story: Surviving WWII and the Bloody Hurtgen Forest*. North Carolina: Lulu Press, Inc., , 2008.

Hernandez, Gwen. *Scrivener for Dummies*. Chichester, West Sussex, England: John Wiley & Sons, Ltd., 2012.

Hill, Clint and Lisa McCubbin. *Five Presidents: My Extraordinary Journey with Eisenhower, Kennedy, Johnson, Nixon, and Ford*. New York: Gallery Books, 2016.

Hill, Clint and Lisa McCubbin. *Five Days in November*. New York: Gallery Books, 2013.

Hill, Clint and Lisa McCubbin. *Mrs Kennedy and Me*. New York: Gallery Books, 2012.

Hvinden, Marlan. *Justice was Swift: Tales of the Old West*. Thompson, ND: Hvinden Publications, year.

Hvinden, Nancy Bergeson. *Scandinavian Holiday Recipes: From the Kitchen of Nancy Bergeson Hvinden*. Thompson, ND: Hvinden Publications, 2018.

Hvinden, Nancy Bergeson. *Growing Up in the Valley: A Nodak Babyboomer Childhood Memories*, Thompson, ND: Hvinden Publications, 2018.

Iseminger, Gordon L. *The Quartzite Border: Surveying and Marking the North Dakota-South Dakota Boundary, 1891-1892*. Sioux Falls, SD: Augustana College, Center for Western Studies. Third ed., 2019.

Iseminger, Gordon L. "Are We Germans, or Russians, or Americans? The McIntosh County German-Russians During World War I", *North Dakota History* 1992 59(2): 2-16.

Larsson, Stieg and Reg Keeland. "The Girl With The Dragon Tattoo." (Millennium Series Book 1). Random House LLC. Swedish Crime Fiction.

Levins, Peter. "When Justice Triumphed," *Daily News*, New York, NY, Sun. News, Oct. 6, 1940, at pp.64,65. Print.

Lindgren, H. Elaine. *Land in Her Own Name: Women as Homesteaders in North Dakota*. Fargo: North Dakota Institute for Regional Studies, North Dakota State University, 1991.

Moorhead Daily News, Moorhead, MN.

Munski, Douglas C. and D. Jerome Tweton, "North Dakota" World Book Online America's Edition, , August 15, 2001. The United States Geological Survey Website.

Nesbø, Jo. *The Snowman: A Harry Hole Novel*." Norwegian Crime Fiction.

Peterson, Lela Atwood. *Selma: Swedish Fortitude on the North Dakota Frontier*. Reynolds, ND: Create Space Independent Publishing Platform, 2015.

Peterson, Lela Atwood. *Pencil Shavings: Growing Up in a One-Room Country School on the North Dakota Prairie*. Reynolds, ND: Lela Atwood Peterson, Woodson Books, 2016.

Peterson, Lela Atwood. *A House Divided: One Family's Struggle to Survive at the Dawn of the Twentieth Century*. Reynolds, ND: Lela Atwood Peterson, Woodson Books, 2019.

Puppe, James. *Dakota Attitude: Interviews from Every Town in North Dakota*. Fargo: Self-published, Printing Forum Publications, 2019.

Raaen, Aagot. *Grass of the Earth*. Northfield, MN: Norwegian-American Historical Association, 1950.

Robinson, Elwyn B. *History of North Dakota*. Lincoln, NE: University of Nebraska Press, 1966.

Rolvaag, Ole E. *Giants in the Earth*. New York: Harper and Brothers, 1927.

Rothman, Lily. *Everything You Need to Ace American History In One Big Fat Notebook*. New York: Workman Publishing, 2016.

Sjowall, Maj and Per Wahloo. "Roseanna: A Martin Beck Police Mystery." Random House LLC. Swedish. Crime Fiction

Schell, Herbert S. *History of South Dakota*. Pierre, SD: South Dakota State Historical Society Press, Rev. Ed., 2004.

Simar, Candace. *Abercrombie Trail: A Novel of the 1862 Uprising*. St. Cloud, MN: North Star Press (2009). www.candacesimar.com.

Simar, Candace. *Pomme de Terre: A Novel of the Minnesota Uprising*. St. Cloud, MN: North Star Press (2010).

Simar, Candace. *Birdie*. St. Cloud, MN: North Star Press (2011).

Simar, Candace. *Blooming Prairie*. St. Cloud, MN: North Star Press (2012).

Simar, Candace, and Angela Foster. *Farm Girls: Reflections and Impressions of Candace Simar and Angela F. Foster*. Brainerd, MN: Riverplace Press (2013).

Simar, Candace. *Shelterbelts*. St. Cloud, MN: North Star Press (2015).

Simar, Candace. *Dear Homefolks*. Aitkin, MN: Riverplace Press (2017).

Simar, Candace. *Escape to Fort Abercrombie*. Waterville, Maine: Five Star Publishing (2018).

Sherman, William C. and Playford V. Thorson, (eds.). *Plains Folk: North Dakota's Ethnic History*. Fargo, ND: North Dakota Institute for Regional Studies, 1986.

Smalley, Eugene Virgil. *History of the Northern Pacific Railroad (1841-1899)*. New York: Wentworth Press, 2016.

Stradley, Scot A. *The Broken Circle: An Economic History of North Dakota* (1993).

State v. Gummer, 51 N.D. 445, 200 N.W. 20 (N.D. 1924).

Teigen, Danielle. *Hidden History of Fargo*. Charleston, SC: History Press, 2017.

Teigen, Danielle. *The Fargo Fire of 1893*. Charleston, SC: History Press, 2020.

Wilder, Laura Ingalls. Rose Wilder Lane (Editor). *Little House on the Prairie* Series.

Winistorfer, Jo Ann B. and Cathy A. Langemo, *Tracing Your Dakota Roots: A Guide to Genealogical Research in the Dakotas*, Second ed. Hazen, ND: Dakota Roots, 2006.

Winistorfer, Jo Ann B. and Cathy A. Langemo, *Tracing Your Dakota Roots: A Guide to Genealogical Research in the Dakotas*, Bismarck, ND: Dakota Roots, First ed., 1999.

Woodward, Mary Dodge. Cowdrey, Mary Boynton (ed.). *The Checkered Years: A Bonanza Farm Diary 1884-88*. Fargo, ND: Cass County Historical Society, Fifth or Later ed., 1988.

Forget-Them-Not

There is someone somewhere in need of your stories.

I hope my genealogy research will assist in your family history research. Remember genealogy is about telling your ancestors' stories. The legacy of your ancestors' rests in your capable hands. You have been chosen to tell their stories.

Thank you for purchasing and reading my series of eight eBooks and eight print books on *Settlers in America from Norway & Sweden*. *Tusen Takk!*

Eileen Tronnes Nelson, Certified Paralegal CP®

Books Coming Soon

BOOKS & PODCASTS COMING SOON

Book 1 *Settlers in America from Norway & Sweden: My Genealogy Techniques May Assist You*

(Print Book and eBook on Amazon).

Book 2 *Settlers in America from Norway & Sweden: Customized Itinerary Independent Travel in Norway & Sweden*

(Currently an eBook on Amazon – need 72 pages minimum for print book).

Book 3 *Settlers in America from Norway & Sweden: Part 1 Photos Traveling in Norway & Sweden*

(Currently an eBook on Amazon-fixing formatting problems for print book).

Book 4 *Settlers in America from Norway & Sweden: Part 2 Photos Traveling in Norway & Sweden*

(Currently an eBook on Amazon-need 72 pages minimum for print book).

Book 5 *Settlers in America from Norway & Sweden: Eleanor Thompson Asphyxiation & Marie Wick Murder & Gummer Trial*

(Print Book and eBook on Amazon, IngramSpark, & Barnes & Noble) (Podcasts on YouTube).

Book 6 *Settlers in America from Norway & Sweden: Johnson Families from Sweden & Tronnes Families from Norway.*

Book 7 *Settlers in America from Norway & Sweden: Documents of Land in Minnesota & North Dakota.*

Book 8 *Settlers in America from Norway & Sweden: Megan Gustafson Murdered in Grand Forks ND.*

Novellas on a variety of topics working on and coming soon.

Ordering information for books and eBooks:

https://amazon.com/author/eileentronnesnelson

QRCode is a link to books and eBooks

https://linktr.ee/eileentronnesnelson

Honor & Remember Eleanor Thompson & Marie Wick

Honor and Remember

Eleanor Thompson

(May 25, 1917-October 8, 1933) &

Marie Petrine Wick

(April 23, 1903-June 7, 1921)

The teenage girls are buried in the Valle Cemetery, rural Grygla, Minnesota. Eleanor is buried near my great grandmother, Johanna Knutsdatter Møgedal.

Valle Cemetery

E leanor Thompson, top left. Marie Wick, bottom right. Valle
Cemetery recording on cloth by Doris Teigland Smeby.

Valle Cemetery.jpg

Valle Cemetery, Rural Grygla, Minnesota.

Epilogue

R eaders please feel free to contact me with questions, comments, or any information concerning Eleanor Thompson, Marie Wick, William Gummer, or anything you wish to share.

Tusen Takk!

Eileen C. Tronnes Nelson

Tronnes.Publishing@gmail.com

About the Author Eileen Tronnes Nelson

Author, Eileen C. Tronnes Nelson, CP®, is a graduate of Nielsville, Minnesota Elementary School; Halstad, Minnesota High School; Minnesota State University Moorhead; & the University of North Dakota. Eileen is a Certified Paralegal, a globally recognized certification by the National Association of Legal Assistants, Tulsa Oklahoma. www.nala.org. Working for 8 years in a Northwood North Dakota law firm, and nearly 40 years with Central Legal Research, University of North Dakota, School of Law, Grand Forks North Dakota. Retiring in July 2015, to research, write, and publish family history. Eileen is a recipient of traditional & contemporary Norwegian cultural skills awards in genealogy, literature, cooking, music, and sports from the Gyda Varden Lodge, Grand Forks North Dakota & Sons of Norway, Minneapolis Minnesota, www.sofn.com, and the Family History Research Award for "Advancing Genealogical Skills" in 2019 from the Heritage Education Commission, Moorhead

Minnesota, www.heritageed.com, converted from a Keynote document, *Settlers in America: from Norway & Sweden* and too large for
publication as one book due to images on each page, thus divided
into 4 books. The first 4 eBooks/paperbacks with subtitles: (1) *"My
Genealogy Techniques May Assist You,"* (2) *"A Customized Itinerary Independent Travel,"* (3) *"Photographs Traveling in Norway,"* (4)
"Photographs Traveling in Sweden." The subtitle of the fifth eBook
& paperback: (5) *"Eleanor Thompson Asphyxiation & Marie Wick
Murder & Gummer Trial"* (Books 1-5 in series of 8 books) (3 genealogy books coming soon). Additionally, Eileen's publications in 2
anthologies, with authors from the Moorhead Friends Writing Group,
Tales from the Frozen North ("Blizzard in North Dakota March 2-5,
1966") (2022) & *Welcome to Effham Falls: Tales from a Small Town*
("Where is Effham Falls? People & Places of the Arrowhead Region")
(2023) (https://moorheadfriendswritinggroup.com/).

https://amazon.com/author/eileentronnesnelson   https://www
.linktr.ee/eileentronnesnelson Tronnes.Publishing@gmail.com

www.ingramcontent.com/pod-product-compliance
Lightning Source LLC
Chambersburg PA
CBHW062154270326
41930CB00009B/1527